FLOYD DELL

Essays from the
FRIDAY
LITERARY REVIEW
1909-1913

R. Craig Sautter, Ed.

december press

A special issue of December Magazine,
comprising vol. 38, no. 2, 1995

Floyd Dell: Essays, R. Craig Sautter, Ed.

ISBN 0-913204-32-3
Library of Congress Catalog Card Number: 94-69575

Manufactured in the United States of America

Cover photo: Floyd Dell, from the Floyd Dell Papers,
The Newberry Library

Published by December Press
Box 302, Highland Park, Illinois 60035

Contents

I wish to acknowledge the contributions of Connie Amon, Joanne and Robert Freeman, Kathryn King, and Norm Streed for their efforts in manuscript preparation; Diana Haskell, Lloyd Lewis Curator of Modern Manuscripts at the Newberry Library for her keen knowledge and preservation of fragile resources; David O. Justice, Dean of the School for New Learning, DePaul University, for his encouragement and the opportunity to teach and write about Chicago literary history; my wife, Sally Reed, for her intellectual and emotional support throughout the duration of my research; Bo for his vigilance and companionship during long and uncertain nights of work; my publisher, Curt Johnson, for his literary expertise and courage in publishing historical scholarship where others thought first of sales and financial gain; and the Society for the Study of Midwestern Literature for its continuing forum for scholars working in this and related fields.

This book is dedicated to all the young, radical Midwestern poets and writers who dare to dream of a more beautiful, just and honest society where art and freedom might thrive.

—R.C.S.

Introduction

When Floyd Dell arrived in Chicago in the autumn of 1908, he carried only twenty dollars and a letter of recommendation in his pockets. Naturally, the influence of the correspondence from Davenport, Iowa, librarian Marilla Freeman to a young *Chicago Evening Post* editorial writer, Charles Hallinan, lasted much longer than the small sum of currency Dell had toiled all summer in George Cram Cook's truck garden to save. Indeed, the introduction directed the 21-year-old-poet-newsman toward a major literary career.

Eventually, Floyd Dell was to become one of the most flamboyant, versatile and influential American Men of Letters of the first third of the 20th century. For many in his generation, he became a symbol of bohemianism, feminism, rebellion, freedom, love and the new modern literature. Certainly the charitable librarian who sent Dell's note of introduction clearly sensed his luminous future as a writer, but her letter speeded him on his way to becoming a major literary critic as well.

Indeed, Dell the young poet, critic, editor, playwright, novelist, social psychologist and reformer found his initial inspiration in the grey stone libraries on the public squares of his small Illinois and Iowa hometowns of Quincy and Davenport, along the Mississippi River. Books offered him exciting and exotic exile from the material world that made him suffer in childhood poverty and deprivation. Soon he was emptying library shelves, absorbing everything from Twain's epic adventures and H.G Well's futuristic journeys to the infidelism of Robert Ingersoll, the fantastic cataclysms of Ignatius Loyola Donnelly and the radical pronouncements of the Russian nihilist movement. For a poor, sensitive, sometimes tormented boy, the public library was a temple of freedom and imagination, the emergent crossroads of literary Europe and America. Books became his passion, his love, his profession.

Dell discovered his poetic soul at an early age. By high school, he recalled, "I was reading English and some other poetry at the rate of one great poet a week. I read and knew vastly by heart Wordsworth, Shelley, Walt Whitman, Kipling, Wilde, the Rossettis, Tennyson, Blunt, Herrick, Heine, Swinburne, Donne, Marvel, Drayton, Shakespeare's sonnets, some Persian and Chinese poetry ...." Like many a tender 19th-century youth, he was seduced by sensuous quatrains of the Fitzgerald translation of the *Rubaiyat*.

He was forced to drop out of high school to enter factory work by a punishing family poverty; the reality of economic survival created a dismal contrast to his realm of poetic marvels. He learned the brutal lessons of economic value in a candy factory where he often burnt flesh from his arms and hands. There he realized that, "I, as a useful worker in a civilization which set a proper value on caramels, had been making more money in that factory than most of the world's great poets had made with their poetry, than any poet was likely to make with his poetry. Certainly I did far better at caramel cutting than Wordsworth ever did by poetry making—he didn't even make enough to pay for his shoe strings, he said, while I paid for my summer's keep ...." Where poetry failed to sustain the body, socialism offered practical hope and comfort against economic exploitation. Dell's developing aesthetic almost naturally joined together impulses of art with the needs of human dignity and economic democracy.

By the time Dell was 16 his poems were appearing in national magazines such as *McClure's, Century, Harper's* and *Mother Earth*. And by the time he departed on rail for the great Midwestern metropolis, he had already written scores of news stories and review columns as a cub reporter on the *Davenport News*. But his brief Iowa journalism career ended abruptly when he was fired for "insolence to the proprietor."

Inevitably, Chicago beckoned him to its experimental stage where an impressive assortment of writers was furiously working away at a new definition of American urban existence. And Dell willingly followed its call with a free spirit that left its mark on the mind of the city and the region. He described that hypnotic impulse which pulled him, along with millions of other country boys and girls, to the surging city along the Great Lake, in an oft quoted conclusion of his first novel, *Moon Calf*, the nation's second best seller, behind *Main Street*, in 1920:

"He saw in his mind's eye, (a map in the rail station) as he tramped the road, a picture of iron roads from all over the Midwest centering in a dark blotch in the corner ...'Chicago' he said to himself ... his trampling steps went to the rhythm of a word that said itself over and over in his mind: 'Chicago! Chicago!'."

During his first months in the city, Dell taught English and helped with plays at Hull House. Even though the *Post*'s Hallinan had no authority to hire Dell, he was charmed by the adventurous and expressive youth and introduced him to other newsmen, including fellow editorial writer and book reviewer, Francis Hackett, a fiery, radical Irishman with modern literary sophistication and an incendiary pen. Before coming to America, Hackett had been an active participant in the "Irish Renaissance." He had been with the *Post* since 1905. When Hackett was named *The Chicago Evening Post*'s Literary Editor in the spring of 1909, an appointment earlier held by Henry

2

Blake Fuller, author of *The Cliffdwellers* and other realistic Chicago novels, he perceptively selected Dell as his assistant. Dell was still 21 years old.

The *Friday Literary Review* first appeared on newsstands as an eight-page supplement to *The Chicago Evening Post* on March 5, 1909. Soon it was available in most major cities in the U.S., and mailed to locations around the country at the subscription price of one dollar a year. It was also sold in London, Paris and Berlin, which may help to explain the *FLR*'s expansive international perspective. In defiance of dominant critical practices, Hackett and Dell proclaimed their first editorial requirement was "to make books interesting." Almost instantly, the *FLR* became an outspoken voice of what has been called the "Chicago Literary Renaissance," and for its rebellious community of poets, novelists, playwrights, artists and critics.

Indeed, at the time Chicago was becoming, as H.L. Mencken later observed, "Literary Capital of the United States." It was an opinion shared by America's leading literary voice, William Dean Howells. In the aftermath of the World's Columbian Exposition of 1893 and up to the time Dell arrived, the city nurtured a growing assortment of writers including George Ade, L. Frank Baum, Francis F. Browne, Clara Louise Burnham, Mary Hartwell Catherwood, Edna Ferber, Eugene Field, I.K. Friedman, Hamlin Garland, Hutchins Hapgood, Robert Herrick, Joseph Kirkland, Ring Lardner, James Weber Linn, Robert Morss Lovett, Edgar Lee Masters, George Barr McCutcheon, John McGovern, Samuel Merwin, Harriet Monroe, Will Payne, Opie Read, Lillian Sommers, Hobart Chatfield Chatfield-Taylor, Stanley Waterloo, Henry Kitchell Webster, Edith Wyatt and others. Theodore Dreiser had already come and gone, returning occasionally to research a new subject. Upton Sinclair had left the city's dark and seering image on the pages of *The Jungle*. Frank Norris had explored it in *The Pit*. Chicago also supported a few literary magazines such as *America*, the *Dial* and the *Chapbook* and publishing companies such as Stone & Kimball.

Among other more obvious traits, Chicago was a city of demanding readers. And with 10,000 U.S. books published each year, these readers needed intelligent guidance. As the sole literary supplement in connection with a daily newspaper outside of New York, the *FLR* quickly earned a reputation as a daring and insightful weekly, among the boldest advocates for a new era in American writing. Yale professor William Lyon Phelps called it, "By far the best purely literary weekly in the United States."

Poet Arthur Davison Ficke whose books were reviewed on its pages and who wrote occasional *FLR* columns, agreed: "The 'Friday Literary Review' was among the liveliest and most informed literary magazines to greet American readers. It defined writing for a new generation of readers as American Letters made its transition from idealized romanticism and respectability to the realism and experimentalism of modernism."

Hackett gained recognition as a fearless editor who mixed social criticism with his aesthetic analysis. The Irish firebrand was in turn satisfied

3

with Dell's expansive literary knowledge, prolific writing abilities and quick editorial judgments. Dell's insights seemed hardly those of a journalistic journeyman. The two worked together in rapid assault on the social and literary provincialism of writers and readers within their reach.

The Chicago Evening Post, located at 12 South Water Street, was a respected and conservative, though witty, daily for the financial and professional set that made the Midwestern economic dynamo go. It had housed political controversy during its 18 years of publication. On its pages, Finley Peter Dunne had created and chronicled his own brand of social criticism with "Mr. Dooley." Yet Dunne's message was conveniently veiled by its barroom setting and disguised with a humorous and heavy brogue. Dooley did not threaten, he merely exposed human and political folly. Readers had a good laugh or cry over Mr. Dooley's philosophical exhibitions.

Hackett's tenure at the *FLR*, however, was a turbulent one. He waged perpetual war against the newspaper's management and the business sensibility of its more traditional readers. The *Post* was not surprisingly uneasy with Hackett's avowed socialism, flagrant attacks on respected social morality and order and with his salutes to dangerous European literary experiments.

Dell described Hackett as "extraordinarily intelligent," of "unflagging zeal," and of "good humor, judgement and skill." He concurred with Hackett's politics. When it came to literature, Hackett's motto, "We are born to revolt," was translated into censure of popular sentimentality, Victorian morality and academic pedanticism. The *FLR* attracted readers across the nation who were ready for forceful expression of fresh literary ideals and who awaited the next assault on the superficialities of too much fashionable fiction, who favored realism over romanticism. Moreover, *FLR*'s radicalism actually sold books. As a result, the supplement brought in abundant book advertising to justify its operations, even if Hackett himself thought nothing of insulting publishers and advertisers who found his viewpoints disagreeable or manners rude.

Hackett rigorously instructed Dell in editorial and deadline tasks, and he initially reserved the full front page reviews and inside editorials for himself. But that left the young writer plenty of hard work filling eight pages of newsprint a week with reviews and notices. Dell pointed out that "doubtless the fact that I could 'review' briefly thirty to a hundred books a week, and still have time to read one book a week and criticize it, had something to do with my having the job."

"Under Francis Hackett," Dell wrote in his 1933 autobiography *Homecoming*, "the *Friday Literary Review* was giving expression to a growing youthful body of American literary taste, which had nourished itself on the best European literature and had civilized modern standards. The growing body of taste had hitherto been voiceless, and was supposed not to exist. Literary criticism was almost entirely either academic or mere puffery;

4

to be alive and to have knowledge of literature was a combination almost unknown; to bring social ideas to bear upon aesthetic products was something very new indeed .... The *Friday Literary Review*, a pioneer in modern civilized criticism in America, gave encouragement to this taste, helped to formulate it ...."

One cannot read Dell's *FLR* essays without encountering a poetic and philosophical lyricism to go along with those social ideals. The prose is intellectually expansive and often profound. Dell's reviews probed for art that was serious and honest, art that was innovative and liberating, art that was dedicated to discovery of the deepest feelings and ideas of individuals and their societies in the new machine age. His underlying style, cynically playful and inventive, often explored an author's themes with intellectual journeys of his own. His linguistic charm and analytic lucidity could not long be hidden on the *FLR*'s inside pages. Soon Dell's reviews were elevated to the front page, alone or sharing space with Hackett.

Dell's first front-page "Book Of The Week" review, extolling "The Idealist, Moncure D. Conway," last of the American Abolitionists, appeared July 16, 1909. His debut foreshadowed a career of reviews that brought the requirements of social and economic freedom to the art he examined. If Hackett found his political ideals in European working men's clubs or Fabian circles, Dell immediately demonstrated his admiration for indigenous American literary and social insurgents as well. After all, his father had been a Civil War veteran and life-long Lincoln Republican and his grandfather had been an Abolitionist farmer. Dell was intently aware of the region's agrarian populist roots and industrial struggles.

In the *FLR* issues that followed, Dell regularly examined origins and developments of the socialist movement in America and Europe. He also probed and promoted the emerging international women's movement and sought to examine psychological implications of changing sexual relations on characters and situations in the literature and society.

But art, as a vehicle of individual and social discovery, and as a celebration of sensuous beauty and psychological veracity, art that was true to life, was his primary fascination. His reviews demanded a literature inherently linked with freedom in living and in writing. Indeed, his reviews still convey a penetrating force and stylistic grace, as well as historical insight, that endures nearly a century later. It could be argued that Hackett and Dell were creating the prototype of the modern book review.

During his five-year tenure, Dell conducted readers on elaborate excursions through writings old and new, of Jack London, H.G Wells, Edward Fitzgerald, Tom Paine, Ralph Waldo Emerson, Friedrich Nietzsche, Mark Twain, G. K. Chesterton, Bernard Shaw, William Blake, William Dean Howells, Theodore Dreiser, George Moore, Ellen Key, William Morris, Yoshio Markino, Arnold Bennett, Jane Addams, Anatole France, Ellen Glasgow, O. Henry, Emma Goldman and hundreds of others. The most prominent and enduring of these are collected in this volume.

Dell also wrote on scores of topics from the history of marriage and the "Little Theater Movement" to Darwinism, and even baseball and the Boy Scouts. Many of his essays were admittedly youthful in their exuberance. But they were undeniably clever and witty, sophisticated and profound, intelligent and wise beyond Dell's years. But few book critics had ever prepared so thoroughly, though unwittingly, for their job. Not surprisingly, Theodore Dreiser told him he was the best critic in America. Later Dreiser drafted him to edit chapters of *"The Genius."*

Along with the front-page "Book Of The Week" review and its center-page line drawing or photograph of the subject, Hackett and Dell developed regular reader sections such as "Literary Small Talk" "The Newest Fiction," "Recent Belles Letters," "Affairs of the Day," "Around the World," "Important Reprints," "Causerie," "Scientific Studies," "Recent Biography," "Magazine Critique," "Poets Minor and Minus," "The Minority Report," "Varied Interest." Dell worked on all columns and thrived on the encyclopedic deadline challenge of putting out the *FLR*.

On page four, weekly unsigned editorials lambasted the latest literary and social buffoonery. Editorials carried provocative and enticing titles such as "The Uselessness of Art," "Should Writers Marry?" "Sterile Culture," "Race Prejudice," "Police Censorship," "Book Reviews and Crime," "The Marriage Shackle," and "Persecuting the Young." In time, Dell wrote most of the editorials. Usually, he also wrote several long, signed reviews on diverse subjects during a single week.

In the "Recent Poetry" column, Swinburne, Lindsay, Wilde, Pound, Masefield gained favor and defense. Ezra Pound wrote Dell in 1909 saying, "I feel almost as if I should apologize for my naive surprise at finding a critic who has considered both the functions of criticism and the nature of the book before him." He confided that Dell was the "one man to whom I can talk, or at whom I can theorize ...." Pound's verse was periodically reviewed, his poems appeared on the editorial page and Dell's March 12, 1913, editorial proclaimed, "Ezra Pound We Salute You."

Dell's encouragements to Vachel Lindsay drew the mystic poet and his "Gospel of Beauty" from Springfield to Chicago where he became a regular guest at the stream of gatherings hosted by Margery Curry, Dell's first wife and a *FLR* reviewer. Lindsay came along to parties on the Indiana sand dunes of Lake Michigan where they all talked ceaselessly and chanted classical and modern lyrics and odes along the beach. The two exchanged poems. In January of 1910, Lindsay wrote Dell, "I consider meeting you, one of the fine adventures of my life, especially meeting you in Rhyme."

Harriet Monroe's *Poetry: A Magazine of Verse*, announced its existence on the September 20, 1912, pages of the *FLR*, and gained enthusiastic editorial support a week later. Dell even delivered *Poetry* a first package of unformed verse by an unknown poet, Carl Sandburg. The work was duly noted and rejected, but was followed a few months later by the famous "Chicago" poems. Dell contributed some of his own verse to the *FLR*'s editorial page, first under his own name, then throughout 1911-1912 in an anonymous satirical series called "Poems of a Young Man."

On January 28, 1910, Dell was promoted to Associate Editor. A year had not yet passed since the review's founding. At the same time, Hackett confided to Dell that he "wasn't going to die old in this editorial desk." Dell was granted greater editorial responsibilities. The two writers worked energetically side by side, until July 28, 1911, when Dell replaced Hackett as *FLR* Editor. Hackett had wearied of his fights with management and of writing about other authors. He left for London to pursue an independent writing career. A few years later in New York, when Dell was editing the *Masses*, he in turn published Hackett's reviews and reports. Hackett later became associated with *The New Republic*.

Under Dell's leadership, the *FLR* refined and expanded its radical critique of society and literature. In one of his first front-page reviews upon assuming editorship, Dell provocatively praised the philosophy of *Rebellion*, a novel by Joseph Medill Patterson, socialist heir to the *Chicago Tribune* and future founder of the *New York Daily News*, endorsing its views on adultery, divorce and radicalism. His review infuriated management.

Dell's *FLR* became even more occupied with questions of feminism. He avidly promoted women writers such as Willa Cather, Ellen Glasgow, Jane Addams and Susan Glaspell. Dell had long hated "the contemptuous degradation of girls in men's minds ...." He despised most men's "implicit attitude of lords of the earth towards a slave class, or sometimes of a hungry tramp toward an apple tree loaded with fruit.... 'That was a good apple' they said with an air of one who has just tossed the core away. Girls were things. And this was an old role for girls, church and state joining in denying them their rights as individuals and employers keeping them in roles of helplessness by cheap wages."

Dell's front page series on "Modern Women," during the "Suffragette Summer" of 1912 highlighted his interest in the "immense and hardly known subject of sex." When a Chicago publisher asked to put out a volume of his poetry, Dell countered with his first of 26 books, *Woman as World Builder*, 1913, a look at "modern women" including Charlotte Perkins Gilman, Emmeline Pankhurst, Beatrice Webb, Margaret Dreier Robins, based on his *FLR* series. These influential essays are also included in this volume. Eventually, Dell's early feminist interest manifested itself in his novels, *Janet March*, 1923, and *Diana Stair*, 1932, which helped promote a new literary image and understanding of American women.

With each review, Dell matured into a more forceful and discerning writer and thinker. His essays were intricate arguments that revealed historical, social, psychological and aesthetic connections in emerging fiction. He argued passionately with the authors he reviewed in imaginary and textual dialogues. He was devoted to writing that told the "truth," as he saw it, against a pervasive social hypocrisy. "Truth-telling," even more than socialism, was Dell's form of radicalism. Yet as a convinced socialist who admired writers like Upton Sinclair, about whom he later wrote a book, his essential freedom of spirit prevented his writings from becoming ideologically dogmatic in the vein of the next generation of radicals. His language was charged with invention and merriment and rebellion. He called for fiction that confirmed the dignity and value of men and women in face of complex mechanical and economic forces and ideals that threatened to dehumanize, indeed, destroy them.

As chief editor, he promptly broadened the *Friday Literary Review*'s base of writing talent. After Hackett's departure, Dell hired his former Davenport mentor and closest friend, George Cram Cook, as Associate Editor. While still in Iowa, Dell and Cook had built a significant intellectual association that shaped both writers. Cook was added to the masthead on November 24, 1911. The summons to Chicago at last liberated an older Cook from the isolation and despondency of working alone in Davenport and pointed him toward his creative destination.

A year and a half later, Cook headed for Greenwich Village where he co-founded the Provincetown Players, along with future Pulitzer Prize dramatist Susan Glaspell, whom he married. The Provincetown Players counted among their number young Eugene O'Neill who was about to revolutionize American theater. When Dell arrived in the Village in late 1913, some of his own whimsical plays, one written for his beloved Edna St. Vincent Millay, were performed and published by Provincetown. Some moved uptown to Broadway, another became a movie. Writing plays was part of community life in the pre-war bohemian Village.

When Cook departed, Dell hired Lucian Cary, originally a Hackett reviewer, whom Dell found brilliant and hard working. Cary became Associate Editor on October 18, 1912, the same date Cook began writing the "New York Letter" column. Dell also built an impressive coterie of *FLR* reviewers. He gave review work to the beautiful and mysterious Margaret Anderson. And it was at one of those notorious bohemian parties in the Dell's 57th street studios on the edge of the remains of the 1893 Columbian Exposition on Chicago's South Side, that Margaret Anderson announced the idea for her *Little Review*, which gained fame, in part, as the first to publish portions of James Joyce's *Ulysses*.

Sherwood Anderson, an unknown advertising copywriter, attended the Dell affairs as well. It was primarily through efforts of Dell and Dreiser that *Windy McPherson's Son*, Anderson's first novel, was published. Fanny Butcher, future book review editor for the *Chicago Tribune*, was another fledgling writer given reviews to pen. Tagore sent correspondences from India. Other reviewers included Van Wyck Brooks, Chicago novelists I.K Friedman, Edith Wyatt and Henry Blake Fuller, poets Eunice Tietjens and

Louis Untermeyer, as well as Dell's future publisher Alfred A. Knopf, who wrote on drama.

By the spring of 1913, the *Post*'s management revolted against the review's onslaughts on traditional culture and society. Dell had picked up the management battle where Hackett left off. Almost every issue of the review renewed the conflict. When the celebrated Post-Impressionist, International Exhibition of Modern Art came to the Chicago Art Institute in 1913, Dell naturally wanted to write about it. But he had been repeatedly warned by superiors that he "was not the political editor and dramatic editor and the music editor and the art editor of the *Post*, but simply and solely the literary editor ...." Fortunately, there was a book on the topic, though there were no copies in Chicago. Dell brazenly reviewed it and the scandalous show on the front page of the March 28, 1913, issue.

Within a month, the *FLR*, as Dell lamented, "lost the dignity of its tabloid independence and was reduced to a mere double page in the body of the *Evening Post*, in an attempt to discipline its wilful modernism." Six months later, while Dell was in New York surveying new fall books with publishers, another of his reviews incited the wrath of the paper's proprietor. In a complicated quarrel that spilled over to the entire staff, several department heads were fired and Hallinan, his patron, quit. When Dell heard about the dispute, he too tendered his resignation. Though the paper sought to retain him, Dell was ready to move on to New York. His experimental marriage with Margery Curry had come to an end and he was eager for greater freedom and artistic engagement writing fiction. He recommended Lucian Cary as the *Post*'s new Literary Editor, with Cary's wife Augusta as Assistant Editor.

From Chicago, Dell ventured East to Greenwich Village, where as Managing and Literary Editor of the *Masses* and *Liberator*, he agitated for social and economic justice and international peace. He continued his career as critic and interpreter of "Books That Are Interesting," as he named his review section in the *Masses*, taking up the slogan he and Hackett had adopted for the *FLR*. In the public press, Dell was often portrayed as a "Prince of the Village," a bohemian free lover. And indeed, his collection of short stories, *Love in Greenwich Village*, 1926, released after he had moved up the Hudson, helped mythologize the dilapidated section of the city as a vagabond haven for artists, writers and other gentle souls.

By 1920, Dell had relocated upstate in Croton-on-Hudson to write 11 popular novels, several Broadway plays and edit diverse collections such as *Daughter of the Revolution and Other Stories by John Reed*, 1927, and pen seminal social volumes such as *Love in the Machine Age: A Psychological Study of the Transition from Patriarchal Society*, 1930. When the Depression dragged on and publishers and producers no longer courted his fiction and plays, Dell accepted work in the New Deal as head editor with the WPA in Washington D.C., and eventually wrote the *Final Report of the WPA*

Program 1935-43 as well as speeches for WPA director Harry Hopkins and John L. Lewis of the United Mine Workers. Dell retired from government work in 1947 and died in the capitol city in 1969, during another season of youthful rebellion, at age 82.

By almost any standard, the *FLR* under Hackett and Dell was a remarkable and bold literary journal, uncommonly honest, critically self-certain, internationally aware, overtly rebellious, often brilliant and illuminating in scope and style. While other book review sections of the time, such as that of *The New York Times*, were still committed to promoting genteel and romantic writing, the *FLR* advocated naturalism, realism and rebellion. And on top of all that, it was a weekly supplement whose insights rapidly multiplied each Friday for nearly half a decade. As readers will soon discover, Dell's *FLR* essays are themselves minor works of art often scaling rhetorical and intellectual heights of critical investigation, evaluation, elegance and insight.

Besides their worth as historical documents of a lyrical and rebellious season of American literature, Dell's reviews also are worth reading as prototypes of the modern book review itself. Dell and Hackett were pioneers of a new genre of intelligent, demanding, sociological and psychological studies and reviews. These works helped establish a style and purpose for the modern book review as we know it, freed from the superficiality and pompous pretense of many of Dell's contemporaries. Dell's work at the *FLR* and the *Masses* elevated his profession of book reviewer to a new level of seriousness of mission and elegance of style, and thereby created new expectations for the modern book review and its readers.

In retrospect, it can also be argued that in his *FLR* columns, Dell also crafted one of America's first coherent and critical interpretations of "modern" literature. In this regard, he developed his weekly critical viewpoint, with its rebellious and probing social sensibility, in chronological parallel with Pound's new experimental aesthetic and prior to Eliot's neo-classicism. And while his attitudes toward literature differ substantially from both these acknowledged aestheticians, Dell's writing is certainly as erudite, compelling and historically, socially and philosophically grounded, and at the time was more broadly read by readers as well as writers, such as Sinclair Lewis who acknowledged its influence.

Dell's best *FLR* writings synthesized the self-conscious convergence of 19th- and 20th-century European and American progressive writing into a social and psychological aesthetic that advocated a more enlightened and humane literature and way of living. Dell was an intuitive and probing critic who was able to intelligently grasp the literary and cultural significance of the books he selected for review and make those connections clear to readers.

It may seem slightly strange now to conceive of realism, revolt and change in a restricted sexual context as radically "modern." Often we mistakenly see "modernism" as a one-dimensional avant-garde phenomenon

10

rather than a real historical process with many paths of exuberance and exploration. Instead of acknowledging many different and conflicting kinds of 20th century modernism, each form evolving from an earlier incarnation, the word has been simplified into a limited and misleading paradigm. Thus we tend to associate modernism solely with post-World War I experimentation of form and disintegration of spirit and forget its realistic and playfully rebellious pre-war origins.

Dell's *FLR* reviews demonstrate that modernism, as it historically unfolded in American literature, was much more complex. There were competing theories, places and approaches working to shape the new literature. While Dell became a symbol of revolt, he was not among the later advocates of literary despair or alienation or a literary nihilism of form without human substance. His style of truth telling was aimed at creating a new idealism that liberated mind and body from false pretense and repressive power and culture. He became an advocate for literature that reasserted man and woman against the chaos of machine and society, that championed love and freedom and veracity. It is this strand of American modernism, that often is lost in our contemporary assessments and which readers will rediscover in the Dell essays that follow. For these historical and literary reasons, these reviews are particularly fascinating and instructive.

This collection, then, brings together a small but representative sample of Dell's *Friday Literary Review* writings. These essays represent primarily front-page "Book Of The Week" reviews of novels whose authors are still widely known to literate readers and whose works can be easily obtained in libraries or quality bookstores. They provide a keen intellectual perspective on classics or near classics from the original time of their publication. This volume also includes Dell's set of six essays on "modern feminists," as well as another series of six front-page essays on Chicago authors. They are reproduced here, without corrective editing (the Latin "Sic" indicates places where some original editing or type errors occurred. The three centered asterisks separating some paragraphs in the text do not indicate deletions but were used in the originals.)

At age 26, Floyd Dell had prospered as a prolific, exciting and insightful writer at the center of a pivotal literary upheaval in American literature. His *FLR* essays had contributed immensely to the public debate, definition and understanding of early modernism and he had added an intellectual and rebellious aesthetic to the turmoil of the Chicago writing scene. Even though his weekly reviews, like all newspaper copy, might have since vanished with the wind (except for yellowing copies in the Newberry Library and Chicago Historical Society), for almost half a decade they inspired and charmed readers and writers, and they did much to elevate American criticism to a new level of influence, distinction and intellectual sophistication.

Through his web of friendships and opus of public opinions, the young writer had shaped currents of America's emerging literature. For these achievements, he stood as defiant symbol for many who shared his spiritual and social yearnings, and an ardent and dangerous enemy to the older order of literature and society that was about to acquiesce. In his few youthful years at the *Friday Literary Review*, Dell had not only become a full-fledged writer, he had served admirably on the front lines of the literary battle for a new fiction and freedom that was sweeping the nation and would help transform its consciousness and concerns.

R. Craig Sautter

ALGERNON CHARLES SWINBURNE

The poetic treasure that the last of England's great poets has bequeathed the world is now so luminous a thing that praise is become superfluous. So secure, indeed, is the fame of Swinburne that it need not be set down to a carping spirit if, even before the shock of his death has ceased to reverberate in the souls of poetry lovers, his work be here treated in the mood of criticism rather than that of eulogy.

It goes without saying that Swinburne's work is not wholly admirable. Without attempting dogmatically to divide the sheep from the goats, it may be possible by indicating the leit-motifs of his poetry to furnish the means whereby to distinguish with clearer vision the magnificently good from the mediocre, the merely clever, the artistically indefensible elements of his production.

Swinburne's poetry derives from many sources: his verbal preciosity came from Gautier, his preoccupation with "sin" from Baudelaire, his sonority and his "terrible and heart-breaking long-windedness" from Hugo; while he took up and carried on, albeit in rather a Gallic fashion, the Republican and revolutionary traditions of Milton and Shelley; and perhaps his wonderful gift of passion was born of his devotion to Sappho, named of him "the supreme head of song."

But of all the phases of this protean shape, the Swinburne of the "Poems and Ballads" is by far the best known. Here he is to be seen in perhaps his truest aspect, as a rebellious and preverse [sic] spirit out of the renaissance—that renaissance which John Ruskin and William Morris damned so heartily, and of which John Addington Symonds pointed out that, in seeking to imitate the healthy animalism of the ancients, the period but called into being curious and devilish orgies that no Greek could have understood. The remark is significant.

The objections raised against the poems on the grounds of morality may be thrown out of court without further ado. The question is wholly an aesthetic one, and the temper of modern art is favorable to the frankest utterances concerning the love-passion. But it is hardly of love in its normal, human aspects that the poet has chosen to speak. Laughter-loving Aphrodite has become

That obscure Venus of the hollow hill,
That thing transformed which was the Cytherean,
With lips that lost their Grecian laugh divine
Long since, and face no more called Erycine—
A ghost, a bitter and luxurious god.

"Poems and Ballads" may be called a monument to a lost opportunity. Swinburne might have anointed with the chrism of poesy the things of the flesh equally with the things of the spirit. Instead, he assured the world, in words curiously like those of some mediaeval saint, that the love and desire of woman is a thing "bitter," "deadly," "shameful." The things of the flesh he has baptized with blood and ashes and, with an anathema far more terrible than any issued by the petty Anthony Comstocks of prose, has well-nigh succeeded in banishing them from the domain of art. And when they are finally welcomed back it will be not because of but in despite the erotic poetry of Algernon Charles Swinburne.

April 16, 1909

THE NEWEST FICTION

The Third Circle, by Frank Norris. Introduction by Will Irwin. [John Lane Company.]

The name of Frank Norris will always bring to some hearts the thrill which is communicated by splendid achievement and the sadness which belongs to the untimely dead. To think of him is to think of a wonderful succession of stories and novels—wonderful in that they cast off one limitation after another and attained even finer and more certain touch: "Moran of the Lady Letty," "McTeague" (greatest of horror stories), "Blix," "A Man's Woman," "The Octopus" (a great novel if there ever was one), and, least notable of all, "The Pit"; it is to forget the fatal destiny that overtook his plans and see him in his potential shape, a towering figure among the great masters of literature.

The basis for all this had been perhaps fully laid when he died; and by an irony of fate he left nothing wholly worthy of his powers. Yet as showing the track by which he climbed, "the way a genius takes to find itself," even his 'prentice work has interest and value. For the publication of the present volume, containing most of the stories he wrote for the San

Francisco Wave in the day before the East awoke to his greatness, there will be many who will be grateful; and the time will surely come when another volume will be called for, containing the rest of his fine early work, down to the last scrap.

"The studio sketches of a great novelist," these have been called. But they have, for all their crudity, an interest of their own. The title story, "The Third Circle," is a horror tale that—by virtue of introducing no actual physical elements of horror, but by suggestion thrice refined—ranks not far below the best in its class. The fault of most of them is serious enough, less in technique than that where they involve moral issues he is unable to keep from taking sides—a most unfair proceeding.

Yet it is a collection of studio sketches that the book will be most eagerly read. "It is," says Mr. Irwin, "as though we saw a complete collection of Rembrandt's early sketches, say—full technique and coordination not yet developed, but all the basic force and vision there. . . . Rough-hewn tales, they are most interesting when compared with that later work which the world knows, and when taken as a melancholy indication of that power of growth which was in him and which must have led, if the masters of fate had only spared him, to the highest achievement in letters."

As an example of the artist who would not skimp his pains, to whom no preparation was too thorough, and whose spirit ever soared triumphant over his mass of carefully collected facts, the least of his work cannot but be an inspiration.

June 11, 1909

THE BOOK OF THE WEEK

THE IDEALIST

Moncure D. Conway: Addresses and Reprints, 1850-1907; published and unpublished work representing the literary and philosophical life of the author. [Houghton Mifflin Company.]

When Moncure D. Conway died, two years ago, in Paris, he closed the line of the abolitionists who wrote so curious and spectacular a page in

American history. And in a sense he was representative of them all, and of all the qualities whereby they were wont to inspire and irritate their fellow men.

At the distance of half a century, we venerate the most splendid and unmanageable of them all, John Brown. But his contemporaries could hardly be blamed for finding his method maddening. His method was that of all idealists, great and small, of Jesus, of Tolstoy, of Moncure D. Conway. Before a tangled complex of legal rights and practical necessities, in which only the mind of a statesman could discern the possibilities of action, he, this John Brown, no statesman, not even a lawyer, not seeing the whole problem at all, ignoring, in fact, all but a single issue, set himself up in judgment and declared for a violent, artificial and impossible solution—for justice.

* * *

Such was the opinion of intelligent contemporaries. But Time was to confute their intelligence. The one issue, the wrongness of slavery, was to weigh in the balance after all against state rights and constitutional provisions; and the violent, artificial and impossible solution, the abolition of slavery, was after all to be adopted.

Nevertheless, the idealist seemed to his fellows a most impracticable sort of person: he was always changing his opinions, and yet in certain situations where it seemed in the blood of man to compromise, he demanded an inhuman consistency. He was forever meddling, and could not rest content with nothing. The view held of him by the man in the street has been very effectively expressed by Hazlitt, in one of his essays:

> He puts everything into a metaphysical crucible to judge of it himself and exhibit it to others as a subject of interesting experiment . . . He strives to overturn all established creeds and systems: but this is in him an effect of constitution. He runs before the most extravagant opinions . . . He tampers with all sorts of obnoxious subjects . . . Persons of this class, instead of consolidating useful and acknowledged truths, and thus advancing the cause of science and virtue, are never easy but in raising doubtful and disagreeable questions . . .

* * *

The actual subject of this description was Percy Bysshe Shelley. We have canonized the poet now, and he can do no wrong. But no doubt most of us would have agreed with Hazlitt at the time; and no doubt there is considerable justification for Hazlitt's view of things.

Though Moncure Conway entered the abolition struggle after the period of martyrdom had ended, he was well within the period of social obloquy, and suffered criticisms to which that quoted above were a kindness.

16

But he survived the hard words, and when abolitionism became popular he went cheerfully on to new heresies. He ended as preacher in possibly the most heretical church in christendom—and one which in spite of that became fashionable.

Dying, he left a host of devoted followers, men and women who had been tremendously influenced by his personality and teachings. It is as a response to the demand by them that this memorial volume has been issued, embodying work representative of all periods of his life.

* * *

Characteristically enough, the anti-slavery advocate was born on a Virginia plantation, the son of a slave owner, and was trained for an innocuous career in the Methodist ministry. A minister he did become; but he was an impressionable young man, and he allowed himself to be influenced by some writings of Horace Mann, who was then fighting for a free public school system. Circuit-riding through Virginia, Conway saw what the state of affairs was there, and wrote a pamphlet which, with the first $50 he could save up, he published.

It was entitled "Free Schools in Virginia, a Plea of Education, Virtue and Thrift Vs. Ignorance, Vice and Poverty." The author was then only 18 years old. He still believed in slavery as a divinely ordained institution, and in the Bible as the inspired word of God. But the seeds of the passion for propagandizing had been implanted in his soul, and his erratic career was determined from that hour.

In this pamphlet, which forms the first selection in the present volume, the young reformer scraped together all the statistics he could find that bore on the subject, and marshaled what seem to us the perfectly obvious arguments in favor of free public schools. Its practical effect was to put him in communication with various reformers. Among them was Horace Greeley, who told him: "Never will Virginia's White children be generally schooled until her Black ones shall cease to be sold."

* * *

The young circuit rider had stopped at a book store to buy Emerson's "Essays," which some one had told him about. At the store all they could produce was Emerson's Algebra, but they ordered the other book. And so he began to imbibe dangerous doctrine. Too many New York Tribune editorials changed his mind about the divine character of slavery, and too much Emerson sapped his belief in conventional religious dogma. So he quit the church, and went to Harvard divinity school, graduating in 1853 as a full-fledged abolitionist; and took a Unitarian pulpit in Washington, D.C.

Here he acquired a reputation for brilliancy that counterbalanced the

17

unpopularity of his opinions. When the war began, at some considerable risk to himself, he went to his old home and brought back with him his father's slaves, setting them free. In 1862 we find him publishing a little book—included in this volume of selections—"The Golden Hour."

* * *

It was addressed to the American people and to Abraham Lincoln, and sought to demonstrate that now was the golden hour to set free the slaves, and so to end the war. It was crystal clear to Conway; he could not see the difficulties that clouded the vision of the President. That he saw no difficulties was his virtue; that Lincoln saw them all, a different and perhaps a greater virtue. It would be trite to suggest that the nation needed, and needs, both virtues.

* * *

His style was not impassioned; it was calm and pitched in low key, with only occasional bursts of rhetoric. So placidly do we now accept the current theories of a "war for the union" that it is worth while to transcribe a passage, representative of their views who abhorred that war:

> Has not this idea of a "war for the Union" its comic side? I once knew of a father's whipping his child because the child did not love him so well as it did its nurse, and it seemed to me an odd way to cultivate filial affection; but is it not so that we are recovering unity with the South? If that Union had not been already dead, surely we have sent artillery enough down there to have killed it several times.

* * *

He did not miss his opportunity of characterizing Boston. It will be perceived that the city he knew, a city of extremes of good and bad, has passed away, taking with it both extremes:

> . . . Boston, where the largest and smallest things are said and done of any place on this continent. In Boston you shall find your noblest and your meanest man; there you shall find the faithful Senator who will stand for Freedom until he is stricken down, and there the creature who will touch glasses with the assassin of his own senator within two squares of the prostrate form. We had brutes enough in Cincinnati to mob Wendell Phillips; but no man who could write a sentence could be found here who would justify it: the mob had to go to Beacon street, Boston, for a defender. . . . But where else could we have found a Phillips?

Because it is put forward as common sense, much of the matter of this pamphlet makes but an ill impression. For it is not common sense to declare that "When our country has an idea in this war, it need only send South a moderate police force." It may be uncommon sense; it may even be true. But common sense is always for the larger battalions.

Only when it comes out as poetry, or as mysticism, does it strike deep. Here is power: "Be not entangled in the illusions which twine about and bind your rulers. Slavery seems to them a strong thing; so mariners have mistaken a fog bank for the Rock of Gibraltar. There is not a mushroom that grows which is not stronger than Slavery, against which every whispering wind, every sunbeam, every leaf, and every human blood drop is conspiring."

And there is an audacity which carries one away in his phrase when he says, asking only that he be not interfered with by United States law: "I challenge the President to permit me—one of the weakest and obscurest friends of Freedom—to liberate the slaves of the South."

Sent to England in 1862 by the Abolition Society to create a public opposition to slavery there which might react favorably in the United States, Mr. Conway came into contact with many of her eminent literary men, and added to the notable list of friendships he had begun in this country. A part of his personality was expressed in his friendships, which came to be world wide, and to traverse every boundary of rank and class.

* * *

In 1863 he became pastor of South Place Chapel, Finsbury, in London, and started there the work which has perhaps been of the most service to the world—the work of humanizing knowledge. His efforts were part of a great movement which turned Spencer, Darwin, Huxley, Tyndall, Clifford and other scientific men from academic work to the task of popularizing and applying the body of scientific knowledge.

To this period belongs "The Earthward Pilgrimage," published in 1870, and included, together with a number of sermons, in this volume. The strength and weakness alike of his method are shown easily in an extract from the "Pilgrimage":

> Science, the one true representative of the Apostolic Succession in this age, reversing all estimates of high and low. Studious rather of actual flies than of possible angels; turning from the infinite to search into the infinitesimal; finding the philosopher's stone in every pebble; circumnavigating the raindrop and reporting its curious tribes; pursuing insects as ardently as suns; reading in flowers the laws of constellations; tracing the bursting of cosmical rings and the generation of worlds in a spinning drop of oil; exploring primeval forests in frost pictures on window panes; following each step in the ascent of the worm to man; showing the consent of solar systems to the motion of a finger—Science has come to this

generation wearing on its head the dust, and has taught us to see in that dust a crown more glorious than ever adorned the brow of royalty.

* * *

This phase of his activity ending with the death of his wife in 1897, he thereafter wrote and published his "Life of Thomas Paine" and "Life of Edmund Randolph," and was at work on a life of Calvin when he died.

During all this time his idealism had carried him farther and farther away from conventional beliefs. Among the addresses which he delivered in this final period are an "Adresse au Congres de la Paix," given at Paris in 1900; an "Address on Sunday Opening of Exhibitions," given before the directors of the Buffalo exposition of 1901; an address on "Dogma and Science" before the Congress of Freethinkers in Rome in 1904, and addresses on "Public Service" and "William Penn," given at Dickinson College, Carlisle, Pa., the last one in the year of his death.

* * *

It is interesting that Andrew Carnegie is an admirer of Conway's writings, and gave to Dickinson College a large sum for building a hall to be called Conway Hall "—in honor of Moncure D. Conway . . . in recognition of his great services in the realms of letters, of reform and of humanitarian effort."

If, as is likely, the present generation finds in the creed of this idealist a lack, an omission to provide for the virile and militant elements of its being, it has failed to understand that more than militant passion which imbued all of his life and glows in the words of his last public utterance: "There can arise no important literature nor art nor real freedom nor happiness among any people until they feel military uniform a livery and see in every battlefield an inglorious arena of human degradation."

July 16, 1909

20

VERSE

The Tramp's Excuse, and Other Poems, by Nicholas Vachel Lindsay. [The War Bulletin, Springfield, Ill.]

Nicholas Vachel Lindsay is one of those who, whether wisely or foolishly, are called "cranks." He is a Y. M. C. A. worker who at present publishes in Springfield, Ill., a diminutive "War Bulletin," of which this book is a special number; and copies of this periodical, including the present volume, are given free to anyone who will, as he says, "write to me and confess that he reads poetry, who will try to read it through twice, who will send me a brief letter when he is done." He is something of an artist; after a fashion, a socialist; more certainly, a religious mystic; and for present purposes it must be added that he is indubitably a poet.

He has a cosmic scheme of his own, a key to some apparent absurdities in his verse. This, like all mystical systems, is too complex and elaborate for immediate explanation. But it may be said that, rejecting the fabric of civilization, he turns to a sacred poverty. "Let a few of us go," he says, "carrying neither purse nor scrip. Let us be healing the sick imaginations, cleansing the leprous minds, raising dead aspirations, casting out the devils of money-lust in those we meet by the way."

It is the joys and sorrows of this mission which he celebrates in most of the poems of the volume. Most impressive are those which tell of the ancient conflict between the love of the ideal purpose and the love of women. To them the wanderer says:

> Though I draw toward you weeping, soul to soul,
> I have a lonely goal beyond the moon.
> Aye, beyond heaven and hell, I have a goal.

And in "The Faces That Pass":

> I turn another way, that has neither tomorrow nor
>   yesterday, renouncing you all. . . .
> Because in my honorable and peculiar journey to a
>   place far from this place, maybe I shall find
>   the truth.
> I know I must travel alone.

In his verse there is also an amount of social idealism and democratic aspiration. Much of this is expressed through the medium of metaphor, as in "The Moon-Worms" and "The Soul of a Spider." But in another poem it comes out, free from obscurity and expressed with fine vigor and beauty. This poem is "The Building of Springfield." Three stanzas may perhaps give some idea of the throbbing, glowing idealism of the whole:

> We should build parks that students from afar
> Would choose to starve in, rather than go home—
> Fair little squares, with Phidian ornament—
> Food for the spirit, milk and honeycomb.
>
> Songs shall be sung by us in that good day—
> Songs we have written—blood within the rhyme
> Beating, as when Old England still was glad,
> The purple, rich Elizabethan time.
>
> Say, is my prophecy too fair and far?
> I only know, unless her faith be high,
> The soul of this our Nineveh is doomed,
> Our little Babylon will surely die.

The volume is embellished with some very curious designs, which are indeed more curious than artistic; and the book itself resembles in appearance a stenographer's note book: altogether a fascinating, unusual, but, it is to be hoped, not altogether a baffling product.

October 29, 1909

THE NEWEST FICTION

Martin Eden, by Jack London. [The Macmillan Company.]

Mr. Jack London is a writer who, more than any other now before the public, requires to be judged by his intentions. Worthy as have been some of his performances, they are not enough in themselves to explain the high reputation he has gained in not the least critical quarters. Against this reputation charges of crudeness, of sensationalism, will not successfully militate. Mr. Jack London is the inheritor of—as yet—unfulfilled renown.

Not to recognize the nobility of Mr. London's intentions is to fail to approach his work in the right spirit. At the risk of appearing to take too seriously a piece of the season's fiction, it may be said that "Martin Eden" is not to be profitably considered with reference to the season's fiction.

Bombastic as it may seem to say so, it is to be considered with reference to "Dr. Faustus" to "Richard III." For "Martin Eden," like each of these, is intended to display in poignant and memorable form the tragedy of ambition.

* * *

It was inevitable that Mr. London should write this tragedy. He has tried it before, in "The Sea Wolf," and made a botch of it; and one who reads the present novel with sympathy may yet feel it to be probable that he will try it again. There is a reason for the fascination which it may be imagined this theme exercises on him. It is not merely that he has—let us audaciously add, like Marlowe—a boyish taste for big and terrible things. But the theme of ambition is peculiarly apposite to his mind. For the modern aspect of ambition is egoism; and egoism, as expressed in Spencer and Nietzsche, is the negation of the democracy in which Mr. London believes. It is, then, as a sociologist as well as an artist that he is interested in the t agic career of the egoist.

* * *

Mr. London's first attempt was, as has been said, unsuccessful. His "Sea Wolf," a sealing captain of giant strength of body and brain, conscienceless, with anti-social instincts, indomitable will and ruthless brutality, made an imposing embodiment of egoistic principles. Too imposing, indeed; for when brought face to face with the cultured, kind-hearted gentleman who represented our altruistic civilization, he wholly overshadowed the latter. In the natural course of events there would have been no tragedy—at least not for the egoist. He would probably even have won the love of the woman for whom the two men were rivals, and lived happily ever after. But this was not at all to Mr. London's mind. He did not intend the giant to win. So a deus ex machina in the guise of apoplexy stepped in to shape the course of events aright. The altruist got the lady and the egoist died miserably.

That was pretty bad. Still, it showed the way to a better treatment of the theme. Mr. London evidently realized that his Nietzschean should be not a repulsive but an attractive figure. And so in this book he has made him, in the person of Martin Eden, a handsome, good-natured young fellow, with genius, hard muscles, a sense of beauty, a capacity for love, and—ambition. It is such a person of whom Mr. London seeks to make a tragic figure.

* * *

Martin Eden starts in the slums and fights his way through life. One fight with another young hooligan, described with poignant horror by the author, is typical.

> There was a loud snap, and Martin's right arm dropped to his side. It was a broken bone. Everybody heard it and knew; and Cheese-face knew, rushing like a tiger in on the other's extremity and raining blow on blow. . . . Martin punched on, with his left hand only, and as he punched, doggedly, only half-conscious, as from a remote distance he heard murmurs of fear in the gangs, and one who said with shaking voice: "This ain't a scrap, fellows. It's murder, an' we ought to stop it."
> But no one stopped it, and he was glad, punching on wearily and endlessly with his one arm, battering away at a bloody something before him that was not a face but a horror, an oscillating, hideous, gibbering, nameless thing that persisted before his wavering vision and would not go away. And he punched on, slower and slower, as the last shreds of vitality oozed from him, . . . until, in a dim way, he became aware that the nameless thing was sinking, slowly sinking down to the rough board planking of the bridge. And the next moment he was standing over it, staggering and swaying on shaky legs, clutching at the air for support, and saying in a voice he did not recognize:
> "D'ye want any more? Say, d'ye want any more?"

Such was the Martin Eden who, returning from a trip as a sailor, met—in one of the many ways possible in America—a beautiful and refined young woman of the middle classes, and straightway fell in love with her. It is at this point, which is the beginning of the book, that the story is most open to criticism. Mr. London does not draw successfully the manners of the bourgeoisie which he so heartily despises; the young woman and her mother are not altogether convincing figures. But since the book is no "novel of manners," this defect, striking as it is, may perhaps be overlooked. What the author requires us to believe is that Martin Eden falls in love with a very ordinary girl, and idealizes her after the fashion of all lovers; further, that the girl, or rather the ideal, awakens the genius that slumbers in this extraordinary young man. He reads and studies and writes. He decides that he will grow worthy of her; he will become a great writer and marry her.

A refined girl may succumb to the charm of a sailor, when he is handsome and intelligent; and this girl is represented as rashly engaging herself to Martin Eden. He studies prodigiously, devouring literature, mathematics and science, and practices at his trade of writing. He cooks in his own room, sleeping only three or four hours a night, and using up great stores of energy. He endures poverty, hunger, sickness. His ambitions are mocked by his relatives. He has temporarily to give up, and earn the money to go on with. The girl secretly disbelieves in him, and urges him to take a position as clerk in her father's office. But never for a moment does he falter, or doubt the achievement of his purpose.

* * *

When Martin Eden goes to the books he finds the philosophy of his life articulated for him by Spencer, and glowing in the cloudy fire of Nietzsche's prose-poetry. He is an individualist, and his career a triumphant exercise of the will-to-power. For he plows his way implacably through all hardships, overcomes all obstacles, goes steadily toward his goal. If people scorn him, he scorns them in turn as "slaves" over whose bodies he shall soon, like Tamburlaine, Ride in triumph through Persepolis.

This time Mr. London does not call on disease to stop his egoist. With a [sic] artistry that should go far to redeem any incidental crudities of the work, he makes the individual will-to-power run counter, not to other wills, but to one of the phenomena of that social psychology of which Nietzscheism takes such scornful account.

Martin Eden, the Nietzschean, attends a socialist meeting and in a speech attacks socialism as "ghetto ethics," "slave-morality," "the philosophy of the unfit." A cub reporter badly in need of copy is present, and writes a foolish story in which Martin Eden is described as preaching revolution. So by an ironical accident the mob is revenged upon him. He is reviled for opinions which he does not hold, and his name made a byword. The sensibilities of his fiancee's family are outraged, and the girl breaks the engagement.

Martin Eden's ideal collapses. It is not that the girl has ceased to love him, but that she never loved him: the girl he loved had never existed. His career is builded on falsehood. Something in him, the motivation of his life, has stopped.

* * *

Then success, bought and paid for with genius, long overdue, arrives at last. The mob reverses its decision and showers adulation upon him. He unloads his old work on the editors and the checks flow in. He is indifferent to it all. Even when the girl comes back and offers herself to him he does not care.

Only he is curious. Martin Eden, genius, went hungry. The same Martin Eden, successful and rich, is invited to dinners. Something more profound than a cynicism comes of this—the knowledge that the mob creates and alters values and that in the mob resides the power which is above power. The mob had taken away the girl he loved, and in mockery it offers her back. Vox populi, vox Dei. His own striving had been ineffectual.

In perfect physical health, with the world at his feet, Martin Eden, egoist, does not know what to do with life. Martin Eden, Nietzschean, is at a loss, tired out, baffled. His will-to-power suffers from fatty degeneration. The individual who lorded it over the crowd shrinks away from the sight of men. His anti-social instincts shut on his soul like a trap. He flees to Hawaii, but on the way realizes that he does not care to go there. Then a thing to do occurs to him. Even as Dr. Faustus let himself be dragged screaming down to hell by devils, as Richard III, warned by ghosts, went forth to the fatal battlefield, so Martin Eden finishes the egoist's career by slipping at midnight through the porthole and drowning silently.

The worth of the book? It is not the best thing the author has done: "The Call of the Wild" is that. But it is the biggest thing he has tried to do. It has faults not easily to be glossed over. But it is epic in its proportions. It is hard to say what its value is. But no one has a right to condemn it for its defects who has not seen the greatness in it.

November 12, 1909

RECENT BELLES-LETTRES

The Romantic Movement in English Poetry, by Arthur Symons. [E.P.Dutton & Co.]

Shelley, in his preface to "The Cenci," said: "I have avoided with great care, in writing this play, the introduction of what is commonly called mere poetry." Symons might have said: "I have carefully avoided, in writing this book, the introduction of what is commonly called mere brilliance."

For Mr. Symons to have succeeded in this is, one feels, itself a feat. For what is commonly called "mere brilliance" may be what Keats with finer discernment termed "isolated verisimilitudes caught from the penetralium of mystery." With these dazzling bits of inconsistent half-knowledge the work of this sheer impressionist has been filled. One has read him, not so much for the scholarship of which he always seemed capable, as for those other brave utterances, those rash interpretations of penumbral things.

* * *

But here is something altogether different—writing which seems addressed not to a partial few, but to the judicious many. His style, its flashing garment of surmise laid by, is revealed in naked muscular certainty. His speech is no longer of things which may be true, but of demonstrable facts. There is no partisanship, but a kind of passionate justice.

26

"The Romantic Movement in English Poetry" is a title likely to mislead. The book is not an essay, nor a series of essays. It is some eighty-odd separate critiques, chronologically arranged, of all the poets who were born before 1800 and survived into the nineteenth century. Good and bad alike, they are duly considered—in a dozen lines, or as many pages. The volume bears witness to years of labor: it embodies the solidest and most valuable kind of critical work. It is astonishing—as though a fay, captured and set to work at a desk, should prove a superior kind of bookkeeper; but it is more than astonishing, it is deeply satisfying. Its author, by virtue of this work, takes rank with the foremost English critics of literature.

Significant, perhaps, of its original quality is the fact that it takes no account of the opinions that have been spun like a mesh around these poets' work since their death. Save Robert Bridges and W. B. Yeats, no present-day writer is mentioned or quoted in the whole volume. The poets' days and verses, their letters and conversations, the criticism of contemporaries—from these materials alone are derived interpretations with a freshness that is as rare as it is welcome in the treatment of these familiar subjects. And along with this impression of freshness is given a sense of finality. Mr. Symons has the air of being at once the first and the last to write of them.

* * *

A new book of criticism must justify itself in our minds by offering us interpretations that are new; and yet the less orthodox the opinion the less we trust it. We should be interested to read of Wordsworth as a sensual egoist or Keats as a fiery radical intent on overturning society; but we would not call that criticism. Mr. Symons' conceptions of the great poets are not really new; if condensed here into a phrase the phrase would inevitably be a hackneyed one. And yet, read at length, they startle and fascinate. Two passages may perhaps convey this peculiar impression; of these one is about Shelley:

> Circumstances meant so little to him that he was unconscious of the cruelty of change to sentiment, and thus of the extent of his cruelty to women. He aimed at moral perfection, but was really of a perfect aesthetic selfishness.

The other passage refers to Keats:

> He was earthly in his love, as in the very essence of his imagination; passion was not less a disease to him than the disease of which he died, or the act of writing verse.

No other than Symons could have written these two passages. They

27

may—as when the present writer first saw them, two years ago—arouse passionate resentment; but they are—as he now believes—fully justified.

Of these eighty-odd critiques, even the shorter notices betray indubitably the hand of the skilled critic; they are adequate and precise. Of the longer ones, some, like the tributes to Hood and to Lamb, are labors of gratitude; others, like those in which he denies greatness to Southey and Scott, show in their reluctant harshness fire [sic] argumentative qualities. Still others are the pure gold of interpretation. There is a fine critique of Blake, distinguished by restraint and justice; one of Wordsworth, written with certitude and sympathy; a rarely intelligent one of Coleridge; one honest and convincing—where most writing is neither—on Landor; a splendidly discriminating one on Byron; with perhaps those on Shelley and Keats as the finest achievements of the book. The more all these critiques are compared with the work of the best modern critics the more sure appears their excellence.

* * *

And this in spite of the fact that they are written to exemplify an antiquated and it must be said a wholly mistaken theory. Mr. Symons represents a reaction against the methods of the literary historian. He has one test for poetry, that expressed in the words of Joubert: "Nothing is poetry that does not transport." He refuses to consider times or manners, adopting as the motto of his book the saying of Blake: "Ages are all equal. But genius is always above the age."

* * *

It is only fair to quote the words in which Mr. Symons states his position. In two paragraphs in his introduction he says:

> Critics or historians of poetry are generally concerned with everything but what is essential in it. They deal with poetry as if it were a fashion, finding merit in its historical significance, as we find interest in an early Victorian bonnet, not because it was beautiful, but because people once thought it genteel. But poetry is a reality, an essence, and is unchanged by any change in fashion; and it is the critic's business to find it where it is, to proclaim it for what it is, and to realize that no amount of historical significance or adaptability to a former fashion can make what is bad poetry in the present century good poetry in any century of the past.
>
> To distinguish poetry where it exists, to consider it in its essence, apart from the accidents of the age in which it came into being, to define its qualities in itself; that is the business of the true critic or student. And to do this he must cast aside all theories of evolution or the natural growth of genius, and remember that genius is always an exception, always something which would be a disease if it were not a divine gift. He must clear his mind of all limiting formulas, whether of *milieu*, *Weltschmerz* or mode. He

28

must disregard all schools or movements as other than convenient and interchangeable labels. He must seek, in short, only poetry, and he must seek poetry in the poet, and nowhere else.

* * *

When Mr. Symons speaks of the "Romantic Movement" he means merely the movement which brought poetry back into its own after what he considers the interregnum of the eighteenth century. Pope he considers an usurper, and his verse something other than poetry. Now it is a thankless task to defend Pope. But, in qualification of praise for Mr. Symons' book, one may perhaps be permitted to express a profound disbelief in all the critical postulates just quoted; to assert that if there be an infallible touchstone for poetry it has not yet been found, and if there is one thing certain about poetry it is that it does have its fashions. The Elizabethan drama was a fashion, the metaphysical mode of Donne was a fashion, the Popian satire was a fashion. Mr. Symons likes the first two and dislikes the last; so do most of us. But that mystery which we so lightly name "taste" has not yet been fathomed and will not be fathomed the sooner for his dogmatizing on the subject.

At all events Taine's methods have come to stay; if Taine applied them clumsily, if Professor Courthope applies them frigidly, the remedy is not rejection, but more intelligent and artistic application. It is vain to cry out against them. Mr. Symons is the champion of a cause hopelessly lost. One could almost mourn the futility of his enthusiasm, but—one has only to read his book to be content that it should be written on a mistaken theory. It has effected its miracle.

* * *

But, one may ask, what are the drawbacks? They are the defects of the book's quality. Mr. Symons has written, better than Professor Courthope could ever write, of poetry in itself. Professor Courthope has written of poetry in its relations. And since it is in its relations that a thing principally exists, for our minds, since it is only in its relations that it can conveniently be apprehended, Mr. Symons has not done us a service of the broadest value. It is his own belief that poetry is not an intellectual but a spiritual entity; that it is not addressed to the dull brain that perplexes and retards, nor is understood so much as felt. However, if one is not content with appreciating poetry, but desires to think about it as well, the less inspired work of Professor Courthope gives that assistance of which "The Romantic Movement" is incapable.

This may or may not appear a great objection. One may prefer to look on poetry as it shines by its own light, or as it is illuminated by exterior facts. But whether one feels that lack of alloy is a fault or a supreme virtue, one is constrained to believe that this work magnificently justifies its existence.

November 12, 1909

RECENT BELLES-LETTRES

Journals of Ralph Waldo Emerson, With Annotations. Edited by Edward Waldo Emerson and Waldo Emerson Forbes. Vols. 1 and 2, 1820-1832. [Houghton Mifflin Company.]

"Take your pen, therefore, and give me the secret history of the sanctuary you call yourself; what new lights illuminate, what fragrant affections perfume it; what litanies are sung; what works are daily done in its industrious recesses, and to what good it is consecrated": These lines, which occur in a letter to a brother, are an expression of Ralph Waldo Emerson's own purpose in keeping these journals, now for the first time exhibited to the public. And it is this alone, the secret history of a sanctuary, that they reveal.

The two volumes now issued deal subjectively with twelve of the most interesting, because formative, years of the poet-philosopher's life. In the time from his seventeenth to his twenty-ninth year Emerson produced no part of his great work, either in prose or verse. He attended college, taught, became a minister, parted from his church; he married and saw his wife laid in her grave. All the while his powers were maturing for an event beyond these happy or tragic accidents. It was a time—to use his own figure—of "eggs, embryos and seminal principles."

* * *

An interest of a different and more general nature will belong to the journals yet to be published, in which will be told the story of friendships among the Transcendentalists and abroad, of life during the great national crisis, of literary and poetic achievement. But in the present extracts from boyish "Wide Worlds" and imitation "Spectators," and the score of successive notebooks kept by teacher and preacher, one may have what will seem to many the rare pleasure of watching a youth with a great future before him "nursing his solitary faculties into self-existence, and making his thoughts and actions his own."

In this word "solitary" is to be found the clew to the peculiar greatness of Emerson. His genius was born of solitude, and he was even ready to acknowledge her his mistress in terms of rhapsodic praise. His journals tell of few walks and talks, but of a thousand solitary hours. He "conversed with truths that had always been spoken in the world, and became conscious of a closer sympathy with Zeno and Arrian than with persons in the house."

* * *

The boy schoolmaster (he was only 18) has given us a picture of the boy student: "I was then delighted with my recent honors, traversing my chambers flushed and proud of a poet's fancies, and the day when they were to be exhibited; pleased with ambitious prospects, and careless because ignorant of the future." It is this flushed poet whom the earliest journals show us: a youth neglecting his Greek and mathematics for Montaigne, Plutarch and Bacon, cultivating at the expense of all other emotions that one which comes from the intense exercise of the intellect, and already forming the basis of his marvelous style. In his seventeenth year he reads "patches of Barrow and Ben Jonson merely because they are authors whose vigorous phrases and quaint, peculiar words may be sought and found, the better 'to rattle out the battle of my thoughts.'"

* * *

It was to be long before actual contact with the world had sifted and proved his book lore and pulpit experience had put into his tone the note of authority which speaks so directly, peremtorily [sic], winningly to our hearts. But it is not so long before the sentences in which he states his immature generalizations begin to take on that bold apothegmatic manner which the astonishing wisdom of his maturity was to justify. And on almost every page one sees, crudely struck out, such ideas as he was to fix in enduring splendor upon his page.

A paragraph of unpromising notes, commencing with "Write on personal independence"—here is the seed from which "Self-Reliance" grew. "Ever since I was a boy," begins a famous essay, "I have wished to write on compensation." Here are the boy's thoughts, to be compared with the man's. The theme recurs again and again; and when in one place he exclaims triumphantly, "Is not the law of compensation perfect?" he answers himself with, "Well, well, old man, hast got no farther? Why, this was taught thee months and years ago."

So one follows the growth of Emerson's interest in biology, in

Swedenborgianism, in German literature, in the oriental classics. We read his comments on Carlyle's article in the Athenaeum: he wonders who their author may be.

Harder to trace is the course of his religious development. He early shocks his aunt by heretical opinion on the subject of the Holy Ghost. As a theological student, he admires Gibbon and Hume for their power of compelling thought, "maugre the skepticism and abominable sneers." As a preacher, .he observes quietly, "I suppose it is not wise, not being natural, to belong to any religious party." It is not, however, until the crisis of his career has come, that he speaks out. He has told his congregation of his repugnance for the communion rite, and proposed a modification; and he is in the mountains awaiting their answer. His journal says:

> Cold, cold. Thermometer says temperate. Yet
> a week of moral excitement. . .
> I have sometimes thought that, in order to be a
> good minister, it was necessary to leave the ministry.
> The profession is antiquated. In an altered age, we
> worship in the dead forms of our forefathers. Were
> not a Socratic paganism better than an effete,
> superannuated Christianity?

* * *

The second volume at least is pervaded by the flavor of authentic Emerson—calmly heretical, vividly inspiring. Among the sentences that demand quotation are these:

> Smother no dictate of your soul, but indulge it.
> No man gains credit for his cowardly courtesies.
> Never so lowly but we remember that we are tenants
> of infinite spaces and survivors of the sun and the stars.
> It is a luxury to be understood.
> Nature notches the edge of the petal and hurls
> the globe in orbits.
> To believe too much is dangerous, because it is the
> near neighbor of unbelief.
> The way for us to be wise is to foresee the great
> tendencies and currents of the universe in the leanings
> and motions of the little straws which our eyes can see.
> We live among eggs, embryos and seminal principles, and
> the wisest is the most prophetic eye.
> Poetry, wise women have said, hath a noble
> inutility, and is loved, as the flowers of the field,
> because not the necessaries, but the luxuries of
> life. . . .
> To be genuine. Goethe, they say, was wholly so.
> The difficulty increases with the gifts of the

individual. A plowboy can be, but a minister, an orator, an ingenious thinker, how hardly!

The world is an academy to the scholar, a butt to the satirist, a church to the devotee, "the scaffold of the divine vengeance" to the Calvinist, good society to the fashionist, a market to the merchant, a conquest to Alexander.

Instead of the old verse, "Speak, that I may know thee," I write, "Speak, that I may suspect thee; write, that I may know thee."

That society is best and unobjectionable which does not violate your solitude, but permits you to communicate the very same train of thought.

* * *

A few jests, some grim and others gay, attract attention by their rarity. "Why," asked Emerson himself, "has my motley diary no jokes?" He answered: "Because it is a soliloquy, and every man is grave alone." He must have written the following in an excetpional [sic] mood.

Burnap was very witty tonight. He said there was one man who had the queerest reputation—Dr. Watts—such a mixture of heathenism and scholastic learning and Calvinism and love and despair and mullygrubs—he was the funniest old cock in the theological walk; that that old Betty should be one of the three legs that support the Trinity, and that the church should go chanting his hymns for centuries, mistaking the effusions of belly-ache for the inspirations of David—was the greatest phenomenon. . . .

"Ah, me," said the mourner to me, "how natural he looked when they had put on his dickey."

The record of Emerson's emotions, in so far as it is to be accepted as faithful, presents a curious difference between his appreciations of love and of friendship. The difference is the same as that apparent in his two essays "Love" and "Friendship." Emerson valued loves only as they exhibited love; but he valued friendships for their own sake.

* * *

Certainly one may discount the exaggeration when he writes thus the history of his heart: "A blank, my lord. I have not the kind affections of a pigeon. Ungenerous and selfish, cautious and cold, I yet wish to be romantic." And again, "When shall I kindle? I was born cold. My bodily habit is cold. I shiver in and out." Yet there is sincere self-revelation in a letter written from the South to a favorite aunt:

> I shall not deny that there are some who take
> such a strong hold of my attention that I am fain to
> quit my stoic fun and fairly go out of my circle and
> shake hands and converse with them. Now I know, my kind
> aunt, with all her electrical imagination, will
> think I am talking of women. Alack-a-day! it surely
> is not so. Woe is me! with all the chivalry that is
> in my soul, backed by all the muse, I pass in cold
> selfishness away from Maine to Florida and tremble
> lest I be destined for a monk. No, I was speaking
> of men....

Friendship was a theme which stirred him. At college, seeming to discern the beginning of friendship, he wishes he could recall at a future period the singular sensations produced at this. Later, writing on friendship, he exclaims: "In God's name, what is in this topic? It encourages, exhilarates, inspires me."

But the first mention in his journals (at least the first as printed here) of the girl who became his wife is the statement, for once severely objective: "I have now been four days engaged to Ellen Louisa Tucker." And it was not until the happiness of first love that he broke through his reticence and forced himself to speak of it. Then he wrote:

> There is that which passes away and never returns.
> This miserable apathy, I know, may wear off. I almost
> fear when it will. Old duties will present themselves
> with no more repulsive face. I shall go again among
> my friends with a tranquil countenance. Again I shall
> be amused, I shall stoop to little hopes and little
> fears and forget the graveyard. . . . Shall I ever
> again be able to connect the face of outward nature,
> the mists of the morn, the star of eve, the flowers,
> the poetry, with the heart and life of an enchanting
> friend? No. There is one birth, and one baptism,
> and one first love, and the affections cannot keep
> their youth any more than men.

These two volumes of Emerson's journals arouse the appetite for more, they stimulate the interest in what it is to be hoped will soon follow. In themselves, since they reveal but little of his life, contain but little of ordinary biographical interest, they are of most value to those having a special interest in Emerson's work. But none can fail to recognize how much this opportunity of self-expression meant to the ungrown philosopher, and how important it really was in the making of an original American.

January 7, 1910

RECENT VERSE

The Poems of Oscar Wilde. Authorized Edition. [John W. Luce & Co., Boston.]

Poems, by Oscar Wilde. With Biographical Introduction by Temple Scott. [Brentano's.]

Two new editions of Wilde's poems attest their author's growing fame. Of these editions both are nominally complete, with uncollected verse, fragments and translations; but the authorized edition contains two hitherto unpublished poems, "Pan" and "Desespoir." Besides which the authorized edition has the better paper, while the other misprints "Wild Flowers" for "Wind Flowers" and omits the dedication of the "Ballad of Reading Gaol." Both editions will do service in representing the poet to a public which is perhaps now ready to accord to his work due appreciation.

"I think," wrote Keats, "that after my death I shall be among the English poets." Wilde, in the bitterest moments of his life, can hardly have doubted that this must be true of himself. His poetic product, as collected in these editions, appears to justify such a belief. There may be aesthetic reasons for rejecting Wilde's work; but with due respect to those who have advanced such reasons it must be submitted that they have not proved their case. To reject Wilde's poetic gifts as negligible is, it would seem, to betray a moral prejudice that in the ten years elapsed since the poet's death should have been cleared up. It ought not to be necessary at this time to insist that in regard to Wilde's verse it is unprofitable and indeed inexcusable to "go behind the returns." Here is a book of beautiful poetry; if it must also be said, of unobjectionable poetry; even, by any legitimate aesthetic standard, of wholesome poetry.

Of the work in this volume part aligns itself unmistakably with the loftiest ethical utterances in English poesy; but perhaps more characteristic is that part which is best termed "unmoral," being concerned almost solely

35

with the poet's feelings in the presence of a world of overpowering loveliness—a succession of cries of joy that pass at times insensibly into cries of pain. It is impossible, one would think, to come to these poems with an open and appreciative mind without being affected deeply by the acuteness with which the poet felt this loveliness and the passion with which he translated it into words.

The poet, as revealed by these poems, was in love with the beauty of earth. He could not speak of the commonplace wonders of day and night without betraying the intensity of his passion, without infecting his verse with the same delicious poison which corroded his nerves. Standing to Keats frankly in the relation of pupil to master, he was imbued with a sense of the loveliness of the world hardly less poignant. The one began a poem with an ecstatic chronicle of things of beauty that are joys forever, "the sun, the moon, trees old and young . . . daffodils, with the green world they live in." The other indulged with sensuous luxuriousness in the same succession of images:

> White lilies in whose cups the gold bees dream,
> The fallen snow of petals where the breeze
> Scatters the chestnut blossom, or the gleam
> Of boyish limbs in water. . . .
> The heron passes homeward to the mere,
> The blue mist creeps among the shivering trees,
> Gold world by world the silent stars appear
>
> And like a blossom blown before the breeze
> A white moon drifts across the shimmering sky. . . .

These myriad lovelinesses of earth composed a ritual which the poet chanted in poem after poem—"The Garden of Eros," "The Burden of Itys," "Charmides," "Panthea," "Humanitad." His emotions became pantheistic, and found expression in strophes such as these:

> We are resolved into the supreme air,
> We are made one with all we touch and see,
> With our heart's blood each crimson sun is fair,
> With our young lives each spring-impassioned tree
> Flames into green. . . .
>
> With beat of systole and of diastole
> One grand great life throbs through earth's giant heart,
> And mighty waves of single Being roll
> From nerveless germ to man, for we are part
> Of every rock and bird and beast and hill. . . .

In Wilde's poems the love passion is a secondary matter. His treatment of it hardly requires comment, save to say that it has none of the conventional Tennysonian reticences. Like Keats, who wrote of love as a "sick longing," a "malady," a "passion both meek and wild," and who described the swoonings and tremblings and "quick sighs vex'd and panting" of his lovers, Wilde described love in its ordinary physical aspects. Yet "Charmides" is by no means so voluptuous as Shakespeare's "Venus and Adonis," or Marlowe's "Hero and Leander." To curb any sentimental inclination to call Wilde's occasional erotics "unmanly" or "exotic," it should be sufficient to keep in mind these two great poems.

* * *

All of this, however, is but one division of Wilde's poetry; another part is of a character so different as to address itself almost to a different audience—at least to a different set of emotions. The change is not merely one from idealistic sensuousness to sensuous idealism; there is in "Eleutheria" and "Rosa Mystica" a distinct and added beauty, the beauty of moral purpose. It is this which gives so commanding a note to the sonnets beginning, "Milton, I think thy spirit hath passed away," and "There was a time in Europe long ago." Another sonnet seems to have every quality which makes for greatness save one, the sonority which is the fitting vesture of nobility; "Easter Day," it is called:

> The silver trumpets rang across the Dome:
>   The people knelt upon the ground with awe:
>   And borne upon the necks of men I saw,
> Like some great God, the Holy Lord of Rome.
> Priestlike, he wore a robe more white than foam,
>   And, kinglike, swathed himself in royal red,
>   Three crowns of gold rose high upon his head:
> In splendor and in light the Pope passed home.
> My heart stole back across wide wastes of years
>   To One who wandered by a lonely sea
>   And sought in vain for any place of rest:
> "Foxes have holes, and every bird its nest,
>   I, only I, must wander warily,
>   And bruise my feet, and drink wine salt with tears."

But the poet's idealism has its highest expression in the magnificent poem, "Ave Imperatrix," with its poignant questionings:

> What profit now that we have bound
> The whole round world in nets of gold,

If hidden in our heart is found
The care that groweth never old?

* * *

Of the other two divisions of Wilde's poetry, one consists of his supreme poetic effort, the one poem in which he fully justified his genius— "The Ballad of Reading Gaol." This poem has established the poet's fame even among those who find his other work too unconscionably derivative. It must be admitted that this somber and intense work is the only boldly original poem he every wrote. It towers over the rest of his product as "The Rime of the Ancient Mariner" over almost everything else of Coleridge. It is the culmination of that youthful quickening of the moral sympathies which he had later deliberately suppressed in favor of his aesthetic sensibilities—a hundredfold more powerful in its renaissance. A profound revelation of pain, it purges the soul with pity and terror and perhaps more than any other modern poem acquaints us with the true significance of the tragic.

* * *

On this great poem comment, necessarily inadequate, is probably superfluous. But of the last division of Wilde's poetry, that in which his inspiration has been found most attenuated: surely it is an unprofitable taste which cannot take pleasure in the fine decorative quality of the verses even the most devoid of thought. Here is a picture, artificial as a satin slipper, and yet strangely "natural."

Under the rose tree's dancing shade
    There stands a little ivory girl,
    Pulling the leaves of pink and pearl
With pale green nails of polished jade.

The red leaves fall upon the mold,
    The white leaves flutter, one by one,
    Down to a blue bowl, where the sun,
Like a great dragon, writhes in gold.

The white leaves float upon the air,
    The red leaves flutter idly down,
    Some fall upon her yellow gown,
And some upon her raven hair. . . .

Formal and fragile at once, like the crystal of a snowflake, this possesses a singular charm. It is the work of a man who knows the secrets of beauty so well he is half contemptuous of them; but it is not mere words, it is a disclosure of the beauty of the actual world. And Wilde's verse, informed as it is in every line with this loyalty to earth, has something in it which makes it too precious not to be treasured.

January 28, 1910

RECENT BIOGRAPHY

Karl Marx: His Life and Work, by John Spargo. [B.W. Huebsch.]

That this should be the first biography of Karl Marx in any language is in itself a little startling. Marx has been dead twenty-seven years, and the modern socialist movement which he founded is quite the most important political phenomenon in the world today: in its extensive literature there are books and books devoted to the exegesis and popularization, the criticism and defense, of Marx's ideas; but, save for a small volume of rather trivial and (as Mr. Spargo shows) somewhat inaccurate "Memoirs" by his friend Wilhelm Liebknecht, there has been no account of his life. In the encyclopedias one finds a minimum of concisely stated facts and dates, and not all of them correct; as to the personality of the man, there are but the vaguest hints generally available. Among his own followers he has largely attained the semidivine and wholly impersonal authority which attaches to the Bible and the dictionary.

It is an opportunity over which a biographer well might gloat. He does not need to furbish up old stories to make them entertaining, or to present us with a new view of his hero; all he tells us is news. Mr. Spargo relates his story very simply, with no attempt at brilliancy or profundity; he picks and chooses among his available materials; he takes a very kindly attitude toward his subject, without idolizing him: for all these reasons he makes a most agreeable biographer—not the final one, for he leaves that place to some erudite and exhaustive German. His book is as readable a biography as one may come across nowadays.

*　*　*

Karl Marx means, to those of us who have occasion to know about him, a great intellect; he was that, truly enough, but one learns from Mr. Spargo that he was a poet, too. It is refreshing to know of him, wasting him (sic) time, at Bonn and the University of Berlin, in every kind of activity but the study of law, which was what he was there for; disappointing an ambitious father and a fond mother by his escapades, his debts, his wild

39

moods; writing poems and plays, planning novels, then burning everything up; overworking at outside studies and probing into metaphysics until he breaks down in health; having a romantic love affair with the daughter of an aristocratic German official, and going nearly distracted over that—a quite human person, this, and a fascinating personality.

His father, a talented Jewish lawyer who had renounced Judaism through entirely worthy motives when Karl was a child, did not know what to make of the lad. His patience completely exhausted, at last he wrote to him in this fashion: "Complete disorder, silly wandering through all branches of science, silly brooding at the burning oil lamp; turned wild in your coat of learning and unkempt hair; and in your wildness you see with four eyes—a horrible setback and disregard for everything decent." He was probably ill at the time he wrote this exasperated comment; a few months later he was dead, the well-loved parent who was one of Karl Marx's three saints—the other two his mother and the girl, Jenny von Westphalen, who became his wife.

At the University of Berlin, Marx made friends with the "Young Hegelians," and gained the affection and respect of such celebrated men on the faculty as Bruno Bauer and Karl Friedrich Koppen. While at Berlin Marx fell under the influence of Ludwig Feuerbach's ideas, which are regarded as forming the connecting link between Hegelianism and Marx's own materialistic philosophy. He planned an academic career at Bonn, but the radical set at the universities gained the disfavor of the government and a policy of repression was inaugrated (sic) which made this impossible. So the young doctor, who had gained his degree with an original thesis on the Epicurean philosophy, turned to political journalism.

Of the Rhenische Zeitung, a new radical daily, he became first contributor, and then editor. The various papers which Marx edited throughout his lifetime had always a remarkable list of contributors, and that, of this earliest venture included Bauer, Koppen, Max Stirner, Moses Hess and George Herwegh, the poet. Already Marx showed an interest in socialism, which then existed in the forms of St. Simonism and Fourierism—utopian aspirations which waited the transforming impress of his realistic hand.

* * *

When the paper was suppressed—Marx's papers were always being suppressed—he went to Paris with his bride, being then 25 years old, and joined a group which included Heine, Bakunin, Proudhon and Cabet. Heine was a close friend, and used to discuss his poems with Marx, one of them, his "Deutschland," being first published in the Vorwaerts.

In Paris Marx also met a young man, Friedrich Engels, who was to be his life-long friend. Engels was the son of a wealthy English manufacturer, had made a study of industrial conditions in England, and, like Marx, had formulated the idea that the working class must organize politically for the overthrow of captalism (sic). The two men at once planned a book, the first of a number they wrote in collaboration. Different in temperament and gifts, these friends were no less different in appearance; they are thus described by Mr. Spargo:

"Marx was rather tall and stout; Engels a little taller, but thin; Marx was so dark that his friends nicknamed him 'Negro'; Engels was a pronounced blonde.

* * *

Marx's head, with its cloud of black or graying hair and beard, is rather well known; some see in the expression of the mouth a characteristic half-sneer, which well accords with his faculty of satire and savage sarcasm. Carl Schurz, who was a little prejudiced against him, leaves a picture of him in debate which is probably not greatly unjust: "Marx's utterances were indeed full of meaning, logical and clear, but I have never seen a man whose bearing was so provoking and intolerable. Everyone who contradicted him he treated with abject contempt; every argument that he did not like he answered either with biting scorn at the unfathomable ignorance that had prompted it or with opprobrious aspersions upon the motives of him who had advanced it. I remember most distinctly the cutting disdain with which he pronounced the word 'bourgeois'; and as a 'bourgeois'—that is, as a detestable example of the deepest mental and moral degeneracy—he denounced everyone that dared to oppose his opinion."

On the other hand, Marx was the gentlest of friends and could be the most patient of teachers. When some one once marveled he replied: "When you have been impatient as long as I have you will not marvel at my patience, Comrade."

* * *

In Paris Marx edited a short-lived radical yearbook, and then the Vorwaerts. When the latter was suppressed and its contributors ordered expelled he went to Brussels. There was a six weeks' visit to England with Engels, in which he read the English economic writings—"gorged himself," said Engels, "with the passion of an insatiable glutton."

The kind of life they lived in Brussels was very significant. It was a preparation for a great future. They organized a German workingmen's club, edited a radical weekly; Marx studied and taught classes of workingmen in political economy and corresponded with the radical leaders of Europe. He and Engels were already planning the political organization of the working class.

"Capital," his great work, was still to be written. But one finds the phase upon which he was now entering more interesting and even more important. Another might have elaborated his theory of surplus value, or at a pinch the Socialist movement could have got on without it. Engels could have set forth the more vital theory of historical materialism. But what Engels could not do, what it seemed it needed a man of Marx's iron will to effect, was the rescuing of the Socialist movement from the bogs of utopianism into which apparently it was hopelessly sunk.

* * *

This was not to be done by writing books on economic theory; it was done, actually, by fighting the utopians one by one and destroying their influence. It was essential that Socialists should stop planning violent insurrections on the one hand and ideal commonwealths across the sea on the other. And when Marx came on the scene practically every leader of power was imbued with one of the two notions. Here was no time for sentimentality about comradeship; it was a matter for fighting out.

The first fight was with Wilhelm Weitling, a single-hearted agitator, in the German Workingmen's Club, a type of the struggles later with Kinkel and Willich in the Communist Alliance and with Bakunin in the International.

The Communist League was formed in London in 1847 as a first step to bring about the political organization of the proletariat. The secrecy and mystery of its parent organization, the International Alliance, were dropped. Hardly had this been effected, however, when Etienne Cabet appeared with his Icarian utopia, and that movement had to be fought if the political movement was not to be sidetracked.

At the second congress of the Communist League was read a program which was practically a first draft of the famous Communist Manifesto; and that epochal document itself was promulgated in 1848, when its authors, Marx and Engels, were respectively 30 and 28 years of age and when a new revolution was breaking out in France. Soon after its publication Marx was arrested and ordered deported.

* * *

Going to Paris, he found himself compelled to fight his old friend Herwegh, who had conceived the romantic notion of organizing a "German legion" in France with which to "carry the Revolution to the Fatherland." It was another friendship sacrificed to the cause, and it was not the last. In Cologne, where he edited the Neue Rhenische Zeitung and where his friendship with Lassalle began, he participated in the revolutionary movement side by side with Willich and Kinkel; but after the failure of the uprisings, the suppression of his paper, his trial for treason and his removal, first to Paris

42

and then to London, he found himself plunged into a bitter struggle with these erstwhile comrades, who were now seeking to turn the movement back into its old ways of conspiratory action. He was at this time in dire poverty, and has been described as "a man who appeared to be haunted; a big, haggard, hopeless-looking man, who seemed to forget his misery only in the intensity of his struggle within the ranks of the Communists." Marx was challenged to a duel, and though he refused to fight, his young friend Schramm barely missed death in an exchange of pistol shots with Willich.

Bakunin, the great apostle-anarchist, he always suspected, and even went so far as to commit what his biographer frankly terms a cowardly action in order to destroy his influence; he spread a report which he knew to be untrue, that Bakunin was a Russian spy. His instinct was right even though his methods were dishonorable, for Bakunin was a secret foe of the International, and that organization had finally to be shattered by Marx and his friends to prevent the anarchist getting control. Hertzen, a friend of Bakunin, was also made a bitter enemy. No wonder, however unjust the idea, that Marx should acquire a reputation for being quarrelsome. Indeed, it is quite plain that he dominated the movement and when he could not dominate he domineered. It is largely owing to the sheer strength of this one man that the movement was kept in the paths in which alone it could achieve success.

In London, where Marx ransacked the British Museum for statistics and wrote "Capital," the family experienced poverty in some of its cruelest phrases (sic): the furniture one winter being attached for rent and the ailing mother and children threatened with being turned out of doors. Marx had for a long time as his only steady income a small salary as correspondent for the New York Tribune. Meanwhile his domestic life was an idyl, and at the lowest ebb of their fortunes he and his wife, who continued to be devoted lovers, would walk up and down the room, hand in hand, singing some cheery song of old times.

He was a devoted father, and very fond of all children, earning the title "Daddy Marx" from those of the neighborhood. His biographer alludes to "the almost Puritanical austerity of his domestic life. No old-time New England Puritan ever guarded the moral atmosphere of his home with greater watchfulness. . . . No ribald song or jest, no 'broad' discussion of topics customarily tabooed was tolerated." In a life that was a mixture of hard literary work and domesticity that as circumstances improved became very pleasant, he continued for the thirty-four years of his life in London.

* * *

The great achievement of his London career, aside from the publication of the first volume of "Capital," was the founding of the International Workingmen's Association in 1864. The story of this organization, which during its life was accused of being responsible for every disorder from a molders' strike in Germany to the Chicago fire, finally came to an end after the Commune, the apocryphal horrors of which were too much for it to shoulder; after the struggle with Bakunin the headquarters were removed to this country, and in 1876 eleven men met in Philadelphia and formally dissolved the organization that had been the terror of every European government.

Marx took an active interests in all international politics, and was, through the trades unions, instrumental in changing the current of British favor from the South to the North in our great civil war. He remained closely in touch with the international socialist movement, and his advice was sought on all occasions by the leaders. Sometimes, as in the case of the union of the German socialist parties in 1875, it was bad and was not taken; and the old man, masterful to the last, was furious.

* * *

Marx's health, undermined by poverty and especially by too much smoking of bad cigars, gave way in his latter years, and when he died he left unfinished the second and third volumes of "Capital"—later completed at the hands of his friend Engels. His wife died in 1881, and two years later, March 15, 1883, Marx died, aged 65 years. He had lived to see his teachings as to tactics carried out in the organization of permanent and more or less powerful proletarian political parties all over the world, and his economic analyses recognized as the most serious indictment of capitalism which it had even been compelled to answer.

There are, accompanying Mr. Spargo's vivid rendering of this story, some forty photographs of the chief persons and places described; these and the letter-press are admirable, but the paper and the binding combine to give the book an unduly cheap appearance, which in the case of such a work one is bound to resent. The volume is one of some 350 large pages, adequate without being exhausting, the kind of work which the intelligent but busy reader will find time to read, as well as one which none who is interested in the socialist movement can afford to neglect.

July 15, 1910

44

RECENT BELLES-LETTRES

Provenca: Poems Selected from Personae, Exultations and Canzoniere of Ezra Pound. [Small, Maynard & Co.]

Though Mr. Pound is an American, he has already received his critical accolade in England. One may have noted, among the very impressive praises that the poet has received in the English press, an occasional note of bewilderment. And a reader, though he have no intention of challenging these praises, may find the bewilderment altogether pardonable. For Mr. Pound is a very new kind of poet. Thinking of the art exhibition just held in London, one might, for want of a better figure, call him a Neo-Impressionist poet. Like the Neo-Impressionist painters, like the Impressionists in their day, Mr. Pound is open to misunderstanding, and even to ridicule. People are saying that one of the Neo-Impressionist pictures was secured by tying a paint brush to a donkey's tail and backing the animal up to the canvas. A jocose little story like that might be invented to explain one of Mr. Pound's poems.

* * *

But though these poems have often an unconventional form, bizarre phraseology, catalectic or involved sentence structure and recondite meanings, yet it is always apparent that the poet knows what he is doing.This sense—the sense that effects which are beyond one's immediate power of comprehension have been exquisitely designed and exactly carried out—is at the base of the pleasure afforded by all art of a high order. It is enough for people of taste to have this feeling (so much more chastened than the patronizing enjoyment they are wont to take in beauty of an accidental sort), to realize that they are in the presence of good art. In this spirit it is that so many critics have given Mr. Pound's work the stamp of their approval, even while admitting that they have not discovered the standards to which it conforms. And it is in their spirit that one more reviewer introduces it to the public.

It may be complained that this is a confession of critical shortcoming. It is hardly less, indeed. Yet one may be somewhat expert in artistic criticism, and fail to understand Whistler when he first appears. One may sincerely admire Moret, [sic] and yet be entirely unable to explain to a skeptic why haystacks should be painted lavender. And one may have acquired, in regard to poetry, that critical vocabulary and manner which add conviction to an otherwise bald and uninteresting confession of admiration—and yet not be able to bring it to bear on Ezra Pound.

* * *

The only thing which can justify Ezra Pound is Ezra Pound. Indeed, one regrets having stood so long with vague and vain explanatory gestures before such a poem as the one which begins thus:

> Bah! I have sung women in three cities,
> But it is all the same;
> And I will sing of the sun.
>
> Lips, words, and you snare them.
> Dreams, words, and they are as jewels.
> Strange spells of old deity,
> Ravens, nights, allurement:
> And they are not;
> Having become the souls of song.
> Eyes, dreams, lips, and the night goes. . . .

And in this "Night Litany" there is a style so lofty, an emotion so limpid, an appeal so direct that it would require a daring or an obtuse mind to pronounce the use of the foreign phrase an affectation or the peculiar arrangement of the lines a vagary:

> O Dieu, purifiez nos coeurs!
>   Purifiez nos coeurs!
> Yea, the lines hast thou laid unto me
>   in pleasant places,
> And the beauty of this thy Venice
>   has thou shown unto me
> Until is its loveliness become unto me
>   a thing of tears.
>
> O God, what great kindness
>   have we done in times past
>   and forgotten it,
> That thou givest this wonder unto us,
>   O God of Waters? . . .

* * *

But no presentation of this poet would be just which did not include a suggestion of the tremendous, the shocking vigor of which he is capable. One stanza will be enough—a stanza from the poem in which there speaks one Bertrans de Born. In a little note at the head of the poem Mr. Pound says: "Dante Alighieri put this man in hell for that he was a stirrer up of strife. Eccovi! Judge ye! Have I dug him up again?" The first stanza of the sestina:

Damn it all! all this our South stinks peace. You whoreson dog, Papiols,
come! Let's to music! I have no life save when the swords clash. But, ah!
when I see the standards, gold, vair, purple, opposing, And the broad fields
beneath them turn crimson, Then howl I my heart nigh mad with rejoicing.

The poet gives expression to the spirit which makes possible such
a poem, in another entitled "Revolt Against the Crepuscular Spirit in Modern
Poetry." It begins:

> I would shake off the lethargy of this our time, and give
> For shadows—shapes of power,
> For dreams men.

And it ends:

> High God, if men are grown but pale, sick phantoms
> That must live only in these mists and tempered lights
> And tremble for dim hours that knock o'er loud
> Or tread too violent in passing them;
> Great God, if these thy sons are grown such thin ephemera,
> I bid Thee grapple chaos and beget
> Some new Titanic spawn to pile the hills and stir
> This earth again.

* * *

Much more might be quoted to show the poet in his moods of
tenderness. And one might regret that this volume of selections does not
include a stirring ballad entitled "The Goodly Fere," which is at the same
time a remarkable reworking of the vein of the Christ-mythus (to use a
convenient term with entire respect) in the fashion of Browning's "Epistle
of Karshish."

That there is in these poems an indebtedness to Browning, also to
Walt Whitman, and perhaps to Henley, as well as to the Provencal poetry
from which the poet's inspiration is so largely derived—these things are
obvious enough. It is a matter of keen regret that something more truly
illuminating cannot be said. But, if the extracts from poems do not at once
settle the matter, the word of the reviewer must be given for what it may be
found to be worth. Ezra Pound is a true poet; his singing has distinctive
spiritual and stylistic qualities which command the most respectful attention;
and to those who approach his work in some humility of spirit it is capable
of giving a deep aesthetic satisfaction.

January 6, 1911

EUGENE FIELD

The Poems of Eugene Field. Complete edition. With portrait. [Charles Scribner's Sons.]

Eugene Field has already been canonized in the nursery. But what one is to think of Saint Eugene's secular poetry, his profane and irreverent newspaper verse, must be another matter. So much this new edition, complete in a single volume, is bound to suggest.

But a reading, or rather a rereading, of this verse gives one confidence. One is tempted to assert that this other verse is better, in its jigging vein, than even dulcet lullabys such as this:

O listen, little Dear-My-Soul,
  To the fairy voices calling,
For the moon is high in the misty sky
  And the honey dew is falling.

Where is the ground for such a preference? Certainly newspaper verse the most clever, rhyming the most facile, are not sufficient. But, as a matter of fact, Field was not surpassingly clever or facile. But in this very newspaper verse one does come unmistakably upon gleams and flashes of a certain rare and intimate spirit—the spirit which manifested itself so wonderfully in some of the Roman lyrists, which we find abundantly in Herrick, in Burns, in Landor: A spirit so fine as to require to be cherished wherever it appears, and valued at its height.

The poets who have this spirit, in making use of autobiographical material, so to speak, do not, like others, transform it into something rich and strange, but render it with a naive and charming literalness. They take the world into their confidence, not about a rapture or an agony, but about some delightful trifle.

* * *

That is why, one feels, the poetry of Field, his newspaper verse, is more certainly enduring metal than that over which some of his contemporaries sweat blood. There is something permanently fascinating in the way he tells the world about his friendships, calling his friends by name and describing the home where he loves to loaf and invite his soul. He relates with infinite gusto his adventures as a book and print and curio collector—recording that he saw some splendid bargains when he was broke in London in the fall of '89, or that in New Orleans one day he "blew in" $20 by 9 o'clock a.m. And his books: what a delightful flavor there is in his talk about bindings and first editions! It is the authentic reality in these things that makes them something more than "fugitive verse."

In smaller matters, too, the same charm persists. The ballad of the washing of the Taylor pup is better than a comic poem; it and "The Delectable Ballad of the Waller Lot" show that unaffected interest in neighborhood affairs which is the source of some of the happiest effects possible in this kind of poetry.

The secret of its charm is the personality which it reveals. At once sophisticated and ingenuous, it extracts a subtle and peculiar interest from memories alike of fashionable London and of old "St. Jo." It turns from blissful reminiscences of midnight suppers with soubrettes to devout little prayers and hymns without a trace of self-consciousness. In all these things there is a spontaneity, a quaint gayety, a tender melancholy, a gentleness of soul, which make it impossible not to become fond of the man who wrote them. Eugene Field lives, a friend and good companion, in all his poems.

Most likeable of all, to some readers, will seem a group of poems of quite different character—the "Echoes From a Sabine Farm." For all their admixture of modernity, these vivacious paraphrases are more successful than any academic translation in giving an impression of the spirit of the Roman poet. Could anything better suggest in English the cheerful Latin heartlessness of Horace:

> Chloris, my friend, I pray you your misconduct to forswear;
> The wife of poor old Ibycus should have more savoir faire.
> A woman at your time of life and drawing near death's door
> Should not play with the girly girls and think she's en
> rapport . . .
>
> 'Tis more becoming, madame, in a creature old and poor,
> To sit and spin than to engage in an affaire d'amour.
> The lutes, the roses and the wine drained deep are not for you;
> Remember what the poet says: "Ce monde est plein de fous."

And, among the pleasanter passages, is this "Invitation to Maecenas":

> Dear, noble friend! a virgin cask
>   Of wine solicits your attention;
> And roses fair, to deck your hair,
>   And things too numerous to mention.
> So tear yourself awhile away
>   From urban turmoil, pride and splendor,
> And deign to share what humble fare
>   And sumptuous fellowship I tender.
> The sweet content retirement brings
> Smooths out the ruffled front of kings.

But he who does not find himself in sympathy with the artifice of these poems is only the more sure to enjoy the simple and open-hearted lays and lyrics written in such a mood as this:

> Little All-Aloney's feet
> Pitter-patter in the hall.
> And his mother runs to meet
> And to kiss her toddling sweet,
> Ere perchance he fall.

Verses superficially like these are published by the thousands every year. They are almost a public nuisance in their affectation, their false sentiment, their utter banality. But one is surely not mistaken in saying that Field's child poems are real poetry, distinguishable in a moment from all such trash by their accent of perfect sincerity. They represent the abandon of a gentle, child-like, child-loving heart, and they have an honorable place in our American literature.

January 13, 1911

AROUND THE WORLD

Anarchism and Other Essays, by Emma Goldman. With a biographic sketch by Hippolyte Havel. [Mother Earth Publishing Association, 210 East 13th St., New York.]

The case of Emma Goldman is an interesting one to a student of modern tendencies in thought. Those who will read critically this volume will find it rather difficult to understand why she should stand to Americans generally as the apotheosis of a sinister danger to civilization. The fact seems to be that the Emma Goldman of the popular imagination does not exist: she is a creation of romantic policemen and reporters. It is true that there have existed dynamic personalities, such as Joan of Arc and Louise Michel, whose voice, whose very presence, has been a menace to the institutions that they opposed: women who could intoxicate men with a high fury, and lead them on to the commission of violent deeds. But nothing seems clearer to the critical observer than that Emma Goldman is not such a woman.

* * *

The real Emma Goldman, as revealed in these writings, is a mild-mannered, earnest woman of the well-known reform type, who is interested in the spread of some very respectable individualistic ideas. There are, it is true, now and then flashes of resentment against the authoritarian methods of the modern state; but you cannot subject the gentlest lady to the stupid police brutalities of which Miss Goldman has been a victim without securing that reaction. Many people besides Anarchists have such feelings; even the orthodox Mr. Chesterton has confessed to moments in which he desires to kill a policeman. But in the main Miss Goldman's utterances are of the sort which may be constantly matched in fashionable pulpits. She urges a theory of the self-sufficiency of the individual to which any number of well-bred and harmless people can easily subscribe.

In the present collection of twelve essays there is one—the last—which dominates all the others in interest; it is on "The Drama: A Powerful Disseminator of Radical Thought." Like most modern readers, Miss Goldman is more interested in the content than in the form of literature; but it is surprising to note how largely literary her interests appear. One suspects that a glance at Miss Goldman's library would show it to be devoted almost exclusively to belles-lettres! One would not wantonly deprive a fellow creature of her robe of martyrdom, but it seems fairly unmistakable that Miss Goldman has missed her vocation; she should have been a popular extension lecturer at one of our up-to-date universities.

* * *

The initial essay of the book is on "Anarchism: What It Really Stands For." The most radical phrases, in this as in the other essays, are quoted from such revolutionary gentlemen as Emerson and Thoreau. She concludes: "Anarchism, the great leaven of thought, is today permeating every phase of human endeavor. Science, art, literature, the drama, the effort for economic betterment—in fact, every individual and social opposition to the existing disorder of things—is illumined by the spiritual light of Anarchism. It is the philosophy of the sovereignty of the individual. It is the theory of social harmony. It is the great, surging, living truth that is reconstructing the world and that will usher in the Dawn." How plain type does give one away! Miss Goldman's alleged inflaming oratory simmers down, in fact, to an optimistic declaration of a belief in the reality of Progress. A City Club pamphlet on housing conditions would be a more incendiary document.

* * *

In "The Psychology of Political Violence" Miss Goldman stoutly maintains that acts of violence are not in conformity with Anarchist teachings. She goes on, however, to express for various political criminals something of that admiration which our school children are taught to give to

51

William Tell, the assassin of Gessler, and John Brown, the bloody desperado of Harper's Ferry.

The other essays in the book are amiable and mediocre expressions of a liberalism in part enlightened and in part already discredited by modern thought. They are upon such subjects as "Minorities versus Majorities," "Prisons: A Social Crime and Failure," "Patriotism: A Menace to Liberty," "Francisco Ferrer and the Modern School," "The Hypocrisy of and [sic-missing line] "Marriage and Love." In "Woman Suffrage" Miss Goldman achieves a distinctly conservative effect by saying that women are getting along all right without the vote!

The volume is prefaced with a spirited biographical sketch by Hippolyte Havel.

February 17, 1911

PROMETHEUS BOUND

The Life of Friedrich Nietzsche, by Daniel Halevy. Translated by J. M. Hone. Introduction by T. M. Kettle, M. P. [The Macmillan Company.]

M. Halevy has achieved the feat of writing soberly and sensibly of Nietzsche. It has been done before, but not often enough to stale the flavor. M. Halevy is neither "for" nor "against." He writes biography as a skillful modern novelist writes fiction, with a discreet detachment.

T. M. Kettle, M. P., who contributes a pyrotechnic sketch of Nietzsche, by way of introduction to this translation, says that "it exhibits him as better than his gospel." From a Christian point of view, perhaps. For, as some readers may be surprised to learn, Nietzsche was in his personal life one of the gentlest of men. He was also an ardent disciple, and a magnificent friend. A poet, an inspired teacher, a stimulating penseur (the English word is too degraded for use), his personality exercises, through the medium of this biography, something of the fascination which Taine and Brandes and a daring few permitted themselves to feel during his lifetime.

If it were for nothing else than the rigor with which this sick and lonely man forced his thoughts into the paths of beauty and strength and joy, his personality would have for us a kind of lofty charm. But the tragic aspect of his career makes it even more impressive. Nietzsche stands to us as a prophet who had endured the terrible austerities of the desert and the mountain peaks, to bring us back a gospel of laughter.

52

                              *   *   *

It is significant that the man who was to invent the grandiose
Superman myth, by which the aristocracy of Europe might be inspired to
rebuild the world, was himself under the influence of a cognate fiction.
Friedrich Nietzsche was of proletarian origin, but he believed devoutly that
he was the descendant of Polish nobles. Born in a German village in 1844,
he quickly exhibited the qualities which were to dominate his whole
life—poetic, philosophic and musical. He was nurtured in Christianity, to
which he said he owed the best experiences of his spiritual life. One must
take that statement seriously. It means that he had the temperament of the
saint, the astonishing combination of egoism and altruism which belongs to
the martyr. He did not come eating and drinking; he hated beer and tobacco.
His joys were chiefly those of the solitary.

But he was not a recluse. There are delightful stories here of the long
walks he would take with some equally youthful fellow-philosopher, and of
the heaven-storming discussions in which they would engage. Nietzsche had
discovered Schopenhauer at the age of 22, and had experienced a tremendous
disillusionment. But he was not saddened, he was invigorated, by his draught
of Truth. The prevailing impression of this period—and it is the key to his
whole life—is one of superabundant spirits, and a dauntless spiritual courage.

In the midst of an unevenly brilliant scholastic career, he was drafted
into the artillery. He became known as the best rider among thirty recruits;
but one day as he was pondering some philosophic problem he fell off his
horse and hurt his side, being thus delivered back to the academic life. He
desired a glorious vacation in Paris, with absinthe, philosophy and the can-
can alternating, but the offer of a chair at Basle, Switzerland, took him
straight there. One reason was that he had just begun an enthusiastic
friendship with Richard Wagner, and the Master lived at Triebschen, near
Basle.

                              *   *   *

It was as a defender of Wagnerian music that Nietzsche made his first
entrance into literature. But "The Birth of Tragedy" signified more than that.
It was the young professor of philology uttering his first defiance to the
pedantic scholarship of Germany. He exalted the primitive religious
enthusiasms at the expense of "reason." In this book was earliest expressed,
under the Dionysian formula, that new mystical evaluation of the positive
qualities of life—joy, strength, beauty—of which his whole philosophy is a
various and perturbing elaboration.

The Wagner-Nietzsche friendship is an example of one great force

                                53

attempting to absorb another, and of the other resisting, until with a great rending both are torn forever apart. It was necessary to his salvation that Nietzsche withdraw himself from the obliterating influence of Wagner, and he accomplished it gently and sadly. In his later years Nietzsche came to regard Wagner as a symbol of all that he opposed, and one of his last books was a savage attack on the musician's memory. But the whole episode is of minor importance.

Nietzsche's philosophic ideas were ripened by his experiences during the Franco-Prussian war. Regarding war at first as a dangerous obstacle to intellectual and artistic progress, he was surprised to find himself being drawn into the patriotic mood of his nation. As he could not fight, being now a Swiss citizen, he joined the hospital service and nursed the wounded. From his patients he caught diphtheria and dysentery, and came home with his health shattered. But he also brought home the conviction that war was a necessity in the ideal state—a philosopher's own reaction. Out of war, he said, flower the positive virtues. It was simply the Dionysian theory taken from art into politics.

The further development of his ideas involved the grand conception of the Superman; the invention of a hierarchy of classes, on the model of the Greek slave-based state; the formulation of the ideal characters of the man and the woman of the future; the analysis of Christianity as a consolatory religion suitable to the slave class; and finally the working out of the ethic of the master class.

A favorite doctrine, the relation of which to his main ideas, it is hard to see, is the Eternal Return. It was probably a piece of deliberate and gratuitous stoicism. For not long after the war Nietzsche's health broke down permanently, his sight and digestion both failing him. Plunged in miseries often the most intense, he did not permit himself the "decadent" feelings of pessimism. He lied gloriously, declaring to the last that life was good. It was a "Non dolet" surpassing that of the Roman woman he admired for him to say: "I shall live this life of exquisite pain over a thousand times, and again and again, forever!"

The rest of Nietzsche's life was that of an invalid, subsisting on a small pension from the university, going about from one Mediterranean resort to another. At first surprised and pained at the hostility or indifference with which his books were received, he grew later to expect this, but never ceased to plan great new works in which future generations would recognize his genius. His periods of weakness left him no strength to work up his notes, and, as he had a deep affinity for the epigrammatic style of writing, he published them in that form, the one perhaps best calculated to produce upon the German public an impression of unintelligibility. It was not that he wrote carelessly; he wielded the most marvelous style of any German writer, and he usually succeeded in his effort to imprison in it "some joyous spirits."

He made friends and gained disciples—one of them a Russian girl—

but his demands upon their friendship were usually too great for their magnanimity, and he lost them one by one. He was compelled to publish his books at his own expense, out of the savings of his meager pension. Always he fought terrible battles with pain and depression—and, after a fashion, won.

"The enormous tension of the intellect, bent on the mystery of pain," he wrote, "shows everything in a new light: and the unspeakable charm of every new light is often powerful enough to overcome all the allurements of suicide. . . . Our pride revolts as it never did before: joyfully does it defend life against such a tyrant as pain, that tyrant that would force us to testify against life. To stand for life in the face of this tyrant is a task of infinite fascination."

It is this quality that makes Nietzsche a fit representative of the modern age, just as the martyr who went joyously to the stake was a type of the middle ages. He is a symbolic personage, a heroic witness to Life, the great Yes-sayer.

* * *

And this very quality widens the significance of Nietzsche's philosophy. Superficially, it is an appeal limited to a circle of aristocratic minds. Actually it rouses and thrills live men everywhere. For what Nietzsche calls the aristocratic virtues are in fact the human virtues. What is to prevent the democrat, the socialist, from sacking this Nietzschian kingdom, and carrying away its treasures to commonwealths of their own?

In fact, many revolutionary minds today acknowledge Nietzsche as their source of their deepest inspiration. They have found that the ideals of power, pride, beauty, joy and communion of free spirits are more operative with them than the ideals of humility, chastity, self-sacrifice and that comradeship which is merely the bedfellowship of misery. They have turned from Christianity to Nietzschianity for the motive force of revolution.

One hesitates, after communing with these splendid conceptions, to return to the sick prophet. Enough that fame came at last, but too late. His mind had already begun to weaken. In 1890 he was taken to a hospital, hopelessly mad, the man who had done some of the profoundest thinking of modern times and had written Germany's finest prose. He died ten years later.

M. Halevy has not set for himself the task of fixing the place of Nietzsche's philosophy in nineteenth century thought. But he has dealt adequately with the man. He has interpreted simply and yet with an accent of grandeur a free and unconquerable spirit.

February 24, 1911

THE BOOK OF THE WEEK

BERNARD SHAW

The Doctor's Dilemma, Getting Married, and the Shewing-Up of Blanco Posnet, by Bernard Shaw. [Brentano's.]

It is thirteen years since the publication of "Plays Pleasant and Unpleasant" gave American readers a new sensation. In those thirteen years Bernard Shaw has produced six of the most impressive examples of contemporary drama; he has written a dozen brilliant and significant prefaces; he has made speeches, submitted to interviews innumerable, and become an international figure. And in all that time a certain proportion of our fellow countrymen have been unaffected by this dynamic presence; they have stood beside Niagara and been unmoved. Without reading Shaw they have disliked him, or have read him without appreciating him. Well! it is too late to do anything for them now. They must swelter in their stupidity. The time has come to criticise: at the risk of giving aid and comfort to the enemy, Shaw must be discussed with reference to his defects rather than to his virtues.

This is all the easier, since in this new volume of plays his virtues are not too much in evidence. "The Doctor's Dilemma" is a farcical satire on the medical profession. "Getting Married" is a clever conversation. "The Shewing-Up of Blanco Posnet" is a pious melodrama. There is here little of the realism of "Widower's Houses," the tenderness of "Candida," the splendor of "Caesar and Cleopatra," or the sheer incisive intellectual power of "Major Barbara." There is verbal wit in plenty; vivid characterization;and an impressive earnestness. But one thing these plays disastrously lack—the spiritual quality which calls forth the reader's sympathy. Without doing violence to anti-vivisectionist principles, on [sic] may dissect them at will.

* * *

"The Doctor's Dilemma" would seem from its title to be a presentation of the very interesting problem which occasionally confronts a physician—whether to kill a patient or cure him. In its simple and most essentially dramatic form, the problem would be this: Has a doctor the right to kill a man who would be, for various reasons, better dead? But Mr. Shaw has complicated the problem by making the man in the case not merely a scoundrel but a scoundrel of genius. He has then modified it by making it necessary for the doctor to choose between saving an old friend and saving the scoundrel. Finally, he has made the doctor fall in love with the scoundrel's wife. By this time it is questionable if a problem exists. Certainly the doctor and his dilemma are pushed into the background, first by discussions in which the absurdity of medical science is self-exposed, and then by the fascinating villainies of the scoundrel of genius. The most interesting thing in the play is the latter's wholly irrelevant death scene in the fourth act. Mr. Shaw calls the play a tragedy—referring perhaps to the fact that the scoundrel's widow marries, not the doctor after all, but another man.

Just as the point at issue is clouded in this play, so is it clouded in "Getting Married." The way to present the problem which arises when people revolt against legal marriage is, obviously enough, to show them dispensing, having dispensed, or about to dispense, with the marriage ceremony. The real factors which enter into the problem are the attitude of society and the reactions of the daring couple to that attitude. The situation has been handled many times, but its materials for treatment are inexhaustible. Mr. Shaw, however, does not attempt to deal with such a situation. Instead, we have this:

Two young people are to be married. The girl's father is an Anglican bishop who—of course—writes anonymous pamphlets attacking legal marriage. The prospective bride and groom do not appear. They are—of course—reading the anonymous pamphlets. When they do appear, they have decided not to get married. Whereupon they sit down at the bishop's suggestion to write out a "marriage contract," after the old Roman style. Several wedding guests take advantage of the opportunity to attempt to rearrange their relations, pursuant to a divorce. But after wrangling for half an hour they find they cannot decide to whom the children shall "belong," and whether the bedroom windows shall be open or shut. So the young people go off and get married anyway, and the wedding guests relapse into their accustomed relationships.

*   *   *

As a mere piece of entertainment, this has some good light comedy to commend it. But as a serious presentation of the modern marriage problem it is frivolous and impertinent. It is possibly the most evasive bit of writing every produced on the subject. For example: One of the wedding guests, colluding with his wife to secure a divorce, has knocked her down in the garden—after digging up the place to make it soft—and gone off chastely to a hotel with a painted woman. Does Mr. Shaw find too distasteful the situation in which a man knocks his wife down and goes off with another woman in earnest?

"The Shewing-Up of Blanco Posnet" deals with an American horse thief, who risks capture and hanging to save a sick child, by turning over the stolen horse to the child's mother. "This little play," it is stated in the preface, "is really a religious tract in dramatic form." It is better than that. It is the most direct and dramatic play in the book. Unfortunately for its interest, however, it represents, not a clash of one human will with another, but the clash of a human will with the divine. There occurs on the stage one "conversion" after another—one submission after another of arrogant, blasphemous men and women to an influence they do not understand that makes for righteousness. It is a real dramatization of "religious experience." But at the same time it seems to indicate the shortcomings of such a theme in drama of this kind. One is rather less edified by the play than might have been expected. And the American reader will be more amused than impressed by the atmosphere and dialogue, as an attempt to envisage our pioneer West.

* * *

But what is it about these plays that makes the devout admirer of Shaw rise from his chair, kick the cat and walk uneasily about the room? What is it that makes him shake his head and say to himself: "No; it won't do!" For these plays are "brilliant"; they are "thought-provoking"; they are all that he has tagged those wonderful plays in the earlier volumes; and yet they are wanting.

If the troubled admirer is rash, he takes down and re-reads one of those wonderful earlier plays; and it is better, but—it, too, is wanting. And so he extends his inquiry. It is no longer merely: What is the matter with these plays? But—

What is the matter with Shaw?

The fact is, we admirers of Bernard Shaw will not have it that he is other than a great man. We think of the creative power which out of the void wrought Candida, Vivie Warren, Ann, Undershaft. We think of the tremendous intellect which has struck out more new ideas than any other man's living. We feel that he ought to make this age one to rival the Elizabethan in great drama. And then we look at his confession: "I am a specialist in immoral and heretical plays." Yes, it is true. Bernard Shaw is only a great specialist.

Why not a great dramatist? One hesitates to give the answer, because it has been said so often that it constitutes a cheap fling. "He does not deal with life."

Well, it is essentially true. Mr. Shaw has never been content with the ordinary dramatic materials. He has persistently sought after exceptional and "odd" types of people for characters. He has created the most bizarre situations. And he has tried to transvalue the old dramatic values. Thus he puts a new meaning into Ambition in "Caesar and Cleopatra," and into Love in "Man and Superman." But are these new meanings true? Was ever any man ambitious in the Shavian fashion? Caesar might have been. And did ever any woman love in the Shavian fashion? Out of our profound knowledge of womankind, let us answer unhesitatingly: No.

The unreality of the eugenic heroine is best shown by the more definite and less vivacious picture of her drawn by Shaw's disciple, Granville

Barker. The girl in "The Marrying of Ann Leete" breaks with her middle-aged and wealthy fiance to marry a healthy gardener; but when they are in their cottage after the wedding, and he wants, not unnaturally, to kiss her, she objects. "We're not to play such games of love," she says. "Think of me—not as a wife—but as the mother of your children." Is anyone deceived for a moment into thinking that this girl exists? In a play of Shaw's, the lovers would have been so busy making epigrams that one wouldn't have noticed whether they kissed or not. But here is the eugenic fiction in its nakedness: and what does it signify as to its original inventor?

It appears to signify that Shaw is, as he calls himself, a Puritan. He gives many indications of being really unable to see the beauty and the importance of sexual love in human life. And a man incapable of appreciating the feelings of ordinary people in so prime a relation as that of sexual love is incapable of writing first-rate drama. And that raises the question of the value of the ideas to propagate which these plays were written. If a drama of marriage that omits the motif of love is artistically worthless, what is the preface worth intellectually that omits the factor of love from discussion?

Mr. Shaw does not precisely omit it. In his 31,000-word preface to "Getting Married" he devotes precisely nineteen lines to it. Some of these lines are worth quoting. Mr. Shaw has just made the point that marriage needs legal regulation, since "society without law, whether between two or two million persons, means tyranny and slavery." He continues:

> If the incorrigible sentimentalists here raise
> their little pipe of "Not if they love one another," I
> tell them, with such patience as is possible, that if
> they had ever had five minutes' experience of love
> they would know that love is itself a tyranny requiring
> special safeguards; that people will perpetrate "for
> the sake of those they love" exactions and submissions
> that they would never dream of proposing to or suffering
> from those they dislike or regard with indifference;
> that healthy marriages are partnerships of companionable
> and affectionate friendship; that cases of chronic
> lifelong love, whether sentimental or sensual, ought to
> be sent to the doctor if not to the executioner. . . .

* * *

This passage is not merely, as a whole, silly; it is significant in its silliness. It means that Mr. Shaw has completely missed the meaning of the great modern movement that has to do with love and marriage. He is in precisely the position of a nineteenth century biologist who would, after the publication of Darwin's book on natural selection, continue to set forth brilliantly his peculiar view on species. The philosophy of James Hinton, of Ellen Key, of Havelock Ellis occupies a similar place in modern sociology, and it is a philosophy in which love is accorded a profound importance. For Shaw to act the one-horse philosopher and cynic and stand apart gibing is to exhibit the serious limitations of his intellect.

However! Here is Shaw and we must take him for what he is—if not as a first-rate playwright or first-rate thinker, then (if a quondam admirer of Shaw can muster up the requisite impudence) as a harmless old fellow with a charming vein of comedy. Mr. Shaw, the author of polite farces and delightful fantasies—it sounds like a false paradox, but it is perhaps a true one. For Shaw's plays, with their "witty dialogue and lively incident," belong in the same honorable category with those of Congreve and Sheridan. "We admire his brilliant dialogue and repartee," some Chambers of the future will say, "and the exuberance of dramatic incident and character; but the total absence of some of the higher sentiments which ennoble life leaves his pages comparatively barren and unproductive of any permanent interest or popularity. His glittering artificial life possesses but few charms for lovers of nature."

On the other hand, some Charles Lamb of the next century may possibly say something like this in his defense: "We have all been spoiled with . . . the exclusive and all-devouring drama of common life. . . . It is altogether a speculative scene of things [in Shaw's plays], which has no reference whatever to the world that is. . . . I am the gayer at least for it."

* * *

In his high fantastic vein (the critic will point out generously), Shaw can achieve "touches of truest pathos." Note the trance speech of Mrs. George in that quaint comedy of "Getting Married":

> When you loved me I gave you the whole sun and
> stars to play with. I gave you eternity in a single
> moment, strength of the mountains in one clasp of
> your arms, and the volume of all the seas in one
> impulse of your souls [sic]. A moment only; but
> was it not enough? I paid the price without
> bargaining: I bore the children without
> flinching: was that a reason for heaping fresh
> burdens on me? I carried the child in my arms:
> must I carry the father, too? When I opened
> the gates of paradise, were you blind? was it
> nothing to you? when all the stars sang in your
> ears and all the winds swept you into the heart of
> heaven, were you deaf? were you dull? was I no
> more to you than a bone to a dog? Was it not
> enough? We spent eternity together; and you ask
> me for a little lifetime more.

And now the dying speech of the scoundrelly artist in "The Doctor's Dilemma":

I know that in an accidental sort of way,
struggling through the unreal part of life, I haven't
always been able to live up to my ideal. But in my
own real world I have never done anything wrong, never
denied my faith, never been untrue to myself. I've
been threatened and blackmailed and insulted and
starved. But I've played the game. I've fought the
good fight. And now it's all over, there's an
indescribable peace. [He feebly folds his hands and
utters his creed.] I believe in Michael Angelo,
Velasquez and Rembrandt; in the might of design, the
mystery of color, the redemption of all things by
Beauty everlasting, and the message of Art that has
made these hands blessed. Amen! Amen! [He closes
his eyes and lies still.]

And so the critic's own valedictory to the plays of Shaw: I have done it. It was hard work. And now it's over, there's an indescribable peace. I believe in Saint-Beauve, and Walter Pater; in the might of analysis, the mystery of judgment, and the redemption of all things by Sincerity everlasting. Amen. Amen.

April 28, 1911

THE BOOK OF THE WEEK
LOVE AND ART

Love's Pilgrimage, A Novel, by Upton Sinclair. [Mitchell Kennerley.]

Upton Sinclair is not an ordinary American author. From the beginning of his literary career he has shown himself to be different—and with a difference not necessarily in his favor. His peculiar interests, methods and personality have been apt to arouse in the public mind suspicions and prejudices. And, indeed, they are rather confirmed than otherwise by this book. Nevertheless it must be stated as a definite conviction that Mr. Sinclair has proved himself to be one of the most vital novelists which this country has produced; and that this book, with all its defects, is one of the most significant of contemporary American novels. It takes rank with Frank Norris' "The Octopus"; with Mr. Howells' under-appreciated study, "April Hopes"; with Mrs. Wharton's "House of Mirth"; with Theodore Dreiser's obscure masterpiece, "Sister Carrie"; and with Robert Herrick's "Together."

"Love's Pilgrimage" is the exposition of a personality. It is a personality easy to dislike, and the method of the exposition is open to severe criticism. But that exposition subserves truth and, less directly, literary art, in such a way as to be beyond the reach of personal distaste and aesthetic cavil alike. It has, in extending the boundaries of our fiction, in taking serious and dignified account of hitherto unexplored regions of life, rendered an authentic service to literature. It challenges the interest of all readers who take literature thoughtfully. It is a book that not only will be read, but deserves to be read.

* * *

The theme is love and marriage: not, however, the typical love and marriage of modern times, which has been so well dealt with by various novelists and dramatists, but a rarer and more poignant experience, seldom touched upon in fiction—that of the artist, or as Mr. Sinclair prefers to call him, the man of genius. This experience is related with a vividness and an intimacy which bring it within the range of popular interest, and give it the broadest emotional appeal.

There is an obvious circumstance in regard to this experience which has no critical significance whatever; but it might better be stated plainly than hinted at or (with seeming studiousness) ignored: the fact that the thing is biographically as well as artistically true; that Mr. Sinclair himself is the subject of this extraordinary study.

Nominally the hero is a young man of weak physique and strong will, who is called by his nickname, Thyrsis; a poet and prose writer to whom the power to create comes only in overwhelming gusts of inspiration, and who is termed by the author a man of genius. One may figure him perhaps as a young Keats, an adolescent Poe, gestating within his soul unique splendors that should dazzle men forever. To this youth, companioned in his solitude by visions, comes a girl. Superficially she is beautiful; but the boy is steeled against beauty. It is no naive romance which develops. The girl has the soul of one of Turgenev's heroines—strong, couragous, [sic] asking only an object worthy its high devotion. Or, at least, so it appears to the youth. So they enter upon a compact: they will "lose themselves, and all thought of themselves, in a common love for something higher"; they will seek this together, and be content with the joy of finding it.

"I take thee, Thyrsis," says the girl, "to be the companion of my soul. I give myself to thee freely, for the sake of love, and I will stay so long as thy soul is better with me than without. But if ever this should cease to be,

I will leave thee; for if my soul is weaker than thine, I have no right to be thy mate."

* * *

An ideal compact, with the odor of tragedy in it even while it is breathed. It might have turned out that he was unworthy of that perfect trust; or that he had been utterly deceived in her. But the real situation to blossom out of this bud is to be understood from these two passages in an exchange of letters. From Thyrsis: "The promise of marriage that I make you is just this: not that I love you—I do not love you; but what I wish the woman to be whom I am to love—that I will make you!" From the girl: "You, you friend, waked me up. . . . Know, you that have a soul which says it lives and suffers—that I can't go to sleep again! . . . If you do not marry me, or if I do not find some man who has your strength and desire for life, and who will take me and help me learn, I shall die without having lived."

Did any youth ever succeed in the task which so many, sublimely confident, set for themselves, of remolding a woman to the heart's desire? Did any woman ever find a man who did not tire too soon of holding the goblet of life to her avid lips? If any, they found scope for their separate egoisms in the ample spaces of luxury; they were not pushed into mutual conflict by poverty.

It is to guard against the most disastrous exigencies of poverty that these two young people adopt a remarkable plan. They have been forced into marriage by the practical impossibility of otherwise continuing their companionship; but they will go on living "like brother and sister." Of course the plan fails after a time; what is surprising is that it is described as for a while succeeding.

The account of the way in which the plan came to be abandoned reveals in the hero depths beneath depths of naivete. But in the consequences of that abandonment, in the problems attendant on an undesired pregnancy, the book touches the issues of common life, and achieves some of its most notable effects in verisimilitude.

In the midst of this poverty, harassed by worries and debts, the young man tries to go on with his work. He finds that perpetual companionship is not so conducive as solitude, after all, to his task of wrestling with visions. He finds that a wife, after all, is a human being, making inescapable demands upon his time and energy. He is confronted with the responsibility which conventionally attaches to a married man, of getting a position; but this he sincerely feels will be fatal to his artistic life. So he struggles desperately along, doing cheap hackwork for the papers; living in a boarding-house, in a tent, in a cabin; going short of food and wearing tattered clothing; nursing a sick wife and taking care of a fretful child—and always, in the intervals, seeking to shape his visions into books and plays. The books are not pub-

63

lished, or fall into the hands of unscrupulous publishers, or do not sell; and all devices for relief, including shameless begging letters to rich men, fail of effect, and he is left "mashed in the stew-pot of domesticity."

At the outset of their troubles the poor youth prays "a prayer without theology or metaphysics—a prayer to the unknown gods." It is "that they might have courage to keep up the fight, that they might be able to hold their love before them, that nothing might ever dim their vision of each other"—a prayer that each one of us, too, prays secretly. But it was only in rare hours that they held the vision. "At such hours he beheld Corydon [the girl] as she was, the flaming spirit, the archangel prisoned in the flesh." But at other times they got on each other's nerves, and quarreled, and hated each other.

In the end—if a book which concludes with the promise of another volume can be said to have an end—the man, long since convinced that his genius had been decoyed by nature into a trap, the trap of sex, turns in a wild anxiety, which masks itself as renunciation, and offers to give up this woman whom he cannot make happy to a man who can. But he fails; and even while he rejoices there is something in him that "sinks back and moans."

* * *

Such is the story. It is here set down not merely without much indication of the emotional power of the original, but without any indication of what it is that really gives the book rank and importance—the sense that here, for the first time in American literature, is a sincere attempt to get the whole of a human life into focus, to render it all faithfully in terms of fictional art.

The main difficulty, of course, is in dealing with the sexual phase of life. Mr. Sinclair has simply disregarded the American conventions. "Love's Pilgrimage" is the frankest novel ever written in America. But it is at the same time one of the most pure-minded books ever written anywhere. Of salacity there is not a trace—though a dash of it might have been welcome, as making the book more human. Something will be said below in criticism of the author's style; but there is no gaucherie in the treatment of sex—it is here that the language is most simple and delicate. And if the author misses some of the beauty of his theme, he will hardly be reproached by the Puritans for that. He has attempted a noble task, and he has, on the whole, achieved a deeply inspiriting success.

But this account, on the other hand, has omitted so far to note those spiritual and stylistic elements which, in the reading, annoy at almost every turn. Not to indicate the sources of this annoyance would be to give a partial impression of the book.

Mr. Sinclair believes in genius. He believes that his hero has genius. "More and more frequently there was coming to him this strange ecstasy, the source of which he could not guess; it was like the giving way of floodgates within him—the pouring in of a tide of wonder and joy. It made him tremble like a leaf, it made him cry aloud and fall down upon the ground exhausted.'' The possession of this kind of nervous system is, according to the theory, the mark of a special faculty which separates one from all the rest of mankind. When one has genius, one should guard it from the corrosive contact of the world; and in order to preserve it in its integrity, one should undergo all manner of sacrifices, and make one's wife undergo them, too. That is the theory upon which this story is founded.

Of course, it is nonsense. Instead of there being a distinct cleavage between what we call the man of genius and the ordinary man, there are infinite gradations of creative ability between the lowest type of intellect, say the Bushman's and Shakespeare's own. But the pragmatical argument is sufficient to adduce. Most people have personal knowledge of the mischievous effects of the genius theory. It works harm in both directions. The young poet who is under its influence is discouraged because he does not have fits, and the natural efflorescence of his soul is checked. On the other hand, the man who has fits and regards their literary result as a divine thing which revision would profane, is shut off from the possibility of first-rate writing.

* * *

Mr. Sinclair's hero illustrates this. Despite all his talk about inspiration, what he actually produces in verse, if one may judge from several pages of excerpts, is a rather trashy sort of juvenilia; while even the books which Mr. Sinclair appears to concur with his hero in thinking "great," do not, as described at length, impress.

Mr. Sinclair himself illustrates the point. His writing is precisely the kind one would expect from a man who believes in "the divine afflatus." Here are the opening sentences of this volume:

> It was the highway of Lost Men.
> They shivered, and drew their shoulders together as they walked, for it was night, and a cold, sleety rain was falling. The lights from saloons and pawnshops fell upon their faces—faces haggard and gaunt with misery, or bloated with disease and sin. Some stared before them fixedly; some gazed about with furtive and hungry eyes as they shuffled on.

There is afflatus here, but it is hardly divine. It is a verbal fault, but a fault which is, in such a work, inexcusable; and its recurrence is one of the reasons why "Love's Pilgrimage is not a great novel.

And Mr. Sinclair is no less wrong-headed in his attitude toward sex than in his attitude toward life. It is annoying to have to appear to be chiefly interested in sexual questions—even though that be the fact; so, as an indication of the critic's reaction, the dogmatic statement must here suffice, that the book mistakenly treats of sex as a thing separable from the rest of life, and inherently hostile to other phases of life. Still more dogmatically it may be pronounced that the artist who starts out with the intention of leaving women out of his life altogether, is indefensible: for he is actually preparing for himself an unnecessary amount of trouble. "All things betray thee who betrayest Me!"

To resume the catalogue of unpleasantnesses, there is the personality that pervades the book. It is a personality that goes far to destroy the sympathy which the situation creates. The author seems to be only half aware how disagreeable the personality of his hero is. He records his hero's faults, and forgives them in the same breath. Thyrsis is an intolerable prig, an abominable egotist, and his domestic manners are insufferable. He makes long speeches to his poor wife, and when she interrupts he says: "I am speaking!" To be a good novelist, one must not merely have the honesty to endow one's hero with characteristics like that, but one must have sensibility enough to realize how horrid they are.

These may seem small matters. But it is at such points at which a writer may be tested for the possession of the spiritual qualities out of which first-rate art proceeds. Mr. Sinclair shows himself wanting in clarity of vision, in sympathy and in judgment. Over against his preoccupation with his hero one sets his violent misunderstanding of the rest of the world. He is, in fact, a sentimentalist.

But if the book is unsuccessful in conveying a true sense of the life which forms the background of its hero's career, in conveying a sense of Life itself, it is singularly successful. Mr. Sinclair is in this regard a better philosopher than artist. He has the sense of the evanescence of life, its hazards and its opportunities, its "infinite preciousness and holiness." This sense it is that makes his chapter on the birth of a child not a mere exercise in realism, but a poignant and exalted revelation. And he has the profound insight to draw the corollary of this sense of life, and define the idea of immortality as "the consummation of all unfaith."

* * *

The value of the book? In answer to that question, these observations are tendered with humble arrogance: No man can be wrong about many things before the value of his art is affected; but there are some things so important that one dare not, as an artist, be wrong about them. These things are not politics and religion; they are art and love. Upton Sinclair is wrong about both. Nevertheless, he has written a book that by sheer sincerity and bravery approaches near to greatness. It opens up new possibilities in fiction for a daring purity of mind.

It is a book that, in our present state of culture, must have required something like heroism in the publisher. But it is the author who will, for the privilege of attempting to tell the truth, pay most dearly. His sacrifice is one that should secure him the gratitude of all sincere lovers of literature and of truth.

May 5, 1911

SPECIAL SUMMER FICTION NUMBER

A LOVE STORY

The Miller of Old Church, by Ellen Glasgow. [Doubleday, Page & Co.]

Ellen Glasgow is an ambitious interpreter of American life. In such books as "The Deliverance" and "The Wheel of Life" she has shown both her sincerity and her capacity; while in "The Romance of a Plain Man," especially, she has revealed her limitations. Undeniably she has many of the qualities that belong to the first-rate novelist. She has the ability not merely to analyze but to synthesize her people—the strength as well as the subtlety of characterization. She has a happy knack at writing dialogue; even when it is apparent that the talkers are "giving themselves away" in fulfillment of the satiric intention of the author, the conversation still remains lifelike. She has true dramatic instinct, and the ready force with which she holds the reader's attention to a situation until its emotional content is exhausted is a thing worthy all admiration. Moreover, one finds in her that important endowment, a sense for contemporary ideas.

In spite of all these qualities, some readers have hesitated to accept Miss Glasgow as more than an exceptionally capable romancer. They have not been able to see in her one of those American writers from whom increasingly better and more truly important work may be expected. Their reason is that Miss Glasgow has not been able to slough off a certain conventionality or crudity of technique. She does not take novel writing with sufficient seriousness, it would seem, to discard the hackneyed in plot and character. She will bring her events to pass in a way that outrages the sensibilities of the cultivated novel reader—and, it may be insisted, outrages literary truth. The coincidence, the unexpected meeting, the happy ending—such devices she uses with a naivete or an unscrupulousness inconsistent with modern standards.

* * *

In "The Miller of Old Church"—which is, if not one of her most largely planned, yet one of her most interesting books—these qualities and limitations are to be seen in striking incongruity. The book contains one of the most tiresomely familiar characters in fiction, the Don Juan—a character, moreover, which Miss Glasgow has not been able to redeem by any novelty of treatment. There is not merely a conventional vengeance wreaked upon this Don Juan by a relative of the girl he has seduced, but it is represented as a replica of one which had been formerly visited upon the young man's uncle. These are minor matters. But in the love story of the Miller and the illegitimate daughter of the slain uncle, which is the real concern of the book, there is an unhappy marriage of the man which has to be cleared away by the most fortuitous and incredible of deaths. Nevertheless, it would seem that the defects of the book bulk much less than its merits. It is an inepitude [sic] of technique and not a fault of vision. The ending, which shows the reconciliation of the lovers, is only apparently a conventional "happy ending." It is not a concession to popular taste, but an essential part of the author's subject. It is here, indeed, in the description of this reconciliation, she exhibits some of her finest literary qualities—her keenest insight into life, her greatest freedom from romantic traditions.

This dual quality certainly diminishes to an extent the enthusiasm which one would feel for the book. One cannot but regret that a writer of Miss Glasgow's powers has rested content with the antiquated elements of her plot. But it is forgivable. In what is essential she has succeeded. She has made a sympathetic, a beautiful, a moving study of one aspect of American life.

* * *

Specially the book tells the story of a high-spirited young fellow (the Miller of the title) sprung from that stock which throughout the South has been rising from the condition of "poor white trash" to that of solid and influential citizenship. This young man is the lover of the girl of illegitimate birth. The book brings in the contrasting type of southern man, the cavalier with exclusively erotic interests. It brings in also the other surviving figure of the ante-bellum period, the delicate and shielded woman, who knows no evil, and who is in her weakness a merciless tyrant.

This last character, the mother of the young Don Juan, is drawn with delicate satire. More fully to explain her devastating influence, she is shown accompanied by her sister, who, being plain and unattractive to men, had to find her destiny in being the other's personal attendant. She had drawn when she was young, and a famous portrait painter who had seen one of her sketches insisted that she ought to go to Paris to study. But, No!

Besides these characters, who are shown in active contrast with each other—and who in their relations exhibit the process which not without pain and violence changes the old into the new—besides these, there are some interesting old people to act as chorus. They sit in the sun or at the "ordinary" and discourse on life and death, religion and love.

But it is the lovers who ocupy [sic] the greatest part of the book. "The Miller of Old Church" is a love story. It is a good love story, veristic and sincere. The girl, Mollie, and, in even a greater degree, the Miller are evoked realistically and appealingly. Their love affair is considered in a way which brings out its deeper value and interest. Their courtship, their quarrels, their heartbreaking estrangement, and after an interval in which the man becomes first a husband and then a widower, their reconciliation—these things are recited with a seriousness which seeks to discover their complete significance in the scheme of life. And, save that there is never once struck the tragic note which resolves the human discords, the effect is worthy of an artist.

June 9, 1911

RECENT BIOGRAPHY

Mary Wollstonecraft: A Study in Economics and Romance, by G.R. Stirling-Taylor. With portraits. [John Lane Company.]

The story of Mary Wollstonecraft is one that might be read by those who profess themselves seriously interested in the subject of the love-passion, with much more profit than the love affairs of Byron, Rachel and the like. The interest in the love-passion is a legitimate interest, which need not be suspected of being merely disguised eroticism; but it would seem that there was very little to be learned from the crude passions of a soldier or the commonplace adventures of a courtesan. In the story of Mary Wollstonecraft, on the other hand, there are matters of real interest to modern readers.

Mary Wollstonecraft was one of the first of "modern" women. Not content with being one among what Havelock Ellis has called "the great and heroic lovers" of the 18th century, she was—if one may accept Mr. Taylor's estimate of her—a thinker of prime importance. She did not merely live, she sought to express life in intellectual terms. Between her intellectual conclusions and her actions, between her ideas and her life, there was sometimes a disparity, a contradiction. And in that contradiction lies the essential fascination of the woman. It is the same as the charm—one may almost call it the tragic charm—of those many women of today whom she prefigured, and whose experience she so largely compassed.

* * *

Those who have only heard of Mary Wollstonecraft are almost sure to mistake her position. She was not—as might be assumed—a special pleader in behalf of her sex. She was the first of that line of thinkers, which today includes Olive Schreiner and Charlotte Perkins Gilman, who have mercilessly satirized women for accepting an artificial segregation from the world. Women are, first of all, human beings; most of the traits called masculine are in reality human, and belong as well to women as to men; the significance of sex has been exaggerated: such was the doctrine of Mary Wollstonecraft. It was a doctrine to which, indeed, her life provided some ironic footnotes. But the importance of her position is as the prime enunciator of this idea, which has been the motif of a hundred wears [sic] of women's struggle since then—and which, after a century of tragic sifting, seems to hold a kernel of essential truth.

* * *

But Mary Wollstonecraft enunciated the doctrine with all the logical rigor and unhesitating enthusiasm of a pioneer. In the same spirit she sought to carry it out in her own life. In part she was certainly successful. For she proved that a woman could earn a living in the so-called masculine pursuit of literature. If Mr. Taylor is to be relied on—and most of Mary Wollstone-craft's books are not readily accessible for proof—she succeeded not merely as a craftsman but as an artist. She wrote a reply to Edmund Burke's "Reflections on the Revolution in France" and exposed the absurdity behind the rhetoric of that much-overrated piece of historical romanticism. This was her "Vindication of the Rights of Men," a pamphlet which appears, from the passages adduced, to have been a most intelligent, brilliant and effective piece of writing. Her novels were probably better than those who have not read them can readily believe. And her "Vindication of the Rights of Woman" is a document which wholly justified the high regard in which she was held by gifted contemporaries.

* * *

But Mary Wollstonecraft had held up independence as the ideal in all things, even in the most intimate relations of men and woman. She disbelieved in the common talk of "constancy." She wrote: "A mistaken education, a narrow, uncultivated mind and many sexual prejudices tend to make women more constant then men." She thought that the mind that can long be "engrossed by one object . . . is weak." This opinion did not proceed from any insensibility to normal feelings: Mary was a beautiful and feminine woman, of a very passionate nature. Going to France to escape from a hopeless love affair with a married man, she met a certain Captain Imlay, who professed radical opinions and fell in love with her. She returned his love unreservedly. It happened that he was the very type of man who could test the "independence" in which the girl believed she believed. He was a man personally charming, intellectually fascinating, but having as "his most marked characteristic," says Mr. Taylor, "a facile and trivial skill in the art of making women love him."

He soon tired of Mary, it seems, and spent much of his time away from her; and it was during one of these absences that she bore him a child. A man who could treat the responsibilities of pregnancy in this way was something not dreamed of in the girl's philosophy. She reacted upon the situation in a very human way; she was unhappy, hysterical, at times verged upon insanity; she tried twice to commit suicide; she wrote him pleading letters, she reproached him for his unfaithfulness, she demanded from him the constancy which before that she had despised as "weak." And, most ironic of all, she held fast to him, and refused to believe that he would not return to her for months after she had discovered his real feelings toward her. She was, in short, "conventional."

* * *

It is this situation, which has been repeated many times in contemporary life, that is the central point of interest in her story. There is, if one may repeat the phrase, a tragic charm in this spectacle. For the girl who had so passionately declared one thing, and now so passionately acts out another, is not "going back on herself." She is but affirming another truth, which though it appears to contradict, does not abrogate the other.

Mary Wollstonecraft had the good fortune to meet, after her recovery from the Imlay affair, with a man of different—and yet not too different—kind. This was William Godwin. Though, for convenience' sake, when she had conceived a child by him, they were married, she reaffirmed her old

71

ideas of independence. She and Godwin lived in different houses and visited each other as friends and lovers. The arrangement had its difficulties, as can be seen from their letters, but it did banish the spirit of custom and familiarity which must be struggled against in the ordinary mutual household. That idyl was ended by the birth of Godwin's child, which was fatal to the mother. The child became the second wife of the poet Shelley.

Mr. Taylor, in relating these things, affects an unnecessary simplicity, which has at times the air of condescension toward the reader. He has not written with the vigor and freshness of his recent book, "Leaders of Socialism." But he has treated the subject sympathetically, with exactitude; and he has been unusually stimulating by his very association of economics and romance.

June 30, 1911

IN THOSE DAYS

Memories and Impressions: A Study in Atmosphere, by Ford Madox Hueffer. Illustrated. [Harper & Brothers.]

Mr. Hueffer does not write like a modern memoirialist [sic]: he does not have, that is to say, the air of responsibility, the worried accuracy, the staidness which mark the ordinary work of this kind. There is an old-fashioned air about the book—it has a spark of the generous flame that kindled in the writings of Boswell, of Casanova, of Cellini. It is, first of all, interesting; its contents were written not with the intention of correcting our misconceptions concerning the Pre-Raphaelites, but out of a hearty conviction that the lives of those men were full of interest.

And so the book has a kind of heroic carelessness which has already called down on it the strictures of critics. Mr. Hueffer has replied to them in his preface, saying: "I really don't deal in facts; I have for facts a most profound contempt. I try to give you what I see to be the spirit of an age, of a town, of a movement. This cannot be done with facts." After that it would be fatuous to discuss the accuracy of the incidents here related. All that one can ask is whether the incidents give a dramatically true picture of the Pre-Raphaelites. Of dramatic truth one who has never seen a Pre-Raphaelite in the flesh is as good a critic as any other.

It is as Mr. Hueffer says: "My impression is that there have been

6,472 books written to give the facts about the Pre-Raphaelite movement. . . . But what I am trying to get at is that, though there have been many things written about these facts, no one has whole-heartedly and thoroughly attempted to get the atmosphere of these twenty-five years.'' Mr. Hueffer has whole-heartedly and thoroughly attempted this task; and it is hardly too much to say that he has splendidly succeeded.

* * *

Certainly "Memories and Impressions" is the only book that calls up in any vivid way the tremendously vital figures of Morris, Burne-Jones, Rossetti, Swinburne, Ford Madox Brown, as they ramped and roared through the literary arena of the time. By dint of not having to conserve the reputation of his heroes, by virtue of not having to reject as probably apocryphal the most interesting stories, by reason of being able to make use of personal memories without revision, he has produced a fascinating record. How Madox Brown kicked a distinguished art critic downstairs, or how a distinguished poet had Madox Brown's address on a label sewn in his coat collar, so that when he was drunk he would be brought there by the cabby and put in a bath to recover; how Rossetti called Ruskin a sneak; how one literary man in a fit of delirium tremens tried to kill a friend, and burst a blood vessel, and how William Sharp, who tried to get a doctor, was arrested because he was covered with blood; how young Bernard Shaw use [sic] to lecture on "The Foolishness of Anarchism," while unscrupulous Anarchists on the edge of the crowd sold that relic of his still earlier youth, a pamphlet entitled "Why I Am an Anarchist"; how Henley cursed the memoirist [sic] up and down, black and blue, for asserting that Sidney wrote "Astropel and Stella," or some such thing; and how—but enough of this. The point is that the book has the high flavor of personality, the tang of adventure.

* * *

And more than this: it is full of the writer's own opinions, ideas, conclusions on all sorts of aesthetic and moral subjects; and these are expressed with a seriousness of manner which partly relieves them of the suspicion of irresponsibility. Mr. Hueffer has not been quite so reckless of his own intellectual reputation as he has of the reputation of that genial, high-spirited crowd of people whom for the most part he celebrates.

There is something pleasant about such writing as this—pleasant if only from its unusualness: "I do not mean to say that the Pre-Raphaelites were any very great shakes. But they cared intensely about their work; they talked about it and about little else. They regarded themselves, indeed, as priests. And without some such beliefs, how can an artist be hardened to do good work? There is no being so solitary, there is no being with so little power of gauging where he stands in estimation of the world.'' Is that first sentence too reckless?

In at least one instance he has been too reckless, and it is an instance which proves his impressions to have been as liable to error as his facts. This is his impression of William Morris as a sentimentalist in his politics. The poet is represented as conceiving of the Co-operative Commonwealth as a matter of Kelmscott printing and Walter Crane pictures—and not much more than that. This idea of Morris as a man incapable of appreciating economics, incapable of having a sound and substantial reason for his politics, is the vulgar idea, but it is an idea which the slightest acquaintance with the facts is enough to dissipate.

* * *

How much more of such falsity of impression there is in this work one can only guess, but one really prefers to set the estimate low. Mr. Hueffer had incomparable advantage, as a child, of association with the ever-fascinating figures of that great generation, and all that he tells us we must take with gratitude. Nor can one but be glad that this new Boswell has one of the best traits of the old, and puts himself, with all his inconsequences and triviality, into the picture. One may find his opinions wrong or inconsistent or impertinent, but the egotism which puts them down in such a book is the quality which gives vitality to biography. And at all events, whether for his memories of men or his ideas about things—or whether for his attitude, half cynical, half sympathetic, and wholly engaging—his book is to be read with unusual and indubitable pleasure.

July 7, 1911

THE APOSTLE

The Apostle: A Drama in Three Acts, by George Moore. With a Prefatory Letter on Reading the Bible for the First Time. [Maunsel & Co., Dublin.]

The portrait of George Moore painted by Manet is illuminating. At first glance it looks like a caricature; and it has all the virtues of the caricature: it presents violently to the attention certain essential characteristics. It shows the man apparently in the most earnest thought or conversation,

74

wholly intent upon an idea; his lips are pursed up, his loose beard is asymetrically scattered away from his face, as though by the intensity of his thought, and his eyes are dark with preoccupation.

It is a picture that is needed to interpret Mr. Moore, or rather to prevent his being misunderstood. For on account of Mr. Moore's sensitivenes [sic] to modern ideas, his faculty of assimilating, embodying, and, in a way, representing an extreme of modern culture—on account of this very sophistication, it needs such a portrait to prove that certain touching simplicities in his literary work are, as one would fain believe, genuine, and that what may seem impudence is often merely this same simplicity.

In the gentle pastime "epater le bourgeois" Mr. Moore has, of course, indulged himself; but many of the things that enrage the Philistines have sprung from no conscious desire on his part to wound them—have sprung, indeed, from his unconsciousness of the crowd, an unconsciousness which if it did not already belong to him as an artist must have speedily become second nature during his residence in France.

The spirit of French art, literary and otherwise, may be likened to the spirit of a club, where a group of men securely sit and discuss their own affairs: outside the window the world goes by, an indifferent spectacle. Mr. Moore, having become accustomed to his club-window attitude, did not depart from it when the English public, on the occasion of the publication of "A Mummer's Wife," threw brickbats through the window. He was surprised perhaps, grieved no doubt, ashamed for his fellow citizens; but when the next big idea came along to make his lips purse up, his eyes darken and his beard fly out centrifugally from his face, the public receded into the depths of his unconsciousness.

* * *

So that when Mr. Moore published this scenario—it is a scenario, by the way, and not a completed play—he did it only for the reason mentioned in his prefatory letter: because he has told the story so often at dinner tables that he was afraid "lest the story might drift so completely into the common consciousness that somebody would imagine he had invented it, and write it in a way that would," as he says, "cause me much unhappiness." And he wrote it, it may be safely affirmed, without meaning to hurt anybody's feelings.

For Mr. Moore, as an artist—and perhaps the most typical and perfect specimen of the genus alive today—dwells in a world where the central story of the Christian faith can be rearranged in any way without a thought of irreverence or malice or even bad taste. So he has rearranged it. He had been told of somebody's theory to the effect that Jesus had not died on the cross, but had succumbed to a cataleptic swoon; and he remembered the old legend which had it that the young Jesus was an Essene monk. "Why, then," he

75

asked himself, "should not Christ have returned to the monastery, having been cured of His wounds at the house of Joseph of Arimathea? Why should not Paul, after a day's preaching amid the Palestinian hills, have knocked at the door of that monastery? What a wonderful meeting that would have been!"

It is a wonderful meeting as Mr. Moore tells it, with his frank admiration for the apostle's energy, courage and attachment to an idea, and his tenderness for the shattered body and lovable soul of the lay brother, Jesus, who retains the marks of a crucifixion in his hands and feet, and the dim memory of old sufferings in his mind. Among the disputatious Essenes, the mystical figure of the humble lay brother and the dynamic figure of Paul stand out impressively.

Very quickly the theme of the drama is developed, in the conflict between Paul and Jesus. Paul takes this man for an impostor, or a snare sent by Satan. He has preached "Christ crucified," and founded the whole Christian religion on that doctrine. If it should get abroad that Jesus had not died, his religion would go to wreck and the world fall back into idolatry. For his part, Jesus rejects the religion that has been founded upon him, and when the memory of his former life has wholly returned, feels anew the call that once drew him out of this monastery. He will go to Jerusalem, though he hang on the cross again, and destroy this new idolatry.

* * *

The last hope which Paul had of proving the man an impostor is destroyed by the testimony of an old woman who was Mary Magdalene.

The conflict ends when Paul becomes overwrought with anger. "O blasphemy! blasphemy!" he says to the man who pretends to be Jesus. "Jesus of Nazareth, the great mediator between God and man, sitteth at the right hand of his father, and it is in his name that I strike thee down." Jesus falls dead.

Aside from the shock which is involved in this ending, the interest of the play consists almost wholly in the presentation of the character of Paul. The monks, with their involved and monotonous discussions of theology, are doubtless intended merely as foils for the two protagonists. The Mary Magdalene is a fluent old woman, with an entirely conventional loyalty and respect for Jesus. She might have been a favorite house servant. And the picture of Jesus is—as Mr. Moore said of Luke's—a disappointment.

"A polished, lifeless narrative, written by a skillful and elaborate man of letters, sleek as Maeterlinck." So he writes of that gospel in his prefatory letter. "In Luke's narrative Christ seems a lifeless, waxen figure, daintily curled, with tinted cheeks, uttering pretty commonplaces gathered from 'The Treasure of the Lowly' as he goes by." The gospel of Matthew he liked better; Christ attains to some reality in it, though it is "a canvas that has passed through the hands of the restorer.''

But it was not until he turned to the gospel of Mark, he says, that he "caught a glimpse of the real Christ, the magnificent young heretic who came up from Galilee to overthrow the priests in Jerusalem.'' Mark, he is certain, "wrote with his eyes on the scenes he describes, though he may not have been an eyewitness to them, and his narrative reveals the same qualities that we admire in Maupassant. He is as concise, as explicit, and as objective. I doubt if a story was ever better told. . . . An admirable narrative, without ecclesiastical introduction, the story beginning as the Frenchman would have begun it: John baptizing a great multitude in the Jordan, Jesus coming to him for baptism, which he receives, forthwith retiring into the desert, and coming out of it forty days after to preach in Galilee.''

* * *

Yet it would seem that Mr. Moore had read the gospel of Mark to little purpose. For his conception of Jesus is still the meek, lowly person, of elegantly simple language and pious sentiments—the ineffectual Syrian minor poet of Renan. He does not once disclose that young healer whom one can see so plainly over Mark's shoulder—haughty, secretive, vain, wilfully ambiguous, mordant, moody, with an eye for a situation and a genius for epigram. There is no lowliness in Mark's Jesus; there is a pride that one may find magnificent or repellant, but that blazes throughout Mark's gospel a vehement and irrepressible flame.

But, not seeing this more heroical Jesus, it was in the Acts that Mr. Moore found the hero of his drama. In the Acts, he felt with relief, we pass from legend to history. That Luke could have written this "marvelous narrative'' Mr. Moore does not believe. Mark might have done so, he thinks; but he prefers to believe that the real author was none other than Paul. In the midst of his confidences, becoming suddenly conscious of the world (at least the world of scholarship) and its opinion, Mr. Moore pàuses for a moment apologetically: "If this prefatory note should fall into the hands of any of your learned German critics, I will ask him to smile indulgently at the criticism of a man of letters who reads the Bible for the first time, and who, through no fault of his own, has been committed to record his impressions. But why should the fear of writing something silly or commonplace stay my pen? Who amongst us has not written something silly or commonplace? And who amongst us dares to say that he will never do so again? So, fortified by the example of my predecessors and contemporaries, I confess that on reading the Acts for the first time my ear was caught by a new voice, and it sounded so clearly out of the words that I could not doubt that Paul was speaking in person. It were impossible for anyone else to catch an individual accent so completely as when Paul bids good-bye to his disciples and friends at Ephesus.''

Then Mr. Moore forgets the world and its opinion again, intent on the personal vision, so vivid and convincing, that he has of the matter. "The narrative of the shipwreck and the journey to Rome could only have been written by a man of literary genius, and there are never two at the same time. The trial at Caesarea is Paul's own rendering of his defense. Of course it is. My pen pauses, for I must wonder how anyone could have entertained, even for a moment, the nation [sic] that Luke 'made it up.' How did he make it up? From hearsay? Blind men and deaf, nowing [sic] nothing of the art of writing!"

The apostle is as real to Mr. Moore as Hamlet, as Don Quixote—with whom, we are reminded, he received an equal number of buffetings, leaving him as unabashed. "In my walks," says Mr. Moore, "Paul rises up before my eyes as clearly as the Knight of the Rueful Countenance, though no word of his personal appearance is given: a man of medium height, about five feet eight or nine, a round head covered with dark curly hair, a short neck, square shoulders, a long body, thick legs, with some belly under his girdle. His large, luminous eyes often look into mine, and sometimes he appears with his shirt open, and there is a great shock of curled hair between his breasts, and his reddish hand goes there, and he scratches as he talks. Sometimes he pulls at his scanty beard petulantly."

The apostle of Mr. Moore's play is really a very convincing presentation of the figure that bustles through the Acts and harangues the early Christians in the Epistles. Such a figure would doubtless—though it would almost seem to argue a defect of imagination—more than that of Jesus, appeal to a man of Mr. Moore's temperament.

For Mr. Moore has the modern, as opposed to the pagan spirit, the attitude toward life that makes a man a novelist rather than a poet. In this he differs strikingly from his fellow countryman, W. B. Yeats. It is not hard to imagine what Mr. Yeats would say of this play. He would say (one imagines): "Why climb up into the misty regions of myth, if what you find there you are to paint in a hard rationalist spirit? Why not confine yourself to women of the theater and convent, and gentlemen of Berkeley Square, whom you will make interesting for us in the best modern fashion. You do not know what a myth is for. It is not to prove or disprove, to examine or rationalize. It is something to believe—to believe voluntarily, because it provides a new vista for the soul. The old Irish, the old Greeks, believed, not as they must but as they chose, for these myths, an intense vivid expression of their emotions and ideas about life, gave them a stronger hold on life's verities."

* * *

And Mr. Yeats would be right. "The Apostle" is a dry and juiceless affair. Mr. Moore's treatment does not unveil any emotion in nude and daring

78

beauty; it does not start any dream or vision; it evokes two gigantic symbols, and leaves them empty of real symbolic significance. And the little shock which the ending gives is no sufficient excuse. Mr. Moore would not have dared to write a play about the myth of Dante and Beatrice which should leave the reader cold; he would not dare to lay hands upon these "huge cloudy symbols of a high romance" without putting them to inspiring use.

That is a thing that has seldom in our English literature been accomplished. Few of our poets have had the power of making new and free and potent use of an old myth—the power upon which rests the singular splendor of the literature of the Greeks. Our Shakespeare lacked it, and turned the myth of Venus and Adonis to trivial use, as he turned that of Joan of Arc to base. Milton had a little of it, and that little, expended upon Satan, kept "Paradise Lost," that poem so rich in purely lyric qualities, from being an overwhelming failure as an epic. Shelley showed somewhat of it in "Prometheus Unbound," Byron somewhat in "Cain." Browning had more of the power than he chose to make use of, but "An Epistle of Karshish" and "Cleon" show what he might have done. But sometimes a phrase reveals the presence of that power: and here is a passage that so reveals it, from Chesterton's essay on "Omar and the Sacred Vine":

> And at the high altar of Christianity stands another figure, in whose hand also is the cup of the vine. "Drink," he says, "for the whole world is as red as this wine, with the crimson of the love and wrath of God. Drink, for the trumpets are blowing for battle, and this is the stirrup cup. Drink, for this is the blood of the new testament that is shed for you. Drink, for I know of whence you come and why. Drink, for I know of when you go and where."

* * *

Does not that liberate the soul? That is the function of myth, and it is the nature of myth that it is fluid, ever susceptible to new and vitalizing treatment, and ever capable of widening the horizons of the spirit.

Another writer who has the power is the new poet, Ezra Pound. In a short poem, entitled "The Ballad of the Goodly Fere" (or Companion), he has done the thing magnificently:

Ha' we lost the goodliest fere o' all
For the priests and the gallows tree?
Aye lover he was of brawny men,
O' ships and the open sea.

When they came wi' a host to take Our Man
His smile was good to see,
"First let these go!" qou' our Goodly Fere,
"Or I'll see ye damned," says he.

79

Aye he sent us out through the crossed high spears
And the scorn of his laugh rang free.
"Why took ye not me when I walked about
Alone in the town?" says he.

Oh we drank his "Hale" in the good red wine
When we last made company.
No capon priest was the Goodly Fere,
But a man o' men was he. . . .

"Ye ha' seen me heal the lame and blind,
And wake the dead," says he,
"Ye shall see one thing to master all:
'Tis how a brave man dies on the tree."

* * *

It is this power, as exercised on the materials of a religion, which makes the religious life one with the aesthetic and the intellectual, which gives a religion enduring value. Christianity has, by losing this power, become a thing apart from the rest of modern life: and the effort of men like Walter Rauschenbusch to re-create the Christian tradition, to invest it with modern emotional significance, acquires from this fact a desperate importance. It does not so much matter that George Moore should be lacking in this power: he can afford to fail here. But here Christianity cannot afford to fail.

August 4, 1911

MARK TWAIN

Mark Twain, by Archibald Henderson. With photographs by Langdon Coburn. [Frederick A. Stokes Company.]

The time has not yet arrived for the writing of Mark Twain's biography. To be interesting, a biography must be, in some sense, news; it must contain facts that we do not know or have forgotten. A welcome biography must be in some measure challenging; it must offer a re-estimate of the subject's worth, or defend the old one vigorously against attack. To

80

write of Mark Twain now, less than two years after his death, is almost inevitably to weary the reader with a repetition of familiar anecdotes, and too familiar laudations.

American [sic] has had less than half a dozen great writers, and Mark Twain is among them: it has been said a thousand times. If someone would only contradict it—as might with much plausibility be done—there would be some virtue in maintaining the proposition. Mr. Archibald Henderson, whose many biographical attempts have revealed him as one of the most assiduous camp-followers of Personality, pleads his gratitude to Mark Twain as the justification for this book. Mr. Langdon Coburn, by some of his exceedingly original and interesting photographs, helps to take the edge off the book's supererogation; the good paper and large type which have been employed to expand it to a sizable volume attracts the eye; and, finally, a workmanlike bibliography of Twainiana at the end cajoles one into good humor.

Mr. Henderson, indeed, is not much worse than inopportune. He is right, in the main, in his opinions of Mark Twain; though he does err here and there, as when he insists that this "brilliant wit" never "dipped his darts in the poison of cynicism, misanthropy or despair." He is not, this biographer, quite hopeless as a writer, though he links cliche to cliche, strews about words like "unique," "incomparable," "supreme" and "imperishable" like the "ad writer" of a circus, and utters such tropes as "remedy the ills of democratic government with the knife of publicity"; not hopeless, it must be insisted, in spite of all this, since one sentence in the book shows some of the artist's feeling for words: "in the laughter of these wild westerners was something at once rustic and sanguinary."

* * *

In that sentence Mr. Henderson almost achieves distinction; and for that, and his pathetically good intentions, he should be forgiven. In the biography of this young southerner there is something at once rustic and in the bloodless sense—sanguinary. It illustrates Mark Twain's American public, and it may help to elucidate Mark Twain himself.

Rustic and hopeful: we Americans were eminently that in the decades in which Mark Twain grew up. It made an atmosphere in which a man like Mark Twain could develop and express his personality to the utmost. It left him free, in a way that our sophistication and cynicism does not leave our writers free today. America believed in Mark Twain, in a generous fashion which only California, it seems, yet retains: it was such a belief as brings out the artist in a man, or ruins him.

We no longer subject our writers to the test of such a dangerous blaze. We have our ideas about Mr. Montague Glass, for instance, and they are judicious; we shall not encourage him to attempt the great American novel; we shall, if we can, keep him doing "Potash and Perlmutter" stories all his life. We appreciate Mr. Glass, but our rustic and sanguinary days are over.

But Mark Twain stood the test: he became an artist. His art was always imperfectly superordinated to his humor, but it is noteworthy that in the tale which brought him his earliest general recognition, the one which gives title to his first published volume, "The Jumping Frog" (1867), there was unmistakable proof that the writer was an artist.

* * *

In regard to this tale, Mr. Henderson neglected an excellent opportunity. He might have commended himself to lovers of truth by showing up the "Jumping Frog" delusion. He quotes Madame Blanc, Mark Twain's first translator, as saying that it is "rather difficult for us to understand, while reading this story, the 'roars of laughter' that it excited. . . ." It is indeed. Jowett once confessed that he saw nothing so terribly funny about the story. And, as a matter of fact, there was nothing so terribly funny to see.

The truth about "The Jumping Frog"—a truth that is merely obscured by Mr. Henderson's inept phrase to the effect that it "fired the laugh heard round the world"—is this. "The Jumping Frog" is a good story. It is, in its form, perfect with a perfection that may be called classic. If it were printed in a newspaper today, it would be copied in every other newspaper in the country, just as it was in 1864. It would bring its author into notice, just as it did then, and it would be translated without much delay. But people would not guffaw, they would not split their sides. For there is nothing about the story to provoke these undignified actions. The story is not that kind of a story. Its humor is of a quiet, even a subtle kind. It can be read and enjoyed perfectly with only the ghost of a smile.

It is true that many of Mark Twain's tales were of the "side-splitting' kind. And it has been hastily assumed by many writers that these represent the humor of Mark Twain, as of America. They do not represent the humor of Mark Twain at its best; and they do not represent American humor at all.

On the basis of Mark Twain's peculiar fondness for burlesque, for extravagance, for gross-dimensional language, there has been erected a wholly false theory of American humor. Now Americans, whether westerners, New Englanders, Kentuckians, or what-not, are practically never heard to indulge in this form of humor. When they read it in "Innocents Abroad" it had to them the surprise of novelty; nor has a generation's familiarity with that book and others implanted it in our minds. The true American humor is more delicate, more human. It is akin to English drollery, to Irish absurdity, to French wit—but the direction in which it varies from these is toward a dryer, if not a subtler, mode of expression. And it is to be found in abundance, alongside his own boisterous humor, in the pages of Mark Twain.

There is an apt illustration of both the coarse materials and the fine methods of American humor in "Huckleberry Finn":

'Store tobacco is flat black plug, but these fellows mostly chaws the natural leaf twisted. When they borrow a chaw, they don't generly cut it off with a knife, but set the plug in between their teeth, and gnaw with their teeth and tug at the plug with their hands will they get it in two; then sometimes the one that owns the tobacco looks mournful at it when it's handed back, and says, sarcastic: "Here, gimme the chaw, and you take the plug!" '

In the same book there is Huck's description of Emmeline, the village poet and artist:

"Everytime a man died, or a woman died, or a child died, she would be on hand with her 'tribute' before he was cold. She called them tributes. The neighbors said it was the doctor first, then Emmeline, then the undertaker— the undertaker never got in ahead of Emmeline but once, and then she hung fire on a rhyme for the dead person's name, which was Whistler. She warn't ever the same after that. . . ."

Emmeline's pictures would show a young woman "leaning pensive on a tombstone on her right elbow, under a weeping willow, and her other hand hanging down her side holding a white handkerchief and a reticule, and underneath the picture it said 'Shall I Never See Thee More Alas.' " Commented Huck: "These was all nice pictures, I reckon, but I didn't somehow seem to take to them. . . . Everybody was sorry she died, because she had laid out a lot more of these pictures to do, and a body could see by what she had done what they had lost. But I reckoned that with her disposition she was having a better time in the graveyard."

* * *

The relations of Literature and Humor, which are apparently not very clear to Mr. Henderson, and which he does not help his readers to understand, deserve all the disentangling they can get. It is sometimes assumed that if a man who is a good laugh-raiser becomes a better and better laugh-raiser, there is a point at which he will be entitled to be called a great writer. This is not the case at all. The ability to make people laugh with arrangements of printed words has no more relation to literature than the ability to make them ill by the same means. The purposes of Literature are other. Literature may be considered as the expression, in a medium perfectly suited to it, of some view of life which, while individual, is broad, sympathetic and just. It is clear that in any broad, sympathetic and just view of life, humor will have some place, a greater or less one according to the view and the viewer. But it will be subordinate to other things. And if it crowds out these other things the view of life will no longer be broad, or sympathetic, or just, and its expression will no longer be literature.

It is, let us say, as desirable that the writer be able to see and represent the humor of life as that the painter be able to see and represent the color of life. But humor without truth is as color without form. The truth should not be stated baldly, any more than form should be defined precisely; but that dash of color apparently laid on with an irresponsible flick of the brush, apparently existing only for the sake of its own hue, must indicate the morphological fact beneath. Humor can no more stand alone than color can. The phrase "great humorist," like the phrase "great colorist," has implications which, when explicated, make it mean—great artist.

It is a felicitous task to point out those of Mark Twain's books which are of real artistic significance. They begin with "The Gilded Age," a book which is of value more for what it attempts than for what it achieves, but which has been neglected of late rather because of the seriousness of its intention than for any better reason. "The Gilded Age," written in collaboration with Charles Dudley Warner, was an effort to give a picture of American life, in all its goodness and badness—but, as the title shows, and naturally enough, especially in its badness, its hypocrisy, its sham, its "bluff." It was an attempt to envisage our rustic and sanguinary civilization. Well, if it failed as a whole, it did not fail in its noblest part: for the character of Colonel Mulberry Sellers, the protagonist of our rustic and sanguinary culture, is one of Mark Twain's finest achievements. A natural-born "promoter," with all the guile and all the naivete of his kind, a mixture of knave and fool, Colonel Sellers is a ridiculous, a pathetic, a rememberable figure. There is one scene in which he invites a friend to dinner; the dinner is of raw turnips, the conversation of millions of dollars. Even if Mark Twain had not meant America by this scene of squalor and unscrupulous idealism, the scene would still have been magnificently true to human nature.

* * *

The next book of significance, attempting less, succeeded. Everyone knows the merits of "The Adventures of Tom Sawyer." Almost everybody knows that later and better book, "The Adventures of Huckleberry Finn," in which the old desire to picture the broader aspects of the American comedy again surged up, to find, this time, successful expression. The third significant book from his hand is "Life on the Mississippi," which, if it has in it less of his humor and less of American life, is nevertheless a masterpiece.

This leaves out of consideration "Puddinhead Wilson," a book nobly intended, but one in which his art broke down; "Joan of Arc," which I have not read; and his "Autobiography," which has been published only in part, and which may well enough, in its complete form, rank with the best of his work.

It is, of course, the books about Tom Sawyer and Huck Finn which rank highest. Never before nor since in American prose has there been writing so true, so original, so powerful and so easy; so admirable in verbal technique, so sure in architectonic, the adjustment of form to content. It is an accomplishment in prose rivaling that of Poe and of Whitman in poetry; excelling, in its own department of prose, in one way or in another, the work of Hawthorne, of Emerson, of Thoreau, of Bret Hart, of Howells, of Frank Norris—and whom have we else to mention?

What of his other books? "Innocents Abroad" is full of the kind of humor for which there is room within the satire-form. The book has been called a satire: but what does it satirize, the old world, or the bumptious visitors from the new? It is a strange thing to say, but the writer lacked the courage of his comic convictions. He thought Europe ridiculous, but he was afraid to go the whole length; he halted half-way and pretended to be making fun of himself.

* * *

In a latter book he returned again to the attack, in the satire "A Yankee in King Arthur's Court." And this book, which Mr. Henderson rightly regards as a failure, shows how wrong Mr. Henderson and others are in taking Mark Twain seriously as a sociologist. Mark Twain satirized the middle ages, but not as he had satirized America. He loved America, after all, but he had no love, no sympathy, for the middle ages. Well, if one despises utterly the middle ages, let him set up something better against it! Mark Twain set up the Boss, a kind of Henry Rogers at once vulgarized and glorified. To prefer the Boss and his milieu to the middle ages argues some defect in intellect and in taste. For it showed that Mark Twain did not understand the ideal he was attacking, it showed him incapable of conceiving a superior idea.

It is easy to take too seriously Mark Twain's ideas. But, one and all, from his quasi-democracy, his pseudo-radicalism, his hysterical fear of Christian Science, his antiquated theological liberalism, his trite mechanistic philosophy, down to his Baconian absurdities—what did they amount to? The fact is that Mark Twain knew American life and could write about it like a master; and below this peak of knowledge to every side there stretched vast abysms of everydayness; ordinary ideas, theories, beliefs, ideals, the kind held by every American citizen, and of no particular importance to anybody.

If the inadequacy of his idealism must be illustrated from his life, rather than from his books, there is the Gorky incident. The less said about this, for Mark Twain's sake, the better. But for a man who pretended to reverence womanhood, and to honor marriage, not to know a real marriage when he saw it, and to assist in the insulting of Madame Gorky, is painfully "human." Nor was his devotion to the cause of Russian freedom such as to stand the test. "Not even his most enthusiastic biographers," says Mr. Henderson of Mark Twain's army career, "have attempted to palliate, save with half-hearted facetiousness, his inglorious desertion of the cause which he had espoused." Let none attempt to palliate this more inglorious desertion.

Could a man of that kind, with that mere human frailty, write great books? The proof, as Mr. Henderson or any other admirer could sufficiently reply to such an objection—the proof is in "Tom Sawyer" and "Huckleberry Finn." Blessed are they that doubt; for, reading these books, they shall be comforted.

August 25, 1911

DIVORCE

Rebellion, by Joseph Medill Patterson. [The Reilly & Britton Company.]

There is not more rejoicing in the courts of heaven over a sinner saved than there will be among judicious novel readers over the publication of "Rebellion." Joseph Medill Patterson was a literary sinner if there ever was one. He is now a sinner saved. His "Little Brother of the Rich" was sentimental, rhetorical, melodramatic. It was bad; it was very bad; it was . . . but why go on?

"Rebellion" is different; it is a real novel, and a good novel. Somehow, in the last three years, Mr. Patterson has learned to write. One can even guess how he learned—it must have been by the beneficent example of Arnold Bennett. There is a character in this present book, a doctor, who "always meant some day to write a true novel, something on the order of 'The Old Wives' Tale,' showing people as they really were. He thought he had the necessary information; and the spectacle of Mr. Bennett's writing has moved him to a kind of happy emulation in the treatment of that information: a treatment at once dry and vivid, orderly and imaginaive, [sic] severe and dynamic. It is a method that leaves aside factitious heroics and insincere pathetics; it calls for all that a writer has of sheer naked ability. That Mr. Patterson could succeed with it—as he has notably succeeded—means much to his native powers.

86

Information—precise, carefully observed, carefully selected, carefully stated facts—are the basis of this book's artistic success.

"Meticulous"? No; that is only another name for "stupid." The realism of the man who knows what he is about is never irrelevant. "Rebellion" is laid in Chicago; Mr. Patterson knows the town, and he could draw pictures, deft, intimate pictures, of a thousand things; and his readers would be pleased, for that matter, since, as some one has remarked, "we're made so that we love first when we see them painted, things we have passed perhaps a hundred times nor cared to see." But Mr. Patterson has drawn such pictures only where they will count. He has stuck to his artist's business of telling about a divorce.

In his first chapter there is a vivid evocation of a saloon episode; and the group of men, their talk, their facile good-fellowship, their way of taking certain things for granted, the expert tact of the barkeeper, the irruption of ward politics in an acute form, the disciplining of a cowardly and drunken henchman—all these things have their bearing, more or less direct, on the theme.

So with the wife of this cowardly and drunken henchman, a working-woman, a stenographer in a downtown office; the chapter in which she is introduced is embellished not at all in vain with a description of the "rectangular room which was over one hundred feet long and half as wide" in which she worked. That rectangular room with its forced ventilation and its castor-mounted desks, has a real relation to the theme.

And Mr. Patterson shows that relation unmistakably. "These details," he says, "were all of profound interest to Georgia, for her desk was the most important thing in the world to her at this time in her life. She delighted in neatness, order, precision, in the adjustment of means to the end. Every morning, just before 9, she punched the clock, which gave her a professional feeling, and hung her hat and jacket in locker 31, which seemed to her a better, a more self-respecting place for them to be than her small, untidy bedroom closet, all littered up with so many things—hers and Jim's."

* * *

These matters, then, bore cogently on that delayed, unpermitted, declined, but always approaching, divorce of hers; and the people who wanted her to stick to her husband till death did them part would better have abolished the modern office building to begin with. At home she could easily enough follow the custom of her kind; but downtown "she was no mean citizen of no mean city."

Comparisons were perhaps dangerous; but comparisons were inevitable. "There were no oaths, no bonds unbreakable." If her employer "had sworn at her, or came ugly drunk into her presence—but that was inconceivable." A good many things went to the making of that divorce, but the office building started it: honor where honor is due.

A woman unhappily married and illicitly in love: shall she stay with her husband or go with her lover? The theme is old; it has been dealt with time without number. And if it is to be made interesting to the sophisticated reader, it must be by virtue of extraordinary truth in the telling.

And this extraordinary truth is just what Mr. Patterson has put into the tale. He has depicted some ordinary Americans as ordinary Americans have seldom before been depicted—with a familiarity and fidelity that in only one or two other American novels can be matched. He has seen these people, and pictured them, as in their most characteristically American moments they see themselves.

There is no tragedy to be discovered in such a view; but there is astringent comedy. When, after Georgia has separated from her husband, her friendship with a young blue-eyed hustler in the same office has blossomed into love, and she has to tell him that she is a Catholic and cannot get a divorce, there was opportunity for a "big scene." Only, these are ordinary Americans, the kind who do not conduct their affairs with much display of emotion. Mr. Patterson could have written a chapter drenched with fictitious tears, windy with counterfeit sighs and black and blue with dishonest emotional spasms; but he didn't. He showed these two young Americans arguing out the matter there on a bench in Lincoln Park, the man reluctantly consenting at last to "pretend" to be only friends as before, and both of them going off with all the grace they could muster to feed the elephant. To a reader used to the ways of books it is astonishing; but it is true enough to American nature.

It was not renunciation, it was common sense; her religion denied the girl the right to have the man for a husband, so she would keep him as a friend. Mr. Patterson, one feels, approves of her attitude. "She managed, being vastly the more expert, to keep him pretending with hardly a lapse throughout the winter." But there are things in human nature—even in American human nature!—deeper than common sense. "She found it more difficult, however, to keep herself pretending." And for the tide of passion, physical and spiritual, that steadily rises in the girl, the author has the same cool and steadfast approval.

There is, at this point in the book, a chapter which may appear to be a digression, since it concerns the girl and her lover not at all, but deals with the girl's "kid brother," a prize fight which he attended and some opinions of the late William James. But it is really to the point; it reveals clearly the philosophy of the book, which is a healthy materialism. The boy who attended the prize fight acquired there, Mr. Patterson tells us, an ambition—the ambition of becoming physically "fit." A struggle began, not yet ended. "His high achievement thus far has been sixth place in a river

Marathon swimming race, his completest failure thirty-six drunken hours in the restricted district." The achievement may or may not move us to admiration; but it was a real achievement. And the failure was a real failure. "With ordinary Americans," Mr. Patterson seems to say, "you need not split any ethical hairs. Good is as visible as green; bad is as obvious as a barber pole. These people are simple, and I am not going to make them out to be complex. I am not going to do any juggling of values in the story of their lives."

* * *

A book's philosophy may make or mar it. A poor, weak, unconvincing philosophy it was that marred so sadly Robert Herrick's "Together," as it has marred many a less promising novel. After much tawdry mysticism in modern fiction one breathes the atmosphere of "Rebellion" with relief. Its emphasis on the plainest physical and spiritual needs of mankind, its passing over of vague, ineffable, quasi and pseudo motivations, give it an appearance of sincerity decidedly refreshing in a literature as stuffed with spiritual pretense as ours. Its simplicity is, in a word, not crude, but distinguished.

But for an accident the book had ended in the middle, when the girl surrendered to herself and agreed to get a divorce. The accident was contrived by the author in order to exhibit the modern and traditional views of marriage in more direct conflict. The man is sent on a special mission to Kansas City, and the girl falls ill with typhoid fever.

Illness does strange things to us: it made this girl renounce her lover and finally to return to her husband. One senses in the author—and it is interesting—a condonation of the girl's action in going back. It looked like a sensible thing. It saved trouble. Besides, her husband has come back from Oklahoma thin and brown and hardened—and, to all appearances, quite cured of his passion for drink. To be sure, Georgia did not love him. But when she herself managed to reconcile herself to living with him, why should a mere author make a racket? "After what she had been through in the past few months, a little more wouldn't greatly matter one way or another. It would certainly be unpleasant to have Jim pawing her again, but she had successfully postponed it much longer than she expected, so now she had better be philosophical about it. . . . Why, therefore, excite her imagination and her sense of horror, and try to make a tremendous hard-luck story out of what after all was a perfectly common and commonplace situation. . . . It was rather ridiculous to think herself a shrinking victim of masculine passion. She had borne this man a child, she was scarred with life, a matron of nearly ten years' standing." It was not ideal, her conduct. But Mr. Patterson does not deal in the ideal. It was human, that is enough.

"Jim," says the author, "was a dipsomaniac, not a villain." He had very good intentions; he loved his wife, and was "faithful" to her; but he

89

relapsed into ward politics, drunkenness, dirtiness and idleness. Mr. Patterson considers him very sympathetically; but he finds nothing in his case which requires a nice girl, against all her instincts, to live with him. Georgia soon regrets her weakness of will in taking him back; but unfortunately she has conceived a child by him. She has to wait for a while. Then, "disencumbered, her strength restored, she would be wholly able to take care of herself and her child. Either she would promptly find another first-class secretarial position or else she would go into business on her own hook"—as stenographer-court reporter-notary public.

But not for several months—"slow months of discomfort, culminating in hours of the acutest agony a human being can suffer and live. She knew. She had been through it once already. But she would never go through it again, after this time. Never. They might say what they liked about race suicide, this was the last for her."

The baby was born, and was marked with the hereditary weakness transmitted by the father. When the child was a few weeks old it fell ill, and in the presence of the mother, the doctor, the priest and the drunken father, died. Considering this scene I will only say that in its realism, its restraint and its power it is quite wonderful.

Thus painfully emancipated, the girl went out again into the world of business. There are some charming chapters dealing with the relationship of the two partners in the firm of Frankland & Connor, of which Georgia was the latter. The characteristic cheerfulness of the American came uppermost in her soul, and her flair for success brought her to prosperity before long. But that wasn't enough. "Frank," she asked that fine old maid, her partner, "do you ever feel like an automaton that's been wound up and has to keep going till it runs down?"

L. Frankland assured her that it was a common human experience. "But what's the use? what's the answer?" Georgia asked querulously. Hear L. Frankland;

> "The answer," she said vivaciously, "for a woman is a man; for a man the answer is a woman. Whoever made us knew what he was about, and don't you forget it."

So Georgia at last concluded; and so concluding, she threw overboard the faith that forbade her to have the man she loved, and procured her divorce.

Mr. Patterson quotes the news item in which the facetious reporter told how "Cupid went down for the count in the courtroom of Circuit Judge James M. Peebles when five couples were legally separated yesterday afternoon between 3 and 4 o'clock—about ten imnutes [sic] for each case. This is said to establish a new record in Cook County for rapid-fire divorce. The cases, which were uncontested, were as follows," etc.

90

The next passage is, I think, the most important in the book. For in it the author relinquishes all claim to special consideration for the case of his heroine, and puts her among the ordinary people who get ordinary divorces. It is a blow between the eyes for the careless reader, who is apt to treat with unthinking cynicism the desperation of people less fortunately mated than himself. It should be read and pondered by all those citizens who have been deceived by the specious arguments of unscrupulous reactionaries in favor of a "uniform" divorce law; by those who have allowed their indignation against the buying of child-wives by middle-aged millionaires to push them into approval for infamous institution of the "interlocutory decree"; by all those who have idly permitted fundamental liberties to be taken from them by ignorant legislatures and an arrogant judiciary, and who read without protest the proposal to enforce by law the most heartless and wicked doctrines that a tyrannical Puritanism can invent:

> Georgia read the item twice and smiled bitterly. So her divorce was one of the "rapid-fire" variety! They said it had taken ten minutes. She knew it had taken ten years.
>
> And Bush, Darroch, those other people—might they not also have walked in Gethsemane? Was this what the papers meant by their humorous account of "divorce mills"? She had received an especially vivid impression of Mr. Darroch and never would forget him. His case had come just before her own. He had spoken in a nasal, penetrating voice, and she heard plainly every word when he testified. He was a short, middle-aged man whose young wife, after ruining him by her extravagance, had run away with a tall traveling salesman. Even after that Mr. Darroch had offered to forgive her and take her back. But she wouldn't come. Then finally he divorced her, as the reporter put it, with record-breaking speed.

* * *

Well, Mr. Patterson has written a remarkable book. He has taken common people, considered them in their own terms and described them in their own idiom—the middle western idiom. This last is in itself an achievement; though Mr. Patterson will be accused of writing "journalese" by those who fail to get the pungency of this natural, living speech. He has treated a great problem with sincerity, power and extraordinary restraint. It remains only for the book to be properly appreciated. If the public does not permit the binding, the paper and the illustrations to dissuade them from buying this masterly work, they will presently be in line for such congratulations as an enthusiastic audience once received from a candid author: "Ladies and gentlemen, you have succeeded!"

October 6, 1911

ARNOLD BENNETT'S EXPERIMENT

Hilda Lessways, by Arnold Bennett. [E. P. Dutton & Co.]

There is rampant among those who read books a heresy which has been pretty well stamped out among those who look at paintings—the curious idea that the public has some rights other than those which the artist chooses to grant it. In its classic form of statement this heresy runs; "I don't know anything about art, but I do know what I like."

The results of allowing the public to dictate to its writers are sufficiently notorious. Mr. Arnold Bennett remarked the other day to a reporter that this dictation constituted "the greatest drawback that an English author has. I don't think the Anglo-Saxon people can expect to have absolutely first-class fiction," he added, "unless they give their authors a free hand, which they have never had since Fielding's day. And there is no doubt that English fiction is not quite equal to that of other countries simply because that of the others is all heart-free."

* * *

Under these circumstances, the rule is that the novelist who takes his art seriously, is the unpopular novelist. That an author should be both popular and serious, that he should venture upon any bold experiment and yet retain his hold upon his public would mean that he was extraordinarily astute as well as extraordinarily daring.

Arnold Bennett is both daring and astute. He has been able to make a departure of the most striking kind in English fiction without—it may be predicted—endangering his popularity. He has just produced two books which, taken together, are comparable in the field of another art to the paintings of such a man as Claude Monet—in that they represent (as Monet's pictures represented) a radical and entirely successful experiment in technique.

He was able to do this by playing upon the public's curiosity. He wished to tell a story of a love affair in two different novels from two different points of view—those of the man and of the woman. It was a magnificent problem in construction; a problem in the working-out of which, in the present state of public taste, he could not hope for any general interest. So he introduced into the first of these books a mystery. Hilda Lessways, a mysterious, reticent, alluring creature, falls in love with young Edwin Clayhanger; there in the Clayhanger printing office she joins with him in the first kiss of love; from Brighton she writes to him in the authentic words of passion: "Dearest, . . . I love you. Every bit of me is absolutely yours. . . ." And then, in only a few days, comes the news that she has married another man!

Why? asked Edwin Clayhanger. And Why: asked the reader, as he counted up anxiously the months that must elapse before he could find out. It was an excellent trick. But the real importance of the book lies outside the trick. It lies in the feat of giving the other side, the feminine side, of the love-story in "Clayhanger."

As Mr. Bennett moves on, in that extraordinary succession of masterpieces that began with "The Old Wives' Tale," he seems to have lost one quality and gained another in each new book. The novel just mentioned remains memorable for its Time effects. In English, at least, there has never been a novel that produced so tremendously the impression of growth and decay. It was like life itself, that moving picture in which, with an illusion of rapidity greater than in any book, one sees one's friends pass from love to sorrow, from strength to weakness, from life to death.

Upon the details of that terrible and curious passage from birth to death this book dwelt just long enough to give the effect of verisimilitude; but not so long as to let one forget the passage itself. In its simplicity the thing was full of tragic beauty and inspiration.

In "Clayhanger" there was a change. Here the incidents, dwelt upon more at length, had a different quality. The people of the other book, who endured life, were succeeded by a man who sought vainly to shape life to his desires. "What Life is" became a tragi-comedy. Edwin Clayhanger caught glimpses again and again of the overwhelming secret which the Bain sisters had only sensed dimly at the end; he momentarily roused himself, but sank back again forgetfully.

That tragi-comedy is gone from the story of Hilda Lessways. She had a gift above ambition. For she enjoyed the savor of existence in all its kinds. She could have said: "In the last resort I do not care whether I am seated on a throne or drunk or dying in a kitchen." Against her palate fine she burst the grapes of remorse and joy and misery, sucking the last drop from each. Always she lived at the top of her energy.

* * *

"The Old Wives' Tale," then, was the story of the endurance of life; "Clayhanger" was the story of the unsuccessful struggle with life; and "Hilda Lessways" is the story of the fierce enjoyment of life. There is another great type to be dealt with—the artist who creates life—and that seems promised in an ensuing work of Mr. Bennett's. Meanwhile, we have something new and vivid in this picture of Hilda Lessway.

Indeed, the fascinating glimpses of this willful and unpredictable young woman in "Clayhanger" hardly prepare one for her intense actuality. When she reads Crashaw's lines:

O, thou undaunted daughter of desires!
By all thy dower of lights and fires;
By all the eagle in thee, all the dove:
By all thy lives and deaths of love;
By thy large draughts of intellectual day;
And by thy thirsts of love more large than they;
By all thy brim-filled bowls of fierce desire—

. . . "it was as if her soul was crying out: 'I also am Teresa. This is I! This is I!'"

Superficially, of course, Hilda is not such a wonderful creature. She is a moody young woman who lives with her mother, who studies shorthand, who assists in launching a Five Towns newspaper, who helps run a boarding-house in Brighton. It is the special magic of realism that this young woman, who might frown at you any day in an elevated train, should be revealed as the object of perpetual and legitimate wonder.

The love story of "Clayhanger," from the point of view of such a person, is necessarily a fascinating matter. It is especially fascinating by reason of the events which constituted the secret of the former book. This secret I unscrupulously divulge: When the girl had kissed Edwin Clayhanger there in the printing office she had already married George Cannon, had grown quickly weary of him and had discovered (with mixed emotions) that he was a bigamist; and it was only her discovery of her pregnancy that cut short her second romance.

* * *

It is Mr. Bennett's triumph as a realist that he can depict so convincingly the virginal quality of this young woman's mind in her second, as in her first, romance. And her hopeless feminine entangling of the motifs of caution and candor—how well that is done! Before her interview with Edwin she wondered: "Would she have the courage to tell him that she was in his society under false pretenses? Could she bring herself to relate her misfortune?" Afterward she composed letters in her head like this: "You see, it was so sudden. I had had no chance to tell you. I did so want to tell you, but how could I? And I hadn't told anybody! I'm sure you will agree with me that it is best to tell some things as little as possible. . . ."

Hilda, it has been said, loves life because it is life; she stands in awe of change because of the inherent wonderfulness of change. In this respect, indeed, she replaces the reader, who was the chief experiencer of the action of "The Old Wives' Tale." But to see someone else deeply affected by a spectacle is not the thing as being yourself affected by the spectacle: and the book of Hilda is correspondingly less poignant than that other truly great novel. It is even less poignant, in a way, than "Clayhanger." For it is only toward the end of the book, after her marriage with George Cannon is at an end, that Mr. Bennett fully enters into the life of his heroine.

Arnold Bennett was Edwin Clayhanger—one perceived no medium of reflection—the man faced the reader directly. But—except toward the end of the book—Arnold Bennett is not Hilda Lessways; one does perceive the medium. Mr. Bennett is, in fact, throughout the book, rather in the way. An observant, even enthusiastic gentleman, he has not that limpid sympathy which is so fine a part of Mr. Galsworthy's literary equipment; nor has he that pungency of personality which redeems Mr. Wells' prejudices. Mr. Bennett is, in short, never greater than his character; sometimes he seems to be standing on tiptoe to measure up to her; but in the latter part of the book writer and subject are one—and then one asks no more, for in her unobstructed view Hilda Lessways is magnificent!

Above all, the book is a woman's vision—or, if you prefer, a feminine view—of life. To read certain chapters in this and the other book side by side (as one is impelled to do after finishing the new book) is to be struck with admiration, and almost with awe, at the precision with which Mr. Bennett has noted the sexual aspect, so to speak, of ideas. He has retold certain conversations, and made of them things as different as the minds of a man and a woman.

Especially has he noted the subtle glamour of masculinity which exists for sensitive women. For Hilda, the young printer had "an exotic and wistful quality." There was "an enigmatic and inscrutable and unprecedented something in his face, in his bearing, which challenged and inflamed her imagination." He had "the inexplicable attractiveness of masculinity, as masculinity is understood by women alone."

Hilda, be it observed, was no improbable romanticist; she had "the inexorable realism of her sex" about facts. It is profitable, in this connection to compare the tenor of the girl's experience with that of Edwin Clayhanger's. We have long permitted our fiction to carry on the absurd tradition of feminine idealism and masculine realism—a tradition which may be sufficiently refuted by reference to the matter of childbirth: in which it is the woman who, characteristically enough, faces the grim reality, and the man who, also characteristically, enjoys its romantic embellishments. Well, in these two books the girl, by the very nature of female existence, deals immediately and practically with a great variety of facts; she lives her life among facts. The man, on the other hand, lives to a great extent among ideas; he has the masculine privilege of generalization. The girl experiences; the man thinks. And it is the man's ideas that fascinate the girl; the faint perfume crushed from experience which in the girl allures the man.

It is not only in Hilda's relations with men that Mr. Bennett understands her femininity; the story of her life at home with her widowed mother shows the same remarkable and unusual insight. One sentence will suffice to quote; "The domestic existence of unmated women together, though it is full of secret exasperations, also has its hours of charm—a charm honeyed, perverse and unique." Who shall say that Arnold Bennett does not understand women?

* * *

There are many fine qualities in the book to which attention might pertinently be called, but one prefers to return to the matter of Mr. Bennett's chief significance—which is, very simply, as a literary artist. "The art of fiction"—the phrase, such is our naivete, sounds like a piece of affectation. Well, before we are through with Mr. Bennett, he will have taught America as well as England better. It may be said (subject to correction only by himself) that Mr. Bennett takes this art seriously. He regards it, not as the by-product of moral or humanitarian enthusiasms, but as an end in itself: precisely as the painter regards painting. He sets himself to serve the art of fiction by formulating and working out untried problems of technique. In writing "Hilda Lessways" he did what is always being done by painters and almost never—consciously—by novelists. He experimented. As for the experiment itself, Wilkie Collins did for cruder and more trivial purposes a similar thing in "The Moonstone." Robert Browning did it, ambitiously enough, in "The Ring and the Book." But where have we the English novelist who cared enough about the art of fiction to attempt the telling of a story from two people's separate points of view in two finished works of fiction?

The fact that Mr. Bennett does care, that he is a conscious and conscientious artist, is the basis of his significance. It is not that he is our best English writer: he is not. It is that he is concerned with his art down to the last comma.

Mr. Bennett is a realist. Wanted—a new definition of realism. There are some people who pretend that realism is a minute description of unimportant details; who pretend even that they find justification of this definition in the writings of Mr. Bennett. In the interview quoted from at the beginning of this review, Mr. Bennett attempted to free the term from its vulgar limitations. "When it comes to the best work," he said, "romanticism and realism are the same thing—they are joined together. When a first-class artist is impressed by anything, he will say, 'This is a romantic thing.' Fielding, for instance, is perfectly truthful, but he shows even in his truthfulness the romantic instinct."

* * *

I do not know of any writings that are more imbued with the sense of the wonderfulness of life than those of Bennett's. When anyone in my hearing speaks of their being "commonplace" I am thrown into a speechless rage. It is to me a sufficient refutation of that libel to quote such a passage as this—which, in its zestful insistence on the truth that underlies the appearance, is perfectly representative of its author's spirit. Hilda is working at a copying press, and a young newspaper man is watching her:

> He was over thirty. He had had affairs with young women. He reckoned that there remained little for him to learn. He had deliberately watched this young woman at the press. He had clearly seen her staring under the gas-jet at the copied letter. And yet in her fierce muscular movements, and in her bendings and straightenings, and in her delicate caressings, and in her savage scowlings and wrinklings, and in her rapt gazings, and in all her awful absorption, he had quite failed to perceive the terrible eager outpourings of a human soul, mighty, passionate and wistful. He had kept his eyes on her slim bust and tight-girded waist that sprung suddenly neat and smooth out of the curving skirt-folds, and it had not occurred to him to exclaim ever in his own heart: "With your girlishness and your ferocity, your intimidating seriousness and your delicious absurdity, I would give a week's wages just to take hold of you and shake you!" No! The dolt had seen absolutely naught but a conscientious female beginner learning the duties of the post which he himself had baptized as that of "editorial secretary."

*　*　*

Here is a man, generous-minded, full of artistic enthusiasms; somewhat lacking, to be sure, in originality—for Mr. Bennett is rather a disciple of George Moore than himself a leader; but gifted with a liking for his work and a capacity for great production; his conscious technique subserved by native ability, by the expertness that comes from much practice, and by amazing architectonic powers: such a man seems bound to exercise on the English and American literature of the present century a dominant, a bracing, a renaissant influence.

October 27, 1911

THE BOOK OF THE WEEK

A GREAT NOVEL

Jennie Gerhardt, by Theodore Dreiser. [Harper & Brothers.]

"Jennie Gerhardt" is the new novel by the author of "Sister Carrie." To some readers this will mean a great deal. To such it is only necessary to say that the new book is a bigger, finer thing even than the old.

There is reason that it should be bigger and finer; it is the work of a man some ten years older, who has lost none of the creative vigor of his twenties. Accordingly it is done with a surer hand, a wider vision, a subtler art. The episode of the going-to-pieces of Hurstwood was, after all, the best thing in "Sister Carrie"; Carrie herself, for all the objective faithfulness with which her career was depicted, showed only the faintest glimpses of her inner life. This new work is above all things the history of a woman's soul.

Jennie Gerhardt, for whom the present book is named, is a girl whose life is lived outside the pale of the conventions. Her story is one easy for a writer to tell sensationally, or is one easy to libel, easy to mistakenly glorify. In taking such a person as his subject, Mr. Dreiser has selected a theme of first-rate importance. In succeeding with it, he has done something which is of profound significance to American literature.

In the columns of a contemporary, a judicious critic, Mr. H. L. Menken [sic] has attempted to evaluate this book. I am in entire accord with his opinion, which puts it as the head of American fiction. But "Jennie Gerhardt" is a book which one would really prefer not to assess in set terms. Anybody may say of any book that it is the "great American novel," and everybody else may treat that statement as incompetent or insincere. What one would like to do is this: To write soberly about the book in such a way that the reader must himself feel what the critic omits to say as to its absolute worth.

* * *

But the very quality of the book makes description difficult. One can only say: Here is a story, a rather unusual story, told in an extraordinarily lucid and sympathetic manner. There are no surprises, no shocks, no bits of splendid writing—just the tale of a woman from girlhood to middle age, in her relations with her mother, her father, her lovers, her child. For perhaps half the volume it is only very interesting. And then it comes upon one that a wonderful thing is being accomplished.

This novelist is dealing with a dozen human beings; and he has very quietly revealed every one of them to us. They live. We know them intimately. And yet there have been no dazzling pages of psychological analysis. There is no brilliancy of character-study. The book is as devoid of this as it is of amazing feats of realistic description. The story moves on, without any straining for effects, without a sign of effort. There is page after page of utterly simple narrative.

And about the middle of the book there comes this sense of the power behind this quiet narrative—the sustained strength, the penetrating vision, the boundless sympathy, the nobility of soul. It is not by minor writers, or by merely clever writers, or by "promising" writers, that such things are done.

Mr. Dreiser is not, in fact, a clever writer. He is weak in the very thing in which a clever writer is strongest—in verbal taste. This was pretty uncertain in "Sister Carrie," in which he would use such phrases as "cultured humans." And the chapter headings, as a distinguished admirer of Mr. Dreiser's regretfully pointed out to me, are what I should call the limit. The present book shows a great improvement. But on the very first page there are phrases which an infinitely lesser writer with a keener taste in the matter of words would have excised with a blush for their banality.

* * *

And yet on that same page there is a sentence which is such as to signify a great deal to the discerning reader. It is of Jennie's mother: "Her eyes were large and patient, and in them dwelt such a shadow of distress as only those who have looked sympathetically into the circumstances of the distraught and helpless poor know anything about."

That sentence signifies that Mr. Dreiser has at his command the power to bend language to the spirit of its content: to call forth a subtle and sympathetic prose music. This power is different from the artificial eloquence, the prose-poetry, which some writers affect: it is, as these are not, a sign of the born artist. I have compared as carefully and fairly as I could certain passages of Mr. Dreiser's writing with certain passages from the writing of one of the most notable of his English contemporaries; and despite its obvious faults it seemed to me that Mr. Dreiser was inherently the better writer.

Be that as it may—Jennie Gerhardt is the daughter of a poor German woman who gets work as a scrubwoman in a hotel at Columbus, Ohio, and who takes home the washing of one of the hotel's guests, Senator Brander. Jennie's father is a glassworker, now out of a job. When this 18-year-old ingenuous girl takes Senator Brander's washing to his room she attracts his attention, and an acquaintance begins, which on the man's part slides rapidly down the scale from paternal benevolence to amorous rashness. He thinks of sending the girl to school, and then marrying her. But he dies suddenly, and Jennie is left with the burden of a fatherless child. She leaves home, and goes to Cincinnati, Ohio, where she is employed as a maid. In this aristocratic home she again attracts the attention of a man, and soon, hoping to relieve the terrible economic situation of her family, becomes his mistress. He is rich and good-hearted, and she hopes that some day he may marry her; so she does not tell him about her child. She lives with him for years, and gains his whole respect. Nevertheless, under pressure of circumstances, he leaves her. Her child dies. She is left neither rich nor poor, neither happy nor miserable, neither rewarded as for heroism nor punished as for sin. That is the story. It is inconclusive, true; but its inconclusivenes [sic] is part of its interest.

The book has a theme: and this theme, again, is difficult to describe by virtue of its simplicity. Starkly put, it is the beauty, and the helplessness, of a generous soul. The whole book is the explication of the inevitable defeat of a woman who asks only to give; and of the loveliness of that doomed nature. It sounds, perhaps, absurd. We have not much sympathy with unselfish people in books. They are either prigs or fools, or both. That is when the author attempts to make a virtue out of a temperamental necessity. Mr. Dreiser makes no such mistake. He looks with a philosophic eagerness upon the spectacle of human life; he sees Jennie, an essentially unselfish girl in a world of essentially selfish people; he knows that she will be exploited, that she is bound to be exploited: and he shows how it happens—that is all.

* * *

He does not blame Jennie's exploiters; nor does he defend them. Selfishness is human. Selfishness can be noble. And even the everyday selfishness of the people among whom Jennie's career unfolds itself is shown to have its aspects of beauty. None of these people were brutes. There was something fine, because it was warm-hearted, instinctive, about the selfishness of the man, Senator Brander, who first took this poor washer-woman's daughter in his arms. There was something exalted about the cruelty of the girl's Lutheran father, when he tried to put her out of his life as hopelessly wicked. There was something beautiful, because violent and daring, about the selfishness of the man, Lester Kane, who made this girl his mistress. And there was something attractive, because frank and open, about the ruthlessness of the society woman who took this man away from the girl at last.

But more beautiful than these aspects of their selfishness, because rarer and more passionate, is the girl's generosity. When she yields to Senator Brander, in her innocent gratitude for the love of such a wonderful man; when the desperate poverty of her family compels her to accept the relation of mistress—a relation instinctively desired but dutifully refused at first—to Lester Kane; when she gives loving service and companionship to this man, who carelessly postpones the legalization of what he has come to consider a real marriage; and when she finally sends him away so that he may not be disinherited—in all this there is an elemental, natural, human quality. It is a positive, not a negative thing; a strength and not a weakness. Jennie never suppresses herself; by such actions it is that she expresses herself.

But in Mr. Dreiser's novel this never becomes abstract: it is always exhibited in a flowing stream of natural events. Jennie goes to Chicago with Lester Kane. The existence of her child is discovered, and the menage for a time is threatened with disruption. Jennie's mother dies. Her father, believing Jennie and Lester are married, comes to live with them. Vesta, the little girl, goes to dancing school, much to her grandfather's dismay. The old man worries because Lester wastes so many matches—five or six to light a single cigar, by chops! It is along this stream that the reader is borne—a journey whose end one foresees, but of which one would not lose a moment.

The melting mood: this, which has been said to be the sign of great art, is what this book continually evokes in the reader. How it is done I do not know; a great part of the effect must be due to the long-sustained simplicity of the narrative, rather than to the quality of any certain passage. Quiet sympathy, it seems, can be prolonged until it reaches the breaking-point of poignancy. Would any piecemeal quotation serve to produce the same effect? It is doubtful. But, for what it will at least show of the author's lucid simplicity, here is a fragment—necessarily lengthy—which tells of Jennie's visit to her father, when she would persuade him to come and live with her and Lester:

> Accordingly she made the trip, hunted up the factory, a great rumbling furniture concern in one of the poorest sections of the city, and inquired at the office for her father [who was a night watchman]. The clerk directed her to a distant warehouse, and Gerhardt was informed that a lady wished to see him. He crawled out of his humble cot and came down, curious as to whom it could be. When Jennie saw him in his dusty, baggy clothes, his hair gray, his eyebrows shaggy, coming out of the dark door, a keen sense of the pathetic moved her again. "Poor papa!" she thought. He came toward her, his inquisitorial eye softened a little by his consciousness of the affection that had inspired her visit: "What are you come for?" he asked cautiously. . . .
>
> "Tell me one thing," he demanded. "Are you married?"
>
> "Yes," she replied, lying hopelessly. "I have been married a long time. You can ask Lester when you come." She could hardly look him in the face, but she managed somehow, and he believed her.
>
> "Well," he said, "it is time."
>
> "Won't you come, papa?" she pleaded.
>
> He threw out his hands after his characteristic manner. The urgency of her appeal touched him to the quick.
>
> "Yes, I come," he said, and turned; but she saw by his shoulders what was happening. He was crying.
>
> "Now, papa?" she pleaded.
>
> For answer he walked back into the dark warehouse to get his things.

Mr. Dreiser writes of meetings and partings, festivities and funerals, as though no one had ever written of them before—freshly, yet without any straining after novelty of effect. The life of Jennie and Lester together is as familiar as a sunset—and as perpetually interesting. He sees everything eagerly, clearly, without prejudice.

* * *

When Lester leaves Jennie, when he marries the cultivated woman of whom he has always been fond, the author does not depart from his attitude of impartiality. It was inevitable. He did not love the girl enough to make this last sacrifice for her. It is true, if he had married her in the beginning, he would not have been put in such a position. But there was no way of knowing what was to come. He had behaved rather sensibly. He had never expected that the affair would have such elements of permanency. And he had behaved rather kindly, too; but his amour propre was offended by the discovery that Jennie had been keeping a secret, the secret of her child, from him—after that, could he marry her? And when he has left her, he is not visited by remorse. He is happy with the other woman—for after all she is of his world, can talk his language. But he is no happier than he was with Jennie; perhaps—he concludes at last—not so happy. His wife is in Europe when a fatal illness overtakes him; he sends for Jennie, and she comes, glad to be able to be of some final service to him. "You are the only woman I ever really loved," he tells her. There is some satisfaction in that confession to Jennie. She knows that he did not love her enough. But he loved her that much, and she is glad.

Meanwhile, Jennie has been left in a gathering loneliness. Her mother had died, and her father. Her lover has gone away. Her little girl succumbs to the typhoid. She is left alone, sad, perplexed, wondering now and then what it all means.

What does it all mean? Mr. Dreiser doesn't say. Life seems to him to justify itself. He does not point to a mistake in Jennie's life or in Lester Kane's, and say that the trouble lay there; that if they had done the right thing there, everything would have gone well. There is no right thing to do. People act according to their natures, and the end makes their actions seem wise or foolish; but there is no way of knowing at the time. There wasn't any mistake in Jennie's life; she lived it well. And the end proves nothing—except that what is going to be, is. Only there is a great sympathy which envelops the history, a sympathy which bathes every incident with a tender light and brings out clearly the tragic outlines of the whole.

Tragedy? The word is loosely used nowadays. It means—what? "Pity and terror" are said to be the emotional effects which distinguish it. "Sympathy and awe" would perhaps be a better rendering of the Greek idea. A Tragedy is the representation of a defeat which brings out the inherent nobility of the defeated one. Nobility is various; it is of one sort in Prometheus, of another sort in Hamlet, of another in the heroine of "The Tragedy of Nan." And Mr. Dreiser's Jennie has an authentic nobility no less—a nobility which nothing but utter defeat could bring out.

Have I conveyed any sense of the power, the truth, the inspiration of "Jennie Gerhardt"? Then perhaps I may say, without saying it in vain: this is a great book.

November 3, 1911

MR. WELLS' SHORT STORIES

The Door in the Wall, and Other Stories, by H. G. Wells. Illustrated with photogravures from photographs by Alvin Langdon Coburn. [Mitchell Kennerley.]

Mr. Wells, before he arrived at his present goal of pre-eminence among English novelists, was a man of many possibilities. He might have remained, as he used to be called, the English Jules Verne—though he was always better than that. He might, as that remarkable book, "First and Last Things," shows, have attained fame as a philosophic essayist. He might have gone on with the sociological prophecy of "Anticipations" and "Mankind in the Making." And he might have been a great short-story writer.

The present volume contains a selection of eight stories made by Mr. Kennerley and used as an occasion to exhibit that publisher's imagination and taste in bookmaking. I do not know anything more beautiful in contemporary bookmaking than Mr. Kennerley's title-pages, and this volume contains one of his finest. . .

* * *

There are all kinds of stories, or almost all kinds, among the eight given here. The one kind that is conspicuously absent is the "slice out of life." If it were needed to show that Mr. Wells is essentially an artist, it could be shown by these stories, which are so much indebted to their form. Mr. Wells preaches one thing and practices another. He recently uttered the heresy that a short story was a jolly piece of writing that could be read in half an hour—or words to that effect. The short story is, of course, nothing of the kind. It is an arrangement of quasi-real events in such a way as to produce a single impression. It is an art-form as definite as the sonnet.

And Mr. Wells has worked pretty generally in accordance with that feeling about the short story. He has started with an idea, and he has invented and arranged his action so as to explicate that idea impressively. Very seldom has he cumbered his writing with details that obscure the significance of his idea. It is true that the idea is not always one of serious permanent interest. Thus, for instance, there is one entitled "The Cone," which is built around the idea of the tremendous heat—300 degrees centigrade—of the cone of a blast furnace. It was an idea that fascinated the curious mind of Mr. Wells; he wanted in some way to show how hot, how terribly hot, 300 degrees centigrade is. So he invented a story—a horrible story. A man is making love to the wife of an iron founder, and the iron founder comes home and discovers it. Pretending to have noticed nothing, the iron founder invites the man to walk with him, promising to show him some "fine effects" in flame and smoke. The husband is insane with jealous rage, and it is his intention to murder the other by throwing him down into the cone. He does it, and the man dies in agony. But not merely in agony—in agony of a particular kind— the kind that only 300 degrees centigrade can inflict. It interested Wells to show just what that would be. He cared nothing for the husband, for the wife, for the illicit love affair. He was interested in making real 300 degrees centigrade.

There is another story almost of the same kind. It is called "The Lord of the Dynamos." A dynamo is a powerful thing. Mr. Wells wanted to show how terribly powerful it is. So he conjured up a savage, a negro not long from Africa, who should worship this power—should worship it as a god, and make a human sacrifice to it, and die a martyr to his religion. With the negro as the helper of a brutal chief attendant of the dynamos, all this was possible. Mr. Wells labors to make it seem likely, but he does not turn it into a simple story of insanity, or revenge. One feels, when one has finished it, above everything else, the terrible power of the dynamo—a thing indeed to inspire worship, and human sacrifice, and martyrdom.

* * *

Again, Mr. Wells wanted to show what the little accidents that astronomers perceive in the heavens would mean to the inhabitants of the planet concerned. He would have some difficulty in working the thing out on just those lines, so he made the earth the victim of such a little accident. He invents a stellar wanderer which invades our solar system and collides with Neptune, making a new star. The story is entitled "The Star." The new star falls into the sun. But in falling it is deflected by Jupiter and in its new path it passes close to the earth. The star grows brighter and brighter, portending an end to the world. It turns night into day, it grows hot, until presently the coming of sunlight is as the coming of a shadow. The ice melts upon the mountains, and there are terrible floods in all the river valleys. The earth is shaken with earthquakes, and whole mountains slide into the sea. The jungles of India are wastes of flame, and China is a waste of water. Whole populations are burned and drowned. A great tidal wave sweeps across the Pacific. But the end of the world has not come. Star and earth approach each other, swing about each other and pass.

And the Martian astronomers, who had watched with keen interest, said: "Considering the mass and temperature of the missile that was flung through our solar system into the sun, ... it is astonishing what little damage the earth, which it missed so narrowly, has sustained. All the familiar continental markings and the masses of the seas remain intact, and indeed the only difference seems to be a shrinkage of the white discoloration (supposed to be frozen water) round either pole."

"The Dream of Armageddon" inweaves with the story of a last terrible world-war the idea of the ruthlessness of love. The man (to whom all these things happen in a succession of strange dreams) is a statesman who might have prevented the war if he had given up his mistress; but he goes to Capri with her, and in the midst of their romance the war breaks. It is a story as beautiful as it is terrible. The new terror and the new beauty that Wells has given to the familiar theme are simply his way of giving the idea, in which he was interested, new force. What a man, even a statesman, will do, when he is in love! He came back to the theme, and treated it at length, in "The New Machiavelli."

* * *

But it is of another story that I wish particularly to speak—"The Country of the Blind." Everyone has heard the saying "In the country of the blind the one-eyed man is king." It occurred to Mr. Wells that this might not be true. He set about passionately showing what the real case would be. He invented a Country of the Blind in South America, a little community cut off from the rest of world, and introduced into it a man who could see. But he felt it necessary to explain how these people came to be blind, and how they had been cut off from the outside world—a long and irrelevant introduction. It is when the mountaineer falls and slides down a precipice and lands safely in the Country of the Blind that the real story begins.

This man finds no disposition on the part of these people to make him king. They make him a slave. Their other faculties are so well developed that they can get along very well without sight. The things that they can do without eyes he cannot do nearly so well with them. He is considered a defective. When he talks about color and mountains and sky, they take him for an idiot or a blasphemer—because their great thinkers have evolved a different philosophy. He falls in love with a girl, and at first she is pleased with his "poetic fancies." But there is opposition to her marriage with such a person, until a blind scientist suggests an operation to cure him. "Those queer things that are called the eyes," he says, "and which exist to make an agreeable depression in the face, are diseased, in the case of Nunez, in such a way as to affect his brain. They are greatly distended, he has eyelashes, and his eyelids move, and consequently his brain is in a constant state of irritation and distraction." A simple operation, he suggests, would remove those irritant bodies, and Nunez would be a sane man, as good as any of themselves.

The girl confidently expects this sacrifice of her lover. She might be a pretty bourgeoise maiden asking her lover to give up writing poetry! For love's sake the man consents. The day approaches. On the last morning he goes out alone.

"He had fully meant to go to a lonely place where the meadows were beautiful with narcissus, and there remain until the hour of his sacrifice should come, but as he walked he lifted up his eyes and saw the morning, the morning like an angel in golden armor, marching down the steeps. . . .

"It seemed to him that before this splendor he and his blind world in the valley, his love and all, were no more than a pit of sin."

* * *

That story, with the ending which I do not indicate here, is one of the finest things that Mr. Wells has ever done—one of the most imaginative, the most poetic, the most symbolic.

And that, if one understands the world rightly, is the key to the interest and value of this form of art. To speak simply, the good short story is a fable, of which the meaning does not end with the story, but extends to the borders of one's experience.

January 5, 1912

ROBERT HERRICK'S CHICAGO

Chicago in Fiction: The First Paper

Concerning no writer more than of Robert Herrick have we the right to ask: What is Chicago to him? And in nearly all of his books, but most definitely in three, the answer is to be found. Those three are "The Memoirs of An American Citizen," "The Web of Life," and "The Common Lot."

It is not merely that in these books are included such historic incidents as the trial of the Haymarket "anarchists," the world's fair and the Pullman strike. It is not merely that Chicago is the background to Mr. Herrick's stirring stories. But Chicago is in each case a moving force in the action, and represents a dynamic principle.

What principle?

To answer that question is to do Mr. Herrick some injustice. For it is to put in harsh and crude sentences what Mr. Herrick has wrought with pains and skills through hundreds of pages to convey. To put it in such terms is to sink Mr. Herrick's art in the consideration of his opinions. Even to quote passages which seem to glow with the writer's personal passion is to do violence to his artistic intention. But that personal passion is an essential part of Mr. Herrick's writing, and must in any case be stated if his work is to be appreciated.

In "The Memoirs" is told, in the first person, the story of a successful pork packer and politician. It begins with his coming into Chicago from Indiana looking for work—but more than that: looking to make his fortune. The year is 1876, in that interval between the two greatest periods of development of American capitalism. There are pictures of the lake front, with its "bums" hounded by vigilant watchman; of the police station and the jail; of the boarding-house, run by a pale slave of a woman whose husband, coming from the country to get rich, has failed, and become a slovenly loafer; of the group there in the little basement dining-room—"strugglers on the outside of prosperity, trying hard to climb up somewhere in the bread-and-butter order of life, and to hold on tight to what we had got." No one, it seems, "ever came to Chicago, at least in those days, without a hope in his pocket of landing at the head of the game sometime. Even old Ma Pierson cherished a secret dream of a rich marriage for one or other of her girls!"

* * *

That boarding-house life, which is one of the most memorable parts of the book, might stand as a symbol of Mr. Herrick's Chicago—a dirty, ugly, disorderly place filled with people too much occupied in "hustling" to see the dirt, the disorder, the ugliness. They are thinking, these people, of getting

107

on; when they to go church, it is a fashionable church, where they can look at the rich people, and talk about them. One of them does protest at last against the dominance of this topic. But she is answered by one of the "hustlers."

> "What else are we here for except to make money?"
> Slocum demanded more bitterly than usual.
> He raised his long arm in explanation and swept it
> to and fro over the struggling prairie city, with its
> rough patched look. I didn't see what there was in
> the city to object to: it was just a place like any
> other—to work, eat and sleep in. Later, however,
> when I saw the little towns back East, the pleasant
> hills, the old homes in the valleys, and the red
> brick house on the elm-shaded street in Portland, then
> I knew what Slocum meant.
> Whatever was there in Chicago in 1877 to live for
> but success?

When the ambitious and rising young man who is the hero of this book is drafted into the jury that is to hang the Haymarket "Anarchists," he is impatient to have it over with. "And then back to business. I suppose the world seemed to me so good a place to hustle in that I couldn't rightly appreciate the complaints of these rebels against society. . . . Guilty or not guilty, these men must suffer for their foolish opinions, which were dead against the majority."

When the World's Fair—the one dream that Chicago had it in her soul to dream—was being realized, this young man begrudged his employer the time he devoted to it. "It made me impatient to have Mr. Dround spend on it his energy that was needed in his own business."

And such a man it is, according to Mr. Herrick, who fits in with Chicago—to whom Chicago gives all that she can of wealth and position and honor.

* * *

In "The Web of Life" Mr. Herrick exhibits the opposing type, the man who has a civic sense, imagination, honor, ideals. This young man is a doctor. He does not like the vulgar pandering to the rich which seems to be the thing in his profession. He does not like the rich, with their ignorance, their tawdry standards, their fatuous pride. He refuses to do what is expected of him, to "make good" in the conventional way. He cuts loose. And Chicago breaks him scornfully—mashes him in misery until he is glad to crawl back and surrender, making the best terms he can. That, again, is Mr. Herrick's Chicago.

The man who figures in "The Common Lot" is neither the born

108

"hustler" nor the born idealist. He is an impressionable fellow, whom Chicago takes and molds to her satisfaction—for a time, until he discovers what thing she has made of him. He is an architect who, in order to stand in with a certain contractor, shuts his eyes to every kind of fraud in the construction work. But when one of his jerry-built hotels burns up before his eyes, and he sees men and women dying in agony, he revolts. Chicago no longer owns his soul. He refuses to "bluff it out" as a good business man is expected to do, but (with his wife's encouragement) makes a clean breast of the whole thing to the coroner's jury. He puts aside success, the success that must be won by lies and murder, and takes his place in the ranks from which he came. He is despised and forgotten. And there, once more, is Mr. Herrick's Chicago.

Or, rather, that is the soul of Chicago. But the body is not different. This young architect, riding down Cottage Grove avenue, can see clearly enough what is the matter with Chicago: "This block, through which the car was grinding its way, had a freakish individuality in sidewalks. Each builder had had his own idea of what the street level should be and had laid his own sidewalk accordingly. There were at least six different levels in this one block. The same blunt expression of individuality was evident in every line of every building. It was the apotheosis of democratic independence. This was not a squalid district, nor a tough one. Goose Island, the stockyards, the Bohemian district, the lumber yards, the factories—all the aspects of the city monstrous by right, were miles away. But Halsted street, with its picturesque mutations of poverty, and its foreign air, was infinitely worthier than this. Sommers shuddered to think how many miles of Cottage Grove avenue and its like Chicago contained—not vicious, not squalid, merely desolate and unforgivably vulgar. If it were properly paved and cleaned, it would be bearable. But the selfish rich and the ignorant poor make bad housekeepers."

He sees it as well in the houses of his friends—"the modern barbarian type that admires hungrily and ravishes greedily from the treasure-house of the Old World what it can get, what is left to get, piling the spoil helter-skelter into an up-to-date American house. Medieval, Renaissance, Italian, French, Flemish—it was all one! Between them they would turn Forest Manor into one of those bizarre, corrupt, baroque museums that our lavish plunderers love—electric lighted and telephoned, with gilded marble fireplaces, massive bronze candelabra, Persian rugs, Goth choir stalls, French bronzes—a house of barbarian spoils!"

* * *

In his hatred of ugliness and disorder, Mr. Herrick reminds one of H.G. Wells. It will be remembered that Mr. Wells wrote about Chicago in "The Future in America." What he said there might almost stand as a summing up of Herrick's opinions.

"Undisciplined"—that, says Wells, is the world [sic] for Chicago. "It is the word for all the progress of the Victorian time, a scrambling, ill-mannered, undignified, unintelligent development of material resources."

But while Mr. Wells intimates that it is a shame, Mr. Herrick feels, with the peculiar moral sensibility of the Puritans, that it is a sin. And there is another difference. "All that is ugly in America," says Mr. Wells, "is due to this, to the shoving unintelligent proceedings of underbred and morally obtuse men. Each man is for himself, each enterprise; there is no order, no provision, no common and universal plan. Modern economic organization is still as yet only thinking of emerging from its first chaotic stage, the stage of lawless enterprise and insanitary aggregation, the stage of the prospector's camp.

"But it does emerge."

* * *

Mr. Herrick does not say, "It emerges." He condemns it as it is, and he has no faith (or so one is constrained to believe) in its future. He sees it as a muddy pathway down to hell, trampled and bloody in a monstrous and useless conflict.

And he sees among the others a few clear-souled men and women who attempt to free themselves, to get out and away from it all. And that effort, even though it be a weak and futile effort, he celebrates in novel after novel with passion and tears. . . . If I am not very much mistaken, the burden of Robert Herrick's writings is: Delenda est—Chicago.

January 26, 1912

"MR. DOOLEY'S" CHICAGO

Chicago in Fiction: Second Paper

Finley Peter Dunne did not, in his Mr. Dooley sketches, tell the whole truth about himself nor about Chicago. Part of Mr. Dooley's talk was local color. Part appears to have been mere brilliant journalism. And Mr. Dunne has more recently found in "The Interpreter's House," in one of our magazines, what seems to him a better medium for expressing his ideas. Nevertheless, in Mr. Dooley is a figure which gives us in bold, clear colors this writer and his Chicago. In bold, clear colors, not somber ones, for it is human nature one sees in Archer road, not the goats and the gas tanks. And after renewing my acquaintance with the "Ar-rchey road" philosopher, I am left with a heightened respect for his creator and some confirmation of the notion that, after Mr. Robert Herrick, the writer who should be interrogated as to what Chicago means to him is Mr. Finley Peter Dunne.

For consider Mr. Dooley. First by comparison. There is in Chicago a publicist whose shrewd observation and delicately ironic comment on current affairs constitute him a person of national interest. Hundreds of thousands of people turn every morning, before they look at anything else in the paper, to see what this man has to say about the news of the day. I refer, of course, to Mr. John T. McCutcheon. Now here is a man of ability and experience, and all that sort of thing. And what is the latest figure which McCutcheon has invented, by and through which to express his ideas on things in general? An astonishing figure, astonishing in its emptiness, its dullness, its tameness: "Dawson, '11"—the most objectionable male prig since the days of Jacob Abbott's Little Rollo.

* * *

What would anybody care about what this adolescent captain of industry of Mr. McCutcheon's might say about Chicago or anything else? Dawson, '11, knows nothing, is nothing, represents nothing save, perhaps, the callow ideal of the business colleges. But Mr. Dooley, sitting back there in his little saloon in Ar-rchey road is a rich and sound personality, with a great deal of experience and an active and original mind; and he represents, as no other figure I know represents, what might be called lower middle-class Chicago.

An Irishman, a Catholic, a saloon-keeper, a semiretired politician, an indefatigable reader of newspapers (and nothing else), a talker, and, above everything else, a satirical observer, Mr. Dooley represents a culture which is of the greatest interest, because it is the culture upon which Chicago may be said to be based. The great public which used to read with delight his weekly discourses to Hennessy did not regard them as something new and strange, but found in them an expression, epigrammatic and racy with his peculiar humor, of their own ideas.

Was it the servant problem? Mr. Dooley talked as a man whose women folk are accustomed to do their own work. He regarded the alleged "problem" with amused tolerance as the vagary of another class. Not that he hated that other class; for he knew that it had in part at least only recently graduated out of Ar-rchey road. "We have a servant problem because, Hinnessy," he said, "it isn't man-ny years since we first began to have servant girls."

Was it divorce? Mr. Dooley took much the same attitude. Divorce was a fad of the rich. Mr. Dooley knew all about domestic unhappiness—perhaps that was one reason that he remained a bachelor. But he spoke for the great mass of people into whose lives divorce does not enter—who have their connubial rows and make them up as best they can—and to whom the existence of children is, for economic reasons, a fact that usually makes divorce entirely out of the question. Since Mr. Dooley first began discussing these things with Mr. Hennessy the situation has been changing, and divorce, from being a privilege of the rich, has percolated down through society until it has reached even Ar-rchey road. But Mr. Dooley's observations remain the clew to a great mass of sentiment on the question here in America.

High finance is another matter that Mr. Dooley regarded from the lower middle class point of view. "It sain't burglary," he told Hennessy, "an' it ain't obtainin' money be [sic] false pretinses, an' it ain't manslaughter. . . . It's what ye might call a judicious selection fr'm the best feature iv them ar-rts."

* * *

Politics he regarded with a friendly if critical eye. Mr. Dooley was not a reformer. Reform was another fad of the rich, a fad with which he could sympathize, but—the reformers were too short-winded to suit him. Reform, he knew, was an avocation, while politics was a vocation. Besides, he did not have—as lower middle-class Chicago does not have—any spark of the reformer's temperament. At best it was a meddling sort of business. It gave Mr. Dooley great delight, when there was talk of the rich having spent all their money at the Paris exposition, to picture the situation when the indigent millionaires came back to Chicago, and had to appeal to the lads at the rollin' mill for help. He imagined a Return Visiting Nurses' Association composed of ladies from Ar-rchey road, who would march into the houses on Lake Shore drive and give the women there instructions about cooking and taking care of babies. "Throw away that oatmeal—'tis no food f'r childer. Run down to the' butcher-shop an' get a nice round steak, an' cook it with onions, an' give the baby the bone to suck."

And he didn't like the life made too smooth and pretty, either. When they talked about reforming the newspapers and not printing anything scandalous, he quoted Father Kelly with approval: "News is sin, an' sin is news. . . . A religious newspaper? None iv thim f'r me. I want to know what's goin' on among the' murder an' burglary set."

With Father Kelly, too, he had the honor to agree as to the proper use of whisky, reporting the matter thus to Mr. Hennessy: "'Whisky,' he says, 'is called th' divvle, because,' he says, 'tis wan if th' fallen angels,' he says. 'It has its place,' he says, 'but its place is not in a man's head,' says he. 'It ought to be th' reward iv action, not th' cause iv it,' he says. 'It's fr th' end iv th' day, not th' beginnin',' he says. . . . 'The minyit a man relies on it fr a crutch, he loses th' use iv his legs. 'Tis a bad thing to stand on, a good thing to sleep on, a good thing to talk on, a bad thing to think on.' "

* * *

And Chicago? Chicago, to Mr. Dunne, is America—the headlines of the story, blacker and harsher than the small type below, but to the same effect. When William Waldorf Astor ceased to be an American, Mr. Dooley went into the subject in a way that lights up all the corners of his creator's mind. "An' whin ye come down to it, I dinnaw as I blame Willum Waldorf Astor for shiftin' his allegiance. Ivery wan to his taste, as th' man said whin he drank out of the fire extinguisher. It depinds on how ye feel. If ye ar-re a tired la-ad an' wan without much light in ye, livin' in this counthry is like thryin' to read th' Lives iv th' saints at a meetin' iv the Clan-na-Gael. They's no quiet fr anybody. They's a fight on ivery minyit iv th' time. Ye may say to ye'ersilf: 'I'll lave these la-ads roll each other as much as they plaze, but I'll set here in th' shade an' dhrink me milk punch,' but ye can't do it. Some wan'll say: 'Look at that gazabo settin' out there alone. He's too proud fr to jine in our simple, dimmycratic festivities. Lave us go over an' bate him on th' eye.' An' they do it.

"Now if I'm tired I don't want to fight. A man hits me in th' eye an' I call fr th' polis. They isn't a polisman in sight. I say to th' man that poked me: 'Sir, I fain wud sleep.' 'Get up,' he says, 'an' be doin',' he says. 'Life is rale, life is earnest,' he says, 'an man was made to fight,' he says, fetchin' me a kick. An' if I'm tired I say, 'What's th' use? I've got plenty iv money in me inside pocket. I'll go to a place where they don't know how to fight. I'll go where I can get something but an argymint fr me money, an' where I won't have to wrassle with th' man that bates me carpets, ayether,' I says, 'fr fifty cints overcharge or good government,' I says. An' I pike off to what Hogan calls th' effete monarchies iv Europe an' no wan walks on me toes, an' ivryman I give a dollar to becomes an acrobat an' I live comfortably an' die a markess! Th' divvle I do!"

"That's what I was goin' to say," Mr. Hennessy remarked. "Ye wuddent live an-nywhere but here."

"No," said Mr. Dooley, "I wuddent. I'd rather be Dooley iv Chicago than th' Earl iv Peltville. It must be that I'm iv th' fightin' kind."

* * *

So is Mr. Dunne—a fighter and a philosopher. His Chicago is the Chicago of Archer road, of Prairie avenue, of the rolling mills, of Dorgan the plumber—all seen in their human, not their picturesque, aspects. It is not a cruel place, as in Mr. Herrick's view, nor a romantic place, as plenty of other writers would make it. It is not ugly, because it is full of men and women and children. It is a place where people work hard in shops and factories and go home, not to an idyllic home, but a human one, and in the evening talk about the election or the neighbors. Mr. Dunne believes in these people. He does not despise their work, nor their homes, nor their conversation. He is an instinctive democrat.

He does not even mind the goats and the gas tanks. But there's the rub! One may forgive him his tolerance of the goats, but one cannot forgive him his tolerance of the gas tanks. A man ought to hate a gas tank. Chicago has been growing, partly by virtue of that hatred, out of the gas tank stage. Mr. Dooley has not noticed it.

February 2, 1912

HENRY B. FULLER'S CHICAGO

Chicago in Fiction: The Third Paper

There is a Chicago which desires to learn—which goes to art classes, and lectures, and abroad—which is anxious, pathetically anxious, to be "up" on everything: and this Chicago is best exhibited in the Chicago novels of Henry B. Fuller.

If in the '70s was pre-eminently Chicago's term of ferocious money-making, as Mr. Herrick tells us, in the '90s was her term of going to school. Then did we study desperately to find out what was good and what was bad in art, music, architecture and what not. Even the "climbing" of the period was in part at least an effort to achieve the good, the true and the beautiful in social relations.

* * *

People had begun to go abroad, and to envy the pervasive taste that comes of a traditional culture. Discontented with the uncertain aesthetic results of our osmotic social process, they set about methodically achieving standards, bit by bit. With what devotion, and with what silent pain, they put themselves in the hands of Theodore Thomas, and Lorado Taft, and the

114

Abbey and Grau Opera Troupe, to be made over. And these aesthetic ministers, like the Mahometan angels of death who prepared the soul for paradise by drawing it out of the body with red-hot pincers, were cruel only to be kind.

Mr. Fuller tells, in "With the Procession," of a visit made by the angular and awkward daughter of an old-fashioned Chicago family to a stately society woman. The episode is one which could hardly be matched at the present time. The idealistic '90s are over and gone!

* * *

"What do you suppose happened to me last winter?" the older woman asks. "I had the greatest setback of my life. I asked to join the Amateur Musical Club. They wouldn't let me in. . . . Well, I played before their committee, and then the secretary wrote me a note. It was a nice enough note, of course, but I knew what it meant. I see now well enough that my fingers were rather stiffer than I realized, and that my 'Twinkling Sprays' and 'Fluttering Zephyrs' were not quite up to date. They wanted Grieg and Lassen and Chopin. Very well, said I, just wait. Now, I never knuckle under. I never give up. So I sent right out for a teacher. I practiced scales an hour a day for weeks and months. Granger thought I was going crazy. I tackled Grieg and Lassen and Chopin—yes, and Tschaikowsky, too. I'm going to play for that committee next month. Let me see if they dare to vote me out again!"

That is not half. The hostess invites her guest into the library: " 'How glorious!' cried Jane, as her eyes ranged over the ranks and rows of formal and costly bindings. It all seemed doubly glorious, after that poor sole bookcase of theirs at home—a huge black walnut thing like a wardrobe, with a couple of drawers at the bottom, receptacles that seemed less adapted to pamphlets than to galoshes. 'How grand,' Jane was not exigent as regarded music, but her whole being went forth toward books. 'Dickens, Thackeray and Bulwer; and Hume and Gibbon, and Johnson's "Lives of the Poets".' "

* * *

Presently these two Chicagoans of the '90s walk into the Grand Salon. This time it is the guest who scores: " 'Hem,' she observed, critically, as her eyes roamed over the specious splendor of the place, 'quite an epitome of the whole rococo period; done, too, with a French grace and a German thoroughness. Almost a real jardin d'hiver, in fact. Very handsome indeed.' "

"You are posted on these things, then?" asks the hostess. "Well," replies Jane, "I belong to an art class. We study the different periods in architecture and decoration."

"Do you?" returned the hostess. "I belong to just such a class

115

myself—and to three or four others. I'm studying and learning right along; I never want to stand still . . .''

* * *

In this same novel there is a young man who has just returned to Chicago after a long stay in Europe, where he has become imbued with continental ideas. Mr. Fuller does not, indeed, approve of his morals, but does approve of his tastes. He is, aesthetically, that to which the Chicago of the '90s aspires.

And through him Chicago pronounces judgment upon itself. The great exposition is just over, and the young man meets halfway "the universal expectation that the spirit of the White City was but just transferred to the body of the Black City close at hand, over which it was to hover as an enlightenment."

* * *

" 'Good,' he thought; 'there's no place it's needed more, or where it might do more good.' The great town in fact sprawled and coiled about him like a hideous monster—piteous, floundering monster, too. It almost called for tears. Nowhere a more tireless activity, nowhere a more profuse expenditure, nowhere a more determined striving after the ornate, nowhere a more undaunted endeavor toward the monumental expression of success, yet nowhere a result so pitifully grotesque, gruesome, appalling. 'So little taste,' sighed Truesdale; 'so little training, so little education, so total an absence of any collective sense of the fit and the proper! Who could believe, here, that there are cities elsewhere which fashioned themselves rightly almost by intuition—which took shape and reached harmony by an unreasoned instinct, as you might say?' "

Truesdale patronized, "so far as he could endure them," the theaters, he visited the art stores regularly, and attended all the good concerts. But he was surprised to find that the city had no promenade, and he missed his beloved cafes. "The cafe, that crowning gem in the coronet of civilization—the name was everywhere, the thing nowhere. Nothing offered save a few large places of general and promiscuous resort, which, under one ameliorative title or another, dispensed prompt refreshment amid furnishings of the most reverberant vulgarity."

Soon after his return home he has a conversation with a "bud" fresh from Michigan. "Where do you suppose I went night before last with Aunt Lydia?" she asks, and goes on in an awe-struck undertone; "To the opera—to 'Rig-o-letto.' Aunt Lydia couldn't get a box—she said they were all taken for the season; but we had seats close to one side, just below the boxes. Such a grand place! Ever since the Auditorium was opened, I've been hoping to see

116

it, and now I have." And Truesdale congratulated her, for he remembered "how he himself had panted for the Scala and for the Apollo at Rome."

* * *

Ah, happy, happy, time! Too happy time, of which the lingering relic is the salon of Mrs. Guffle, celebrated by our esteemed contemporary, B. L. T. This Chicago is not the apocalyptic sociological beast of Mr. Herrick; it is the scene of a tragi-comedy of manners.

* * *

Or a tragedy, if you like: for if Mr. Fuller's Chicago aspired, it was because she was vile. Chicago was sordid, with a sordidness that defeated every attempt at reaching something better. She was drab, with a hopeless drabness. That word sums up the impression which Mr. Fuller's two Chicago novels convey. It is not essentially a wicked city, but it is perhaps worse than wicked. Certainly it seems to have grated upon Mr. Fuller more than Nineveh could have done.

"The Cliff Dwellers" and "With the Procession" are collections, half-satirical, half sympathetic of middle-western ugliness of speech and action. They reveal "miles of flimsy and shabby shanties and back views of sheds and stables; of grimy, cindered switch-yards, with the long flanks of freight houses and interminable strings of loaded or empty cars; of dingy viaducts and groggy lamp posts and dilapidated fences whose scanty remains called to remembrance lotions and tonics that had long passed their vogue; of groups of Sunday loungers before saloons, and gangs of unclassifiable foreigners picking up bits of coal along the tracks; of muddy crossings, over roads whose bordering ditches were filled with flocks of geese; of wide prairies, cut up by endless tracks, dotted with pools of water, and rustling with the dead grasses of last summer, then suburbs new and old—some in the fresh promise of sidewalks and trees and nothing else, others unkempt, shabby, gone to seed; then a high passage over a marshy plain, a range of low-wooded hill, emancipation from the dubious body known as the Cook County Commissioners—and Hinsdale." This last is hardly enough to compensate for the monotonous others!

* * *

It is really too bad that Mr. Fuller ever wrote of Chicago. For he is a master of a delicate irony, for which a theme like that of "The Chevalier of Pensieri Vani" is vastly better suited. He should have conceived fiction in such languid and evasive terms as has Anatole France. But Mr. Fuller has not so conceived fiction. He has adopted our robustious English mode of

117

novel-writing, filled, as it is, with irrelevancies which can exist only by sheer vitality; he has gone in for genre painting and phonographic conversation. Think what you will of the result, it involves a misuse of peculiar and rare abilities. I wish he would give us a great talker, a philosopher after his own heart, an American Bergeret—it were worth a dozen Chicago novels!

February 9, 1912

JOSEPH MEDILL PATTERSON'S CHICAGO

Chicago in Fiction: The Fourth Paper

Not all of our writers hate Chicago. The city, and what the city stands for, has its friends. Joseph Medill Patterson is among them. In fact, Mr. Patterson belongs to a group of people who officially believe in the city.

This group of people regard nothing as so foolish as the cavil which tender-minded people make at the iniquities of modern civilization. They see something in civilization besides iniquity. They are the modern inheritors of the old theory of progress—but it is not in the coming-to-be of a vague beatitude that they believe, as but in a precise evolution of a specific future out of the specific present. If the present—they say—were not as it is, with all its iniquities, the future, with all its glories, could not come to pass.

This refers, of course, to the Socialists, of whom Mr. Patterson is one. The fact of Mr. Patterson's politics is of considerable importance to us. For he writes like a Socialist—that is to say, optimistically.

* * *

There is a superstition to the effect that Socialists are pessimistic. That superstition is easily explained. Socialists in their talk and their journalism are continually insisting on various phenomena of the times—such as starvation and diamond dog collars—which are depressing to the ordinary reader. He thinks: "What melancholy folk these Socialists must be!" But there is where he is mistaken. These things are not depressing to the Socialists; they are, on the other hand, encouraging. They are, to him, the signs of change. He believes that when society has come to such a state as that it must be on the point of a revolution. In these terrible stories of the extremes of modern society he sees a meaning to which the ordinary reader is blind—and he is cheered by it.

* * *

There, in vulgar terms, is a statement of the Socialist temperament. It is a temperament that leads one to look courageously on the most sordid and heart-breaking facts, seeking there a clew to the happy destiny of mankind. Mr. Patterson has that temperament. You will not find him, like Mr. Herrick, denouncing civilization, the city, the machine. He will not be heard calling Chicago a plague spot, or a monster, or a whirlpool. On the contrary, for exact reasons, he will give it a discreet blessing.

The elevated train, the newspaper—but here you shall see his heroine (in that fine novel "Rebellion") riding in one and reading the other: "Each morning as Georgia entered the elevated train and spread open her paper she cast off centuries, being transformed from a housewife to a 'modern economic unit.'"

Is that transformation a bad thing or is it a good thing, in the opinion of Mr. Patterson? "She smiled at the morning cartoon. . . . She always turned to the insurance notes next. It was her Duty to be Well Informed and Interested in the Success of Her Employer, for His Success was Hers. She hadn't been to business college for eight weeks not to know that. Next a peek at Marion Jean Delorme's column of heart throbs, which she frankly regarded as dissipation, because she enjoyed it and everybody who read it called it common.

"By this time home and its squabbling; its everlasting question of how far a pay envelope can stretch; her sullen contemplation of Jim's alcoholism [Jim was her husband]; and irritability at her mother's pottering way had vanished into the background of her mind, where they slept through her working day. She engaged herself with more appealing problems and a larger world. She deplored the litter of torn-up streets and the thunder of the loop, instead of the litter of the breakfast dishes and the squeak of the hinge. Not that clean dishes are less meritorious than clean streets, but, to minds such as hers had grown to be, less captivating. To change desks downtown was more fun than to change chairs at home."

* * *

Chicago, Mr. Patterson seems to say, is very likely to be better than the homes of its people; very likely to be the finest influence in the lives of those people. This young wife, Georgia, for instance, "was a citizen of no mean city" throughout the day: at the lunch club where she co-operated; in the big, white-tiled vestibule of her building, where she exchanged ten words of weather prophecy with the elevator starter between clicks; in the restroom

119

where they talked office politics, and shows, and woman suffrage, as well as beaux and hats; behind her machine, which rattled $20 a week by your own ten fingers and no man's gratuity."

"There were no oaths, no bonds unbreakable, no church to tell her that she couldn't change her job, as it tells the housed and covered women who get this bread by wifehood."

A discreet way of saying that the city does tend to "break up the home"—and a suggestion that such homes ought to be broken up!

* * *

The city destroys religion, too. Georgia's "belief was orthodox [Catholic], but it did not hold her as vividly as it held the old folk in the old days. Had she lived nearer to the miracles of the sun going down in darkness and coming up in light; or thunderstorms and young oats springing green out of black, with wild mustard interspersed among them like deeds of sin; of the frost coming out of the ground; and the leaves dying and the trees sleeping; she would perhaps have lived nearer to the miracles of bread and wine, of Christ sleeping that the world may wake.

"But she lived in a place of obvious cause and effect. When the sun came down, the footlights came up to you if you had a ticket, and man's miracle banished God's, even though you might be in the flying balcony and the tenor almost a block away. Thunderstorms meant that it was reckless to telephone; oats, wheat and corn, something they controlled on the board of trade; the melting of the snows showed the city hall was weak on the sewer side—what else could you expect of politicians?—the dying leaves presaged the end of the Riverview season and young Al's excitement over the world's series. . . . God may have made the pansies, but He did not make 'the loop.' His majesty is hidden from its people by their self-sufficing skill, and they turn their faces from Him. West Siders do not pray for universal transfers"— and Mr. Patterson is rather glad they don't.

* * *

Is Chicago a place of dirt? Superficially, perhaps, but within its big office buildings it is a miracle of cleanliness and neatness, suggests Mr. Patterson. The desks in the place where Georgia worked were "mounted on castors so that they could be wheeled out of the way at night, while the tiled floor was being washed down with hose and long-handled mops. . . . Rubber disks, hinged against the desk and set to the floor, held them in place during working hours. Narrow, black, right-angular marks showed where each desk belonged, and where, exactly, it must be moved back when the nightly cleaning was finished. These details were all of profound interest to Georgia, for her desk was the most important thing in the world to her at this time of her life.

"She delighted in neatness, order, precision; in the adjustment of the means to the end. Every morning just before 9 she punched the clock, which gave her a professional feeling, and hung up her hat and jacket in locker 31, which seemed to her a better, a more self-respecting place for them to be than her small, untidy bedroom closet, all littered up with so many things—hers and Jim's. Chicago and [sic] exemplar of neatness and order!

The novel "Rebellion" is written about the theme of a woman's divorce. In this matter, too, Chicago figures. It is Chicago, the great city, the focus of modernity, which takes hold of Georgia, and makes her marry the man she loves—that makes her discard the religion in which she has been reared, and all the customs of her people, in order to do it. Chicago will not let her alone; it forces her to be modern.

Chicago redeems us from superstition, from custom, from ignorance, from provincialism; it provides us, as nothing else can, efficient means for the performance of work; it provides us likewise with leisure, pleasure, companionship, stimulus: so one understands Mr. Patterson to say. Let there be drawn a continuous, never-ending line, to represent the course of mankind through time; that which is already drawn is history; and that blank space ahead, the future. But the point of the line, the point which bores into the future, the living present—that is Chicago.

* * *

It is Mr. Patterson's attitude toward the present, as exemplified in his attitude toward Chicago, that makes his novel "Rebellion" so interesting. Mr. Herrick mourns over what is, as though it ought to be something else. Mr. Patterson has a better philosophy, if not so good a literary style: and his writing is accordingly more valid.

But as to Mr. Patterson's literary style, which has been called mere journalism: it is at least adequate to the making of a powerful novel. What more can one ask? If the greatest novels use a whole orchestra of verbal instruments, they justify their use. But to demand an orchestra, to add to it a zylophone [sic], a tom-tom and a calliope, and then to make no sufficient use of this aggregation of instruments (by which trope it is intended gently to suggest the disparity between the stylistic means and the fictional effects of various American novelists)—this is hardly the thing. Better the journalistic penny-whistle of Mr. Patterson, upon which can be played a moving music of love and death and change.

February 16, 1912

THEODORE DREISER'S CHICAGO

Chicago in Fiction: The Fifth Paper

The poetry of Chicago has been adequately rendered, so far, by only one writer, and in only one book. The book is, naturally enough, that one which Frank Harris declared in the London Academy to be "The best story, on the whole, that has yet come out of America," to wit: "Sister Carrie," by Theodore Dreiser. It is the most real, the most sincere, the most moving, of all the books with which we have dealt, or are likely to deal, in this study of "Chicago in Fiction." And it is real and moving greatly by virtue of being poetic.

A good deal of the magic of a great city is that which lingers in the mind from one's first experiences in it. And the true story of adventure in Chicago begins somewhere else. Not to tell how it felt to leave the old town is to omit something of a distinct relevance to the story of Chicago. There is less of Chicago, in whole novels, ostensibly about the life of this city, than there is in the opening paragraph of "Sister Carrie":

"When Caroline Meeber boarded the afternoon train for Chicago, her total outfit consisted of a small trunk, a cheap imitation alligator-skin satchel, a small lunch in a pepper box and a yellow leather snap purse containing her ticket, a scrap of paper with her sister's address in Van Buren street and four dollars in money. It was in August, 1889. She was 18 years of age, bright, timid, and full of the illusions of ignorance and youth. Whatever touch of regret at parting characterized her thoughts, it was certainly not for advantages now being given up. A gush of tears at her mother's farewell kiss, a touch in her throat when the cars clacked by the flour mill where her father worked by the day, a pathetic sigh as the familiar green environs of the village passed in review, and the threads which bound her so lightly to girlhood and home were irretrievably broken."

* * *

And then there is the coming into the city. This, like the other, has been done before in American fiction, but not in the way of Mr. Dreiser. For he writes as one who will not slur the beauty of any emotion, though it were as common as a sunset: "They were nearing Chicago. . . . To the child, the genius with imagination, or the wholly untraveled, the approach to a great city for the first time is a wonderful thing. Particularly if it be evening—that mystic period between the glare and gloom of the world when life is changing from one sphere or condition to another. Ah, the promise of the night. . . . Though all humanity be still inclosed in the shops, the thrill runs abroad. It is in the air. The dullest feel something which they may not always express or describe. It is the lifting of the burden of toil."

Carrie goes to her sister's home. "Minnie's flat, as the one-floor resident apartments were then being called, was in a part of West Van Buren street inhabited by families of laborers and clerks, men who had come, and were still coming, with the rush of population pouring in at the rate of 50,000 a year. It was on the third floor, the front windows looking down into the street, where, at night, the lights of grocery stores were shining and children were playing. To Carrie, the sound of the little bells upon the horse-cars, as they tinkled in and out of hearing, was as pleasing as it was novel. She gazed into the lighted streets when Minnie brought her into the front room, and wondered at the sounds, the movement, the murmur of the vast city which stretched for miles and miles in every direction."

* * *

That passage is significant. We have writers who would be so interested in the sociological significance of the location of Minnie's flat that they would forget all about Sister Carrie. Others would romance about the girl until one sickened of the unreality and threw the book across the room. Others would be so preoccupied with the destiny of Sister Carrie that that would find a moral suggestion in everything they dealt with. Mr. Dreiser kept his head and used it.

He kept his head no less in the description of the factory-room into which Carrie went to work: "The firm of Speigelheim & Co., makers of boys' caps, occupied one floor of the building, fifty feet in width and some eighty feet in depth. It was a place rather dingily lighted, the darkest portions having incandescent lights, filled with machines and work benches. At the latter labored quite a company of girls and some men. The former were drabby-looking creatures, stained in face with oil and dust, clad in thin, shapeless, cotton dresses and shod with more or less worn shoes. Many of them had their sleeves rolled up, revealing their bare arms, and in some cases, owing to the heat, their dresses were open at the neck. They were a fair type of nearly the lowest order of shop girls—careless, slouchy, and more or less pale from confinement. They were not timid, however, were rich in curiosity, and strong and daring in slang."

We are in the habit of forgiving injustice in writing because it is committed on the side of the angels. If a writer has a social sense, he can nowadays be forgiven almost anything. But to the city, which gives this willing little country girl no means of support save back-breaking toil at four dollars and a half a week, and to the man who takes advantage of her situation to make her his mistress, Mr. Dreiser can be fair.

He first shows us this man in his favorite restaurant and his favorite saloon: "Drouet was not a drinker in excess. He was not a moneyed man. He craved only the best, as his mind conceived it, and such doings seemed part of the best. Rector's, with its polished marble walls and floor, its profusion of lights, its show of china and silverware, and above all, it [sic] reputation as a resort for actors and professional men, seemed to him the proper place for a successful man to go. He loved fine clothes, good eating, and particularly the company and acquaintanceship of successful men. When dining, it was a source of keen satisfaction to him to know that Joseph Jefferson was wont to come to this same place, or that Henry E. Dixie, a well-known performer of the day, was then only a few tables off. At Rector's he could always obtain this satisfaction, for there one could encounter politicians, brokers, actors, some rich young 'rounders' of the town, all eating and drinking amid a buzz of popular, commonplace conversation. . . .

"His preference for Fitzgerald and Moy's Adams street place was another yard off the same cloth. This was really a gorgeous saloon from a Chicago standpoint. Like Rector's, it was also ornamented with a blaze of incandescent lights held in handsome chandeliers. . . . Drouet for one was lured as much by his longing for pleasure as by his desire to shine among his betters. The many friends he met here dropped in because they craved, without, perhaps, consciously analyzing it, the company, the glow, the atmosphere which they found. One might take it, after all, as an augur of the better social order, for the things which they satisfied here, though sensory, were not evil."

It is not cleverness, that produces such an account as this. "She conceived a true estimate of Drouet. To her, and indeed to all the world, he was a nice, goodhearted man. There was nothing evil in the fellow. He gave her the money out of a good heart—out of a realization of her want. He would not have given the same amount to a poor young man; but we must not forget that a poor young man could not, in the nature of things, have appealed to him like a poor young girl. Feminity affected his feelings. He was the creature of an inborn desire. . . . In his good clothes and fine health he was a merry, unthinking moth of the lamp. Deprived of his position and struck by a few of the involved and baffling forces which sometime play upon man, he would have been as helpless as Carrie—as helpless, as non-understanding, as pitiable, if you will, as she."

* * *

To say, as was said above, that "Sister Carrie" is a poetic novel is perhaps to invite misunderstanding. It may have warned the reader to look out for a caterwauling prose-poetry, or a heaping up of tremendous rhetoric. But the term means neither one thing nor the other.

What it means is this: that the writer must have his materials, not merely at his fingers' ends, but in his mind long enough to undergo a subtle reconstitution, flowing forth at last in currents of their own and inappropriate verbal rhythms. He must have in solution, as it were, all the thoughts, gestures, actions of his characters, and all the scenes among which they move until they crystallize in the right words. In such a way, surely, comes "Fraternity" and "Evelyn Innes."

There are fine novels that are not poetic, such as Mr. Bennett's; and there are fine novels that, by virtue of the partial unfamiliarity of their materials to the author's mind, are poetic only in flashes: "A Mummer's Wife" is such a one. But to achieve a poetic effect with the diverse elements of a changing life in a great city is a wonderful achievement.

* * *

Mr. Dreiser has not looked to see the badness of the city, nor its goodness; he has looked to see its beauty and its ugliness, and he has seen a beauty even in its ugliness. And in doing that he has given us, there is little doubt, the Chicago of the whole middle West—a beacon across the prairies, a place of splendor and joy and triumph, the place toward which the young faces turn and the end of the road along which the young feet yearn to tread.

February 23, 1912

B. L. T.'S CHICAGO

Chicago in Fiction: The Sixth Paper

Besides those who come to Chicago for money, are those who come for fame: they come, these sweet flies, as to the musk rose, full of dewy wine. And if it is no musk rose, but a fly trap—then there is a story to tell. It may be told in many and various ways. Mr. Bert Leston Taylor in "The Charlatans" (1906) tells it in a way of his own.

It is a beautiful, golden-winged, unsophisticated fly that he chooses for his heroine: in plain terms, a girl of 18 from a village in a neighboring state. Her mother, "when a girl, had shown a taste for music"; and now that Hope shows a similar talent her mother will not let it wither uncared for. The little girl practices ("on rainy days and in the winter time, with industry and enthusiasm"); and a lady from the city, who hears her play, bids her throw away her "Silvery Waves" and "Monastery Bells"—she will send her some real music. Comes Czerny, Bach and Beethoven. More practice. Says a music teacher: "You should have a wider field." Hope turns the leaves of the annual catalogue of the Colossus Conservatory of Music. There is figuring by Farmer Winston, some correspondence, and at last the railway ticket is bought.

* * *

The Colossus: "the largest conservatory of music in this or any other land; it had more departments, more world-renowned instructors, more educational methods than any other; the conservatory building reached nearer to heaven and contained more studios than any other; it graduated more students" . . . and so on! "Come unto us," it exhorted, using the voice of Dr. Erdmann, its president, "and learn to express your soul!"

A boarding-house in Atwood street is the girl's base of operations; a house with "an ill-lighted hall, through which wandered dismally the ghosts of innumerable boiled cabbages." She is companioned there by a fat music teacher, Mme. Jesurin, who is a countess but does not use the title; who adores Wagner and ham sandwiches and Bouguereau.

Hope goes to the Colossus and makes friends among the students, who inquire: "Do you screech, scrape or scramble?" She scrambles, it seems. She talks with Dr. Erdmann, who has a curious ring on his finger and an eye for pretty girls.

* * *

And then to her first concert, and is thrilled; also edified by the interpretive notes written for the program by Dr. Dudelsack: "And then again, when, pregnant by the sun's warm beams, the mountains do with diamonds teem, the dancing nymphs (woodwind doubled above and below) to play invite; and peasants young and old surcease of sorrow seek in laughter, frolic song . . ."

It looked like perfectly good English!

There, too, she sees handsome young Churchill West, the musical critic of the Post, and (as any experienced novel reader can tell) her fated lover. When they become acquainted later, he tells her many interesting things, among them this: "Contrary to tradition, the wealthy patrons make less noise when the orchestra is playing than the so-called music-lovers up here in the gallery." Incidentally, he remarks that the ordinary student "ought to be back on the farm, helping her mother with the housework. Oh, I beg your pardon!"

She had turned scarlet!

* * *

There are valuable lessons lasting fifteen minutes each, in which the students imitate waves breaking on a beach; and pat the top of their heads

126

with one hand while they rub their stomachs with the other; and other harmless, necessary things. Meanwhile, Dr. Erdmann is strangely assiduous in his attentions, making her accept a fine piano and some costly private lessons.

The critic of the Post, I regret to say, is not assiduous; but he reads to Hope some poetry of George Meredith's, which is a good thing for any young woman. She is much affected. "Had he thrown down the book at that moment and held out his arms, she would have made the leap." Instead, he read more Meredith. Critics are sometimes very stupid, aren't they?

While this young man is making up his mind another young man with lots of money proposes marriage. The money at home has run out, and Hope is strongly tempted (oh, weak and wicked girl!) to sacrifice him to her career. But things take a jarring turn. Dr. Erdmann's favorite pupil (on whose hand Hope has recently seen that curious ring) drowns herself. Hope understands. In the school concert that evening she expresses all her grief and shame and rage in her rendering of a Brahms rhapsody. Then she packs up and goes back to the farm.

*   *   *

And then—

The rest is fiction. But I am glad to say that before the critic of the Post follows her out to the farm to express his mature decision he has had a windfall.

Much delightful talk of music, a little satire, a very ordinary vein of romance, a touch of tragedy and some realism in disguise—this last a disciple's tribute to Meredith: such is "The Charlatans." It is done with a light touch, which is in itself pleasant; but the satire is too tender. Mr. Taylor, like a French duelist, feels that honor is satisfied once he has "pinked" his subject. Charlatanism is never once dealt a dangerous wound.

His Chicago is the Chicago of absurd efforts to attain a pretentious culture; but it is no less the Chicago of innocent-hearted artists. It is a place of cruel exploitation of the ambitious; but it is the place where young men read "Love in the Valley" to their sweethearts.

March 1, 1912

RECENT BELLES-LETTRES

The Collected Works of William Morris, with introductions by his daughter, May Morris. The first twelve volumes. [Longmans, Green & Co.]

The achievement of William Morris as a man of letters is not fully represented, of course, in the twelve volumes so far issued in this collected edition of his works. But these volumes do indicate, partly by virtue of the prefaces by his daughter, something of even more importance concerning his career. These imposing volumes are, as the prefaces show, the by-products of a life taken up with other things—in Morris' view and perhaps also in ours, more important things.

More important than that lovely series of romances in verse, "The Earthly Paradise"? More important than that flaming epic, "Sigurd the Volsung"? What piece of hangings, what illuminated manuscript could be more important than these? The question is unanswerable: but it is unfair. It is Morris' literary career as a whole which is to be compared with his career as a handicraftsman and as a prophet of handicraft. In this latter respect he is of prime importance: and the making of poems may well stand second in a man's life to the task of bringing back, by precept and example, a beauty and a joy almost lost from the world.

* * *

Consider the situation in the time of Morris. Handicraft was crushed by the impact of the factory system. With the ascendency of the machine, the device of division of labor and the conflict between "speeding up" and "soldiering," and the old artist's joy in work had disappeared. So much for the industrial aspects of the matter, of which everyone is very well aware. On the spiritual side—using that phrase to mean roughly the ideals and aspirations, as distinguished from the institutions and practices of men—the situation was worse. Men's ideals were only a glorification of the factory system. In so far as men dreamed, they dreamed of an extension of the factory system to the last details of existence. They thought that progress consisted in doing away with all effort except the pressing of buttons.

Even the socialists—the most puissant dreamers of the time—were under the spell. They had inherited from their forbears, the Utopists, a faith in the machine. They only wanted the state to own the machine: so long as there was no exploitation of one class by another through private ownership of the machine, they did not care how complex and elaborate and world-embracing the machine became. They desired an end to work—they would have enslaved the machine, even as their masters had enslaved them: forgetting for the time the saying that if one end of a chain is fastened to the

128

wrist of the slave, the other end is fastened to the wrist of the master. In short, they imagined a mechanical wilderness, and called it the co-operative commonwealth.

* * *

If the world was to be awakened from this gross illusion, it must be by an extremist. It required a man who would make no terms with the machine whatever: one who would go his own way, regardless of the trend of the times, regardless of common sense, and of consistency. Only such a man could stamp his ideals upon a world whose best deeds and whose finest dreams were alike hostile.

Cynics have laughed at the democratic pretensions of a man whose products could only be enjoyed by the rich. But the man out of his time and against his time, cannot but be inconsistent. Morris' books and hangings, the toys of an idle class, are yet the connecting link between a sane past and a sane future.

All this may seem to imply that Morris was quite right about the machine: that the future will go back to the ways of the middle ages. Of course he was wrong—splendidly wrong; and the future, in part because of that magnificent intransigency of his will, will make a good use of the machine. But the nineteenth century needed a man more mediaeval than the middle ages: and found him in Morris.

* * *

All this takes us a good way from Morris' poetry: but no further than it took Morris. He was not the man to preach handicraft: he went and did it. He became—what? A designer, an engraver, an illuminator, a scribe, a dyer. He worked, not played, at it. His daughter prints an extract from one of his letters which fairly has the odor of hard exertion upon it.

"Please," he says, "I shall want a bath when I come home: you may imagine that I shall not be very presentable as to color: I have been dyeing in the blue vat today: we had to work at 130 degrees, and a hot work it was, as you must keep the goods clean under the surface of the bath. It will be a difficult matter to arrange dyeing the shades: our vat is too strong at present for quite light shades. I have been red-dyeing, also, but have not tackled the greens and yellows yet: I must try to do something in them before I go: I set myself too much work to do: that is a fact. . . ."

The way he went into the business of dyeing is characteristic of the man. He started in with the ordinary dyes. "In the matter of color," writes his daughter, "he was dependent on the best that could be got in the ordinary way of trade, and it was a serious thing when costly hangings sent out by the firm were found to have faded: experiments had to be made as to what weaving materials then obtainable could be relied on, and only those used; but it was not possible for anyone with his gift of color to allow himself to be hampered forever in this way, and the tricky and fugitive nature of the brilliant and sometimes beautiful sniline [sic] dyes made him more and more determined to find out the old methods for himself, and to make stuffs at once both beautiful and durable. He approached the matter from the standpoint of an artist whose ideal in color was found in the carpets and fabrics of Asia Minor and Persia. This meant that the old formulas had to be rediscovered; old books on the art of dyeing had to be studied, vegetable dyestuffs imported, old dyes, who had a tradition dating from before the general adoption of the modern processes, questioned, practical work done in an established dyeing business, his own dyeshop set up at Queen Square for experiments—the letters of these two years are full of it.''

In the end, according to Mr. Mackail, ''he and Wardle [with whom he became associated] actually restored dyeing to the position of an important industry.''

*   *   *

Then there was his work in illumination. His daughter gives a list of thirteen projected works, some of which were finished and some left incomplete at this death—but, even so, a staggering lot of work. ''I have dwelt,'' she writes, ''on these written and painted books, because I think that though people know vaguely that my father had worked a little at illumination, they need to have before their eyes such a list as I have given to realize the amount of sheer physical labor he got through, in the course of scribe's work alone; as to what he schemed out, no man's life could possibly be long enough to bring to a conclusion a tithe of the work of various kinds he would have liked to carry through.'' It is hard, even so, to realize what the work meant. ''I have watched,'' says Miss Morris, ''his firm, broad hand as it covered a gold square half an inch in size with wee flowers formed of five pin points of white laid with the extreme point of a full brush. The least wavering would have meant a jog or a blot, but the blossoms grew with the ease and surety that one associates with a Chinese craftsman who has spent his life with a brush in his hand.''

*   *   *

This is not the picture of a literary man. ''I am very hard at work,'' he wrote, ''at one thing or another; firm's work, for one thing. I should like very much to make the business quite a success, and it can't be, unless I work at it myself. I must say, though I don't call myself money-greedy, a smash on that side would be a terrible nuisance; I have so many serious troubles, pleasures, hopes and fears that I have not time on my hands to be

130

ruined and get really poor; above all things it would destroy my freedom of work, which is a dear delight to me.''

Incidentally, Morris organized a Society for the Protection of Ancient Buildings, and interfered belligerently with many a rash "restorer"; he was, says his daughter, continually "hurrying down into the country with Mr. Thackeray Turner to see a church threatened with destruction.''

How did he do it all? Did he never rest? "It is difficult,'' says his daughter, "for people who did not know him to realize the intensity and the swiftness with which he worked, nor with what unconcern he could put off the work of the moment and 'idle' with friends.''

* * *

And his literary work? "My father did his writing in rest hours and on holidays—sometime working at night when all the household had long since been asleep. The business hours of the day were passed in the ordinary occupations of designing and the hundred and one details of overseeing his working people.''

So that his poems were almost literally what he entitled one collection of them—"Poems by the Way." Some were translations intended for a series of volumes to be printed by himself; some were verses written for pictures, tapestry and embroidery and printed in various exhibition catalogues; others were done "as a distraction in the midst of more important production''; and, latterly, some were "made to order for Socialist needs.''

It is almost unfair to repeat one little anecdote about the origin of "Goldilocks and Goldilocks": "During the printing of 'Poems by the Way' Emery Walker went into my father's study,'' says Miss Morris, "and heard that the volume was all set up and only made so many pages; it was too thin, and father a little bothered; he thought they 'could not charge 2 guineas for that.' They parted, and Walker came in to dinner the same night, and afterward my father said: 'Now I'll read you what I've written to fill out the book,' and forthwith chanted this pretty fairy poem to his wondering and amused crony.''

* * *

I suppose I am but a middling Morrisite—if, indeed, I am a Morrisite at all. For his gospel of work I love him as much as any man this side of idolatry. But some of his writings I cannot read and some I cannot understand. I have no patience with those who pretend to find Browning "obscure": but every time I read "The Defense of Guenevere" the mystery grows deeper. And whatever it means, it is a pretty poor poem. Thus one extreme: as for the other, I regard, "Sigurd the Volsung" as being one of the greatest of modern English poems—for sustained narrative vigor and emotional force. I know of no equal.

"Sigurd the Volsung" (which occupies the twelfth great volume of this edition) was the intense flowering of Morris' passion for northern mythology. He had nourished it by a visit to Iceland, the "Journals" of which make up the seventh of these volumes. Other volumes, the seventh and tenth, testify to the same passion: one contains translations of the Grettir and the Volsung and Niblung sagas; the other paraphrases of "Three Northern Love Stories" and a translation in meter of "Beowulf." Miss Morris admits that the "Beowulf" must be reckoned among his few failures." It is better to reckon the whole lot of these northern translations as the preparation for his noble poem "Sigurd the Volsung." Failure had better be reserved for his translation of the Aeneid: anyone less competent by reason of his peculiar virtues to translate a Latin poem could hardly be discovered.

* * *

In a previous notice of this edition an attempt was made to express the pleasure which one takes in its physical form—its blue-gray boards, its paper labels, its large pages, good paper and clear type. Perhaps all that may be taken for granted—an edition of Morris without some of the qualities for which his name stands would be a sin. The distinct interest of this edition, aside from the fact that it will include Morris' whole work, is in the biographical prefaces of Miss May Morris, with their quotations from conversations and letters. There is a happy note in Miss Morris' writing which does as much as anything else to put one in intimacy with the exuberant personality of her father. There are illustrations, showing illuminated MSS, and borders and the poet's first drafts of various poems—all that delights in a biography; and there are portraits, both from paintings and from photographs. The paintings of the women are, of course, all Rossetti-fied; but in the photographs they are livably human. To return for a moment to the subject of Morris' "Sigurd": It is interesting to observe his anger at Wagner for making an opera of the legend. It is, he wrote to Buxton Forman, "Nothing short of desecration to bring such a tremendous and worldwide subject under the gaslights of an opera: the most rococo and degraded of all forms of art—the idea of a sandy-haired German tenor tweedledeeing over the unspeakable woes of Sigurd, which even the simplest words are not typical enough to express!''

* * *

One can (if one be not a besotted Wagnerite) sympathize with him. And yet to condemn Wagner is to set a high standard of achievement in art. Did Morris him- [sic] reach such a height? This "Sigurd" could have been better. My father worked harder than ever this year, 1876," writes Miss

Morris; "experiments in dyeing became always more absorbing, and 'Sigurd' was being written."

One pays for practicing what one preaches. "Sigurd" and the dye-vat: surely the poem would have been better if he had left the dyeing to Mr. Wardle! And yet—one is glad he didn't.

February 16, 1912

THE HISTORY OF CHICAGO

Chicago: Its History and Its Builders, by J. Seymour Currey. In five volumes. Illustrated. [The S. J. Clarke Publishing Company, Chicago.]

One reason for knowing the history of Chicago is that the history of Chicago is the history of the Middle West. And the history of the Middle West is, to a larger extent than the school textbooks have ever permitted us to discover, the history of the nation.

If these three large volumes (the other two are devoted to biographies) were merely a manifestation of civic egotism, an undigested record of local incident, a storehouse of antiquarian fact, I should not be calling them to public attention. They are more than that. Mr. Currey, who possesses the most expert and detailed knowledge of the incidents of our pioneer, historical, commercial and social history, has in addition to this a true historical sense, which enables him to set all these facts in an orderly relation, a fascinating perspective.

There have been other histories of Chicago—I have painful memories of them. Not being by temperament an archaeologist, I object to digging through stratum after stratum of rubbish to find what I want to know. Perhaps those previous histories have everything in them; if one looked faithfully one might perhaps discover a long lost relative! But in this work Mr. Currey has brought order out of chaos; one is able to lay one's finger at once on any significant fact; and, above all, there is a clear relation of facts to political and economic movements of national importance.

The connection of Stephen A. Douglas with Chicago, the visits and speeches of Lincoln, and the Republican convention of 1860 are obviously significant and interesting matters; and with these Mr. Currey deals fully and adequately. More important is his treatment of such a matter as the Rivers and Harbors Convention of 1847. The chapter on this convention is in a measure a contribution to that new history of America which is being written by such men as Professor William E. Dodd (in "Statesmen of the Old South") and A. M. Simons (in "Social Forces in American History").

* * *

The Rivers and Harbors Convention was one of the most important skirmishes in that long contest between the commercial system of the North and the slave system of the South, which finally broke out in open civil war. No account of that contest is true which does not take it into consideration; while in the industrial development of the Middle West, and of Chicago in particular, it is an epochal event.

The panic of 1837, after a fever of speculation in land values and of fabulous internal improvements in the Middle West, marked the close of the period when the interests of the Middle West and of the South were allied. From then on the hostility increased, and with the election of Polk in 1844, the South came into control of the national administration. It held that control until the election of Lincoln in 1860, and it used the administrative machinery in every possible way to advance its sectional economic interests, and to hamper and destroy those of the North and Middle West. Pursuant to this policy, Polk embarked on a program of imperialism for the benefit of the South, and succeeded in adding to the national domain a million square miles of new territory, into which it was expected and intended to introduce slavery. At the same time, the President, who had devoted millions to these conquests and purchases, vetoed, in 1846, a beggarly appropriation of $80,000 to improve the harbors at Racine, Little Fort, Southport, Milwaukee and Chicago. The object was simply to check the industrial development of the commercial system of the Middle West.

* * *

There was a rebellious protest by the Middle West—and that rebellious protest was the Rivers and Harbors Convention of 1847. Chicago, then a little town of less than 20,000 population, was chosen as the meeting place. Into that little town poured a flood of people greater than the entire population of the town, assembled to protest against the tyranny of the South, and to formulate a constructive policy that would set the Middle West free to achieve its potential prosperity. There were 10,000 delegates, "the largest deliberative body ever assembled." Horace Greeley was there to report the proceedings for the New York Tribune, and Thurlow Weed for the Albany Evening Journal. The convention sat three days, and its action, though failing of immediate results in the next congressional session, was the declaration of political war between the Middle West and the South, and the beginning of Chicago's new commercial development. "It is," says Mr. Currey, "one of

134

the greatest events of our history . . . a great wave wash of the fast-rising tide which has carried Chicago forward to its destiny, and within fifty years from the time that convention was held has made her the metropolis of the West, a city of two million inhabitants, and the second city in the Union.''

But thus violently to condense Mr. Currey's historical background is to do a certain injustice to his narrative, which is fluent and often dramatic.

Peculiarly interesting to the Chicagoan is the account of the Fort Dearborn massacre. I do not know how generally that episode in its details is known. But those details do serve to differentiate it from the type ''Indian massacre'' tale, and, as related by Mr. Currey, invest it with emotional force. A photograph of the original order by General Hull to evacuate the fort is reproduced, with comments on that officer's ignorance of the situation; and the moral quality of Captain Heald, which would not permit him any independent action, but which sent him out with the garrison and the women and children to an inevitable and unnecessary death, is properly exhibited.

It is certainly not generally known that any part of the Revolutionary war was fought on Chicago soil: but such is the fact. It was not much of an ''action,'' perhaps, but four lives were lost in it, and a number of prisoners taken. It seems that a party of seventeen Americans from Cahokia captured Fort St. Joseph from the British, but were overtaken on their return at some spot now within the limits of Chicago and were defeated.

''It would be interesting,'' writes Mr. Currey, ''to know the precise location of this so-called 'battle,' and if it can be definitely ascertained it should be suitably marked with a monument.''

* * *

The instinct which leads men to mark the spot where an historic event took place has been identified, and rather convincingly, with the instinct which leads a man to keep and cherish some token of his beloved. Perhaps a lover ought not to need a ribbon or a glove to remind him of his love—but it does stimulate the imagination. To walk over the battlefield of Waterloo, says Hilaire Belloc, gives one a feeling about that battle than can be gained in no other way. Certainly those Americans who died where now perhaps the flare of steel mills lights the sky were part of the event which made us, for better or for worse, a new nation. Until we can visit the site of that little battle, and think of those resolute Yankee traders who rather than see their profits diminish, created a revolution—until such time the best thing one can do who wishes to exercise his historical imagination is to take a drink in the saloon which stands on the site of old Fort Dearborn, and think of the young pioneers who marched out to certain death, north along the lake shore, one August morning a hundred years ago.

* * *

But modern Chicago is by no means neglected in this history. There are full and vivid accounts, some of them contributed by writers to whom acknowledgment is made in the preface, of educational, musical, religious and industrial growth. There are chapters on the Chicago Fire, the World's Fair, the Pullman Strike, and other episodes. I note a few very interesting pages on Hull House and other settlements. There is also a chapter on "Socialism and Anarchism in Chicago" which contains the first complete account of these movements in Chicago from the beginning until the hanging of the Haymarket "Anarchists." Upon closer inspection, I discover that this chapter was written by myself, so I had better say no more about it.

If Chicago has not been loved by her people as other cities have been loved by theirs, it is perhaps because Chicago has seemed too large. But, by giving us a few significant places which stand symbolically for the whole, history serves to make the large small; Greece is Athens, Athens is the Acropolis. Even the "loop," nuisance as it is, has perhaps helped us to envisage our town, and so helped us to love her. The history of Mr. Currey's—one wishes it were accessible in a popular form in a single volume—will help more.

* * *

But perhaps I am wrong in thinking that Chicago has not been loved. Here in these three volumes are found many signs of that fierce patriotism which grows firmly in the soil of industrial success, and which comes to defy fire, flood and failure: such are the gradual achievements of artistic, musical, scientific and educational advantages against overwhelming setbacks and discouragements. Truly, there is no lack in this record of a high faith in Chicago: there is, on the contrary, an insistence on its beauty, its possession of the elements of happiness, its magnificent possibilities.

May 10, 1912

MODERN WOMEN

Charlotte Perkins Gilman: The First Paper

First, let me betray a secret: the secret, that is, of the apparent indifference or even hostility of men toward the woman's movement. The fact is, as has been bitterly recited by the rebellious leaders of their sex, that women have always been what men wanted them to be—have changed to suit his changing ideals. The fact is, furthermore, that the woman's movement of today is but another example of that readiness of women to adapt themselves to a masculine demand.

Men are tired of subservient women; or, to speak more exactly, of the seemingly subservient woman who effects her will by stealth—the pretty slave with all the slave's subtlety and cleverness. So long as it was possible for men to imagine themselves masters, they were satisfied. But when they found out that they were dupes, they wanted a change. If only for self-protection, they desired to find in woman a comrade and an equal. In reality they desired it because it promised to be more fun.

So that we have as the motive behind the rebellion of women an obscure rebellion of men. Why, then, have men appeared hostile to the woman's rebellion? Because what men desire are real individuals who have achieved their own freedom. It will not do to pluck freedom like a flower and give it to the lady with a polite bow. She must fight for it.

* * *

We are, to tell the truth, a little afraid that unless the struggle is one which will call upon all her powers, which will try her to the utmost, she will fall short of becoming that self-sufficient, able, broadly imaginative and healthy minded creature upon whom we have set our masculine desire.

It is, then, as a phase of the great human renaissance inaugurated by men that the woman's movement deserves to be considered. And what more fitting than that a man should sit in judgment upon the contemporary aspects of that movement, weighing out approval or disapproval! Such criticism—which will not be attempted, save in the most casual way, in these articles—is not a masculine impertinence, but a masculine right, a right properly pertaining to those who are responsible for the movement and whose demands it must ultimately fulfill.

Of the women who represent and carry on this many-sided movement today, the first to be considered from this masculine viewpoint should, I think, be Charlotte Perkins Gilman. For she is, to a superficial view, the most intransigent feminist of them all, the one most exclusively concerned with the improvement of the lot of woman, the least likely to compromise at the instance of man, child, church, state or devil.

* * *

Mrs. Gilman is the author of "Women and Economics" and several other books of theory, "What Diantha Did," and several other books of fiction; she is the editor and publisher of a remarkable journal, the Forerunner, the whole varied contents of which is written by herself; she has a couple of plays to her credit, and she has published a book of poems. If in spite of all this publicity it is still possible to misunderstand the attitude of Mrs. Gilman, I can only suppose it to be because her poetry is less well known than her prose. For in this book of verse, "In This Our World," Mrs. Gilman has so completely justified herself that no man need ever be afraid of her—nor any woman who, having a lingering tenderness for the other sex, would object to living in a beehive world, full of raging, efficient women, with the men relegated to the position of the drone.

Of course, I do but jest when I speak of this fear; but there is, to the ordinary male, something curiously objectionable at the first glance in Mrs. Gilman's arguments, whether they are for co-operative kitchens or for the labor of women outside the home. And the reason for that objection lies precisely in the fact that her plans seem to be made in a complete forgetfulness of him and his interests. It all has the air of a feminine plot. The co-operative kitchens, and the labor by which women's economic independence is to be achieved, seem the means to an end.

And so they are. But the end, as revealed in Mrs. Gilman's poems, is that one which all intelligent men must desire. I do not know whether or not the more elaborate co-operative schemes of Mrs. Gilman are practical; and I fancy that she rather exaggerates the possibilities of independent work for women who have or intend to have children. But the spirit behind these plans is one which cannot but be in the greatest degree stimulating and beneficent in its effect upon her sex.

* * *

For Mrs. Gilman is, first of all, a poet, an idealist. She is a lover of life. She rejoices in beauty and daring and achievement, in all the fine and splendid things of the world. She does not merely disapprove of the contemporary "home" as wasteful and inefficient—she hates it because it vulgarizes life. In this "home," this private food-preparing and baby-rearing establishment, she sees a machine which breaks down all that is good and noble in women, which degrades and pettifies them. The contrast between the instinctive ideals of young women and the sordid realities into which housekeeping plunges them is to her intolerable. And in the best satirical verse of modern times she ridicules these unnecessary shames. In one spirited piece she points out that the soap-vat, the pickle-tub, even the loom and wheel, have lost their sanctity, have been banished to shops and factories:

> But bow ye down to the Holy Stove,
> The Altar of the Home!

The real feeling of Mrs. Gilman is revealed in these lines, which voice, indeed, the angry mood of many an outraged housewife, who finds herself the serf of a contraption of cast iron:

> . . . We toil to keep the altar crowned
> With dishes new and nice, And Art
> and Love, and Time and Truth,
> We offer up, with Health and Youth, In
> daily sacrifice.

Mrs. Gilman is not under the illusion that the conditions of work outside the home are perfect; she is, indeed, a socialist, and as such is engaged in the great task of revolutionizing the basis of modern industry. But she has looked into women's souls, and turned away in disgust at the likeness of a dirty kitchen which those souls present.

Into these lives, corrupted by the influences of the "home," nothing can come unspoiled—nothing can enter in its original stature and beauty, she says;

> Birth comes. Birth—
> The breathing re-creation of the earth!
> All earth, all sky, all God, life's sweet deep whole,
> Newborn again to each new soul!
> "Oh, are you? What a shame! Too bad, my dear!
> How well you stand it, too! It's very queer
> The dreadful trials women have to carry;
> But you can't always help it when you marry.
> Oh, what a sweet layette! What lovely socks!
> What an exquisite puff and powder box!
> Who is your doctor? Yes, his skill's immense—
> But it's a dreadful danger and expense!"

And so with love, and death, and work—all are smutted and debased. And her revolt is a revolt against that which smuts and debases them—against those artificial channels which break up the strong, pure stream of woman's energy into a thousand little, stangant [sic] canals, covered with spiritual pondscum.

It is a part of her idealism to conceive life in terms of war. So it is that she scorns compromise, for in war compromise is treason. And so it is that she has heart for the long, slow marshaling of forces, and the dingy details of the commissariat—for these things are necessary if the cry of victory is ever to ring out over the battlefield. Some of her phrases have so militant an air that they seem to have been born among the captains and the shouting. They make us ashamed of our vicious civilian comfort. . . .

Mrs. Gilman's attitude toward the bearing and rearing of children is easy to misunderstand. She does seem to relegate these things to the background of women's lives. She does deny to these things a tremendous importance. Why, she asks, is it so important that women should bear and rear children to live lives as empty and poor as their own? Surely, she says, it is more important to make life something worth giving to children! No, she insists, it is not sufficient to be a mother: an oyster can be a mother. It is necessary that a woman should be a person as well as a mother. She must know and do.

* * *

And as for the ideal of love which is founded on masculine privilege, she satirizes it very effectively in some verses entitled "Wedded Bliss":

> "O come and be my mate!" said the Eagle to the Hen;
> "I love to soar, but then I want my mate to rest
> Forever in the nest!" Said the Hen, "I cannot fly,
> I have no wish to try, But I joy to see my mate careering
> through the sky!" They wed, and cried, "Ah, this is Love, my
> own!"
> And the Hen sat, the Eagle soared, alone.

Woman, in Mrs. Gilman's view, must not be content with Hendom: the sky is her province, too. Of all base domesticity, all degrading love, she is the enemy. She gives her approval only to that work which has in it something high and free, and that love which is the dalliance of the eagles.

June 28, 1912

MODERN WOMEN

Emmeline Pankhurst and Jane Addams: The Second Paper

A few months ago it was rather the fashion to reply to some political verses by Mr. Kipling which assumed to show that women should not be given the ballot, and which had as their refrain:

The female of the species is more deadly than the male!
But it seems that no one pointed out that this fact, even in the limited sense in which it is a fact in the human species, is an argument for giving women the vote.

For if women are—as Mr. Kipling says—lacking in a sense of abstract justice, in patience, in the spirit of compromise, if they are violent and unscrupulous in gaining an end upon which they have set their hearts, then by all means they should be rendered comparatively harmless by being given the ballot. For it is characteristic of a republic that its political machinery, created in order to carry out the will of the people, come to respond with difficulty to that will, while being perfectly susceptible to other influences. Republican government, when not modified by drastic democratic devices, is an expensive, cumbrous and highly inefficient method of carrying out the popular will; and casting a vote is like nothing so much as casting bread upon the waters. It shall return—after many days. By voting, by exercising an infinitesimal pressure on our complex, slow-moving political mechanism, one cannot—it is a sad fact—do much good; but one cannot—and it should encourage the pessimistic Mr. Kipling—one cannot, even though a woman, do much harm.

* * *

This is not, however, a disquisition on woman suffrage. There is only one argument for woman suffrage: women want it; there are no arguments against it. But one may profitably inquire, What will be the effect of the emergence of women into politics upon politics itself? And one may hope to find an answer in the temperament and career of certain representative leaders of the woman's movement. Let us accordingly turn to the accredited leader of the English "votes for women" movement, and to the woman in the American movement who is best known to the public.

That Miss Jane Addams has become known chiefly through other activities does not matter here. It is temperament and career in which we are immediately interested. What is perhaps the most outstanding fact in the temperament of Miss Addams is revealed only indirectly in her autobiography: it may be called the passion of conciliation.

Miss Emmeline Pankhurst has by her actions written herself down for a fighter. She has but recently been released from Holloway jail, where she was serving a term of imprisonment for "conspiracy and violence." In a book by H. G. Wells, which contains a very bitter attack on the woman's suffrage movement (I refer to "Ann Veronica"), she is described as "implacable"; and I believe that it is she to whom Mr. Wells refers as being "as incapable of argument as a steam roller broken loose." The same things might have been said of Sherman on his dreadful march to the sea. These phrases, malicious as they are, contain what I am inclined to accept as an accurate description of Mrs. Pankhurst's temperament.

No one would call Mrs. Pankhurst a conciliator. And no one would call Miss Addams "implacable." It is not intended to suggest that Miss Addams is one of those inveterate compromisers who prefer a bad peace to a good war. But she has the gift of imaginative sympathy; and it is impossible for her to have toward either party in a conflict the cold hostility which each party has for the other. She sees both sides; and even though one side is the wrong side, she cannot help seeing why its partisans believe in it.

* * *

"If the under dog were always right," Miss Addams has said, "one might quite easily try to defend him. The trouble is that very often he is but obscurely right, sometimes only partially right, and often quite wrong, but perhaps he is never so altogether wrong and pig-headed and utterly reprehensible as he is represented to be by those who add the possession of prejudice to the other almost insuperable difficulties in understanding him."

Miss Addams has taken in good faith the social settlement ideal—"to span the gulf between the rich and the poor, or between those who have had cultural opportunities and those who have not, by the process of neighborliness." In her writings, as in her work, there is never sounded the note of defiance. Even in defense of the social settlement and its methods of conciliation (which have been venomously assailed by the newspapers during Chicago's fits of temporary insanity, as in the Averbuch case), Miss Addams has not become militant. She has never ceased to be serenely reasonable.

But when one comes to ask how powerful Miss Addams' example has been, one is forced to admit that it has been limited. There are two other settlement houses in Chicago which are managed in the spirit of Hull House. But all the others—and there are about forty settlement houses in the city—have discarded almost openly the principle of conciliation. They are efficient, or religious, or something else, but they are afraid of being too sympathetic with the working class. They do not, for instance, permit labor unions to meet in their halls. The splendid social idealism of the '80s, of which Miss Addams is representative, has disappeared, leaving two sides angry and hostile and with none but Miss Addams believing in the possibility of finding any common ground for action. One event after another from the Pullman strike to the Averbuch case has brought this hostility out into the open, with Miss Addams occupying neutral ground, and left high and dry upon it.

It is the fact that Miss Addams has not been able to imbue the movement in which she is a leader with her own spirit. Her career has been successful only so far as individual genius could make it successful. If one compares her achievement to that of Mrs. Pankhurst, one sees that the latter is startlingly social in its nature.

For Mrs. Pankhurst has called upon women to be like herself, to display her own Amazonian qualities. She called upon shopgirls and college students and wives and old women to commit physical assaults on cabinet ministers, to raid parliament and fight with policemen, to destroy property and go to prison, to endure almost every indignity from the mobs and from their jailers, to suffer in health and perhaps to die, exactly as soldiers suffer and die in a campaign.

And they did. They answered her call by the thousands. They have fought and suffered, and some of them have died. If this had been the result of individual genius in Mrs. Pankhurst, transforming peaceful girls into fighters out of hand, she would be the most extraordinary person of the age. But it is impossible to believe that all this militancy was created out of the void. It was simply awakened where it lay sleeping in these women's hearts.

Mrs. Pankhurst has performed no miracle. She has only shown to us the truth which we have blindly refused to see. She has had the insight to recognize in women generally the same fighting spirit which she found in herself, and the courage to draw upon it. She has enabled us to see what women really are like, just as Miss Addams has by her magnificent anomalies shown us what women are not like.

Can anyone doubt this? Can anyone, seeing the lone eminence of Miss Addams, assert that imaginative sympathy, patience and the spirit of conciliation are the ordinary traits of women? Can anyone, seeing the battle frenzy which Mrs. Pankhurst has evoked with a signal in thousands of ordinary Englishwomen, deny that women have a fighting soul?

* * *

And can anyone doubt the effect which the emergence of women into politics will have, eventually, on politics? —Eventually, for in spite of their boasted independence the decorous example of men will rule them at first. But when they have become used to politics—well, we shall find that we have harnessed an unruly Niagara!

In women as voters we shall have an element impatient of restraint, straining at the rules of procedure, cynical of excuses for inaction; not always by any means on the side of progress; making every mistake possible to ignorance and self-conceit; but transforming our politics from a vicious end to an efficient means—from a cancer into an organ.

This, with but little doubt, is the historic mission of women. They will not escape a certain taming by politics. But that they should be permanently tamed I find impossible to believe. Rather they will subdue it to to [sic] their purposes, remold it nearer to their hearts' desire, change it as men would never dream of changing it, wreck it savagely in the face of our masculine protest and merrily rebuild it anew in the face of our despair. With their aid we may at least achieve what we seem to be unable to achieve unaided—a democracy.

Meanwhile let us understand this suffrage movement. Let us understand that we have in militancy rather than in conciliation, in action rather than wisdom, the keynote of women in politics. And we males, who have so long played in our politics at innocent games of war, we shall have an opportunity to fight in earnest at the side of the Valkyrs.

July 5, 1912

MODERN WOMEN

Olive Schreiner and Isadora Duncan: The Third Paper

I hope that no one will see in the conjuncture of these names a mere wanton fantasy, or a mere sensational contrast. To me there is something extraordinarily appropriate in that conjuncture, inasmuch as the work of Olive Schreiner and the work of Isadora Duncan supplement each other.

It is the drawback of the woman's movement that in any one of its aspects (heightened and colored as such an aspect often is by the violence of propaganda) it may appear too fiercely narrow. That women should make so much fuss about getting the vote, or that they should so excite themselves over the prospect of working for wages, will appear incomprehensible to many people who have a proper regard for art, for literature, and for the graces of social intercourse. It is only when the woman's movement is seen broadly, in a variety of its aspects, that there comes the realization that here is a cause in which every fine aspiration has a place, a cause from which sincere lovers of truth and beauty have nothing really to fear.

Mrs. Olive Schreiner stands, by virtue of her latest book, "Women and Labor," as an exponent of the doctrine that would send women into every field of economic activity; or, rather, the doctrine that finds in the forces which are driving them there a savior of her sex from the degradation of parasitism. In behalf of this doctrine she has expended all that eloquence and passion which have made her one of the figures in modern literature and a spokesman for all women who have not learned to speak that hieratic language which is heard, as the inexpressive speech of daily life is not heard, across space and time.

Miss Isadora Duncan stands as representative of the renaissance in dancing. She has brought back to us the antique beauty of an art of which we have had only relics and memento in classic sculpture and decoration. She has made us despise the frigid artifice of the ballet, and taught us that in the natural movements of the body are contained the highest possibilities of choregraphic [sic] beauty. It has been to many of us one of the finest experiences of our lives to see, for the first time, the marble maiden of the Grecian urn come to life in her, and all the leaf-fringed legends of Arcady drift across our enamored vision. She has touched our lives with the magic of immemorial loveliness.

But to class Olive Schreiner as a sociologist and Isadora Duncan as a dancer, to divorce them by any such categories, is to do them both an injustice. For they are sister workers in the woman's movement. They have each shown the way to a new freedom of the body and the soul.

* * *

It will perhaps be possible, later in the series, to show how fully the woman's movement is a product of the evolutionary science of the nineteenth century. Women's rebellions there have been before, utopian visions there have been, which have contributed no little to the modern movement by the force of their tradition and ever-living spirit. No Joan of Arc has led men to victory, no Lady Godiva has sacrificed her modesty—nay, even, no courtesan has taught a feeble king how to rule his country—without feeding the flame of feminine aspiration. But it is modern science which, by giving us a new view of the body, its functions, its needs, its claim upon the world, has laid the basis for a successful feminist movement. When the true history of this movement is written it will contain more about Herbert Spencer and Walt Whitman, perhaps, than about Virginia Woodhull and Tennessee Claflin. In any case, it is to the body that one looks for the Magna Charta of feminism.

The eye—that is to say—is guarantor for the safety of art in a future regime under the dominance of women; and the ear for poetry. These have their functions and their needs, and the woman of the future will not deny them.

* * *

It is the hand that Olive Schreiner would emancipate from idleness. She knows the significance of the hand in human history. It was by virtue of the hand that we, and not some other creature, gained lordship over the earth. It was the hand (marvelous instrument, coaxing out of the directing will an ever-increasing subtlety) that made possible the human brain, and all the vistas of reason and imagination by which our little lives gain their peculiar grandeur.

And this hand, if it be a woman's in the present day, is doomed to the smallest activities. "Our spinning wheels are all broken . . . Our hoes and grindstones passed from us long ago . . . Year by year, day by day, there is a silently working but determined tendency for the sphere of women's domestic labors to contract itself." Even the training of her child is taken away from the mother by the "mighty and inexorable demands of modern civilization." That condition is to her intolerable; and it is on behalf of women's empty hands that she makes her demand: "That, in that strange new world that is arising alike upon the man and the woman, where nothing is as it was, and all things are assuming new shapes and relations, that in this new world we also shall have our share of honored and socially useful human toil, our full half of the labor of the Children of Woman."

* * *

And what of Miss Duncan—what is her part in the woman's movement? In her book on "The Dance" she tells a story.

> A woman once asked me why I dance with bare feet,
> and I replied, "Madam, I believe in the religion of the
> beauty of the human foot"—and the lady replied, "But
> I do not," and I said: "Yet you must, Madam, for the
> expression and intelligence of the human foot is one
> of the greatest triumphs of the evolution of man."
> "But," said the lady, "I do not believe in the
> evolution of man." At this said I, "My task is at an
> end. I refer you to my most reverend teachers, Mr.
> Charles Darwin and Mr. Ernst Haeckel—" "But," said
> the lady, "I do not believe in Darwin and Haeckel—"
> At this point I could think of nothing more to say.
> So you see that, to convince people, I am of little
> value and ought not to speak.

146

But rather to dance! Yet it is good to find so explicit a statement of the idea which she expresses so nobly in her dancing. For, as the hand is the symbol of that constructive exertion of the body which we call work, so is the foot the symbol of that diffusive exertion of the body which we call play. Isadora Duncan would emancipate the one as Olive Schreiner would emancipate the other—to new activities and new delights.

And if such work is not a thing for itself only, but a gateway to a new world, so is such play not a thing for itself only. "It is not only a question of true art," writes Miss Duncan, "it is a question of race, of the development of the female sex to beauty and health, of the return to the original strength and the natural movements of woman's body. It is a question of the development of perfect mothers and the birth of healthy and beautiful children." Here we have an inspiriting expression of the spirit which, through the poems of Walt Whitman and the writing of various moderns, has renovated the modern soul and made us see, without any obscene blurring by Puritan spectacles, the goodness of the whole body. This is as much a part of the woman's movement as the demand for a vote (or, rather, it is more central and essential a part); and only by realizing this is it possible to understand that movement.

* * *

The body is no longer to be separated in the thought of women from the soul: "The dancer of the future will be one whose body and soul have grown so harmoniously together that the natural language of that soul will have become the movement of the body. The dancer will not belong to a nation, but to all humanity. She will dance not in the form of nymph, nor fairy, nor coquette, but in the form of woman in its greatest and purest expression. She will realize the mission of woman's body and the holiness of all its parts. She will dance the changing life of nature, showing how each part is transformed into the other. From all parts of her body shall shine radiant intelligence, bringing to the world the message of the thoughts and aspirations of thousands of women. She shall dance the freedom of women.
. . .

"She will help womankind to a new knowledge of the possible strength and beauty of their bodies, and the relation of their bodies to the earth nature and to the children of the future. She will dance, the body emerging again from centuries of civilized forgetfulness, emerging not in the nudity of primitive man, but in a new nakedness, no longer at war with spirituality and intelligence, but joining itself forever with this intelligence in a glorious harmony. . . .

"Oh, she is coming, the dancer of the future; the free spirit, who will inhabit the body of new women, more glorious than any woman that has yet

147

been; more beautiful than the Egyptian, than the Greek, the early Italian, than all women of past centuries—the highest intelligence in the freest body!''

* * *

If the woman's movement means anything, it means that women are demanding everything. They will not exchange one place for another, nor give up one right to pay for another, but they will achieve all rights to which their bodies and brains give them an implicit title. They will have a larger political life, a larger motherhood, a larger social service, a larger love, and they will reconstruct or destroy institutions to that end as it becomes necessary. They will not be content with any concession or any triumph until they have conquered all experience.

July 12, 1912

MODERN WOMEN

Beatrice Webb and Emma Goldman: The Fourth Paper

The careers of these two women serve admirably to exhibit the woman's movement in still another aspect, and to throw light upon the essential nature of woman's character. These careers stand in plain contrast. Beatrice Webb has compiled statistics, and Emma Goldman has preached the gospel of freedom. It remains to be shown which is the better and the more characteristically feminine gift to the world.

Beatrice Potter was the daughter of a Canadian railway president. Born in 1858, she grew up in a time when revolutionary movements were in the making. She was a pupil of Herbert Spencer, and it was perhaps from him that she learned so to respect her natural interest in facts that the brilliancy of no generalization could lure her into forgetting them. At all events, she was captured permanently by the magic of facts. She studied working-class life in Lancashire and East London at first hand, and in 1885 joined Charles Booth in his investigations of English social conditions. These investigations (which in my amateur ignorance I always confused, until half an hour ago, with those of General Booth of the Salvation Army!) were published in four large volumes entitled "Life and Labor of the People." Miss Potter's special contributions were articles on the docks, the tailoring

148

trade and the Jewish community. Later she published a book on "The Co-operative Movement in Great Britain." Then, in 1892, she married Sidney Webb, a man extraordinarily of her own sort, and became confirmed, if such a thing were necessary, in her statistical habit of mind.

*   *   *

Meanwhile, in 1883, the Fabian Society had been founded. But first a word about statistics. "Statistics" does not mean a long list of figures. It means the spreading of knowledge of facts. Statistics may be called the dogma that knowledge is dynamic—that it is somehow operative in bringing about that great change which all intelligent people desire (and which the Fabians conceived as Socialism). The Fabian Society was founded on the dogma of statistics as on a rock. The Fabians did not start a newspaper, nor create a new political party, nor organize public meetings; but they wrote to the newspapers already in existence, ran for office on party tickets already in the field, and made speeches to other organizations. That is to say, they went about like the cuckoo, laying their statistical eggs in other people's nests and expecting to see them hatch into enlightened public opinion and progressive legislation.

Some of them hatched and some of them didn't. The point is that we have in this section of Beatrice Webb's career something typical of herself. She has gone on, serving on government commissions, writing (with her husband) the history of Trade Unionism, patiently collecting statistics and getting them printed in black ink on white paper, making detailed plans of the abolition of poverty, and always concerning herself with the homely fact.

*   *   *

At the time that Beatrice Potter joined Mr. Booth in his social investigations there was a 16-year-old Jewish girl living in the German-Russian province of Kurland. A year later, in 1886, this girl, Emma Goldman by name, came to America, to escape the inevitable persecutions attending on any lover of liberty in Russia. She had been one of those who had gone "to the people"; and it was as a working girl that she came to America.

She had, that is to say, the heightened sensibilities, the keen sympathies, of the middle class idealist, and the direct contact with the harsh realities of our social and industrial conditions which is the lot of the worker. Her first experiences in America disabused her of the traditional belief that America was a refuge where the oppressed of all lands were welcome. The treatment of immigrants aboard ship, the humiliating brutalities of the officials at Castle Garden, and the insolent tyranny of the New York police convinced her that she had simply come from one oppressed land to another.

She went to work in a clothing factory, her wages being $2.50 a week. She had ample opportunities to see the degradations of our economic system, especially as it affects women. So it was not strange that she should be drawn into the American labor movement, which was then, with the Knights of Labor, the eight-hour agitation, and the propaganda of the Socialists and the Anarchists, at its height. She became acquainted with various radicals, read pamphlets and books, and heard speeches. She was especially influenced by the eloquent writings of Johann Most in his journal Freiheit.

* * *

So little is known, and so much absurd nonsense is believed, about the Anarchists that it is necessary to state dogmatically a few facts. If these facts seem odd, the reader is respectfully urged to verify them. One fact is that secret organizations of Anarchists plotting a violent overthrow of the government do not exist, and never have existed, save in the writings of Johann Most and in the imagination of the police: the whole spirit of Anarchism is opposed to such organizations. Another fact is that Anarchists do not believe in violence of any kind, or in any exercise of force; when they commit violence it is not as Anarchists, but as outraged human beings. They believe that violent reprisals are bound to be provoked among workingmen by the tyrannies to which they are subjected; but they abjure alike the bomb and the policeman's club.

There was a brief period in which Anarchists, under the influence of Johann Most, believed in (even if they did not practice) the use of dynamite. But this period was ended, in America, by the hanging of several innocent men in Chicago in 1887, which at least served the useful purpose of showing radicals that it was a bad plan even to talk of dynamite. And this hanging, which was the end of what may be called the Anarchist "boom" in this country, was the beginning of Emma Goldman's career as a publicist.

Since 1887 the Anarchists have lost influence among workingmen until they are today negligible as a factor in the labor movement. The Anarchists have, in fact, left the industrial field more and more and have entered into other kinds of propaganda. They have, as it was euphemistically stated in a recent editorial in The Evening Post, especially "gone in for kissing games."

And Emma Goldman reflects, in her career, the change in Anarchism. She has become simply an advocate of freedom—freedom of every sort. She does not advocate violence, any more than Ralph Waldo Emerson advocated violence. It is, in fact, as an essayist and speaker of the kind, if not the quality, of Emerson, Thoreau or George Francis Train that she is to be considered.

Aside from these activities (and the evading of our overzealous police in times of stress) she has worked as a trained nurse and midwife; she

150

conducted a kind of radical salon in New York, frequented by such people as John Swinton and Benjamin Tucker; she traveled abroad to study social conditions; she has become conversant with such modern writings as those of Hauptmann, Nietzsche, Ibsen, Zola and Thomas Hardy. It is stated that the "Rev. Mr. Parkhurst, during the Lexow investigation, did his utmost to induce her to join the Vigilance Committee in order to fight Tammany Hall." She was the manager of Paul Orlenoff and Mme. Nazimova. She was a friend of Ernest Crosby. Her library, it is said, would be taken for that of a university extension lecturer on literature.

*   *   *

It will thus be seen that Emma Goldman is of a type familiar enough in America, and conceded a popular respect. She has a legitimate social function—that of holding before our eyes the ideal of freedom. She is licensed to taunt us with our moral cowardice, to plant in our souls the nettles of remorse at having acquiesced so tamely in the brutal artifice of present day society.

I submit the following passage from her writings ("Anarchism and Other Essays") as at once showing her difference from other radicals and exhibiting the nature of her appeal to her public:

"The misfortune of woman is not that she is unable to do the work of a man, but that she is wasting her life force to outdo him, with a tradition of centuries which has left her physically incapable of keeping pace with him. Oh, I know some have succeeded, but at what cost, at what terrific cost! The import is not the kind of work woman does, but rather the quality of the work she furnishes. She can give suffrage or the ballot no new quality, nor can she receive anything from it that will enhance her own quality. Her development, her freedom, her independence, must come from and through herself. First, by asserting herself as a personality, and not as a sex commodity. Second, by refusing the right to anyone over her body; by refusing to bear children unless she wants them; by refusing to be a servant to God, the State, society, the husband, the family, etc; by making her life simpler, but deeper and richer. That is, by trying to learn the meaning and substance of life in all its complexities, by freeing herself from the fear of public opinion and public condemnation. Only that, and not the ballot, will set woman free, will make her a force hitherto unknown in the world, a force for real love, for peace, for harmony; a force of divine fire, of life giving; a creator of free men and women."

There is little in this that Ibsen would not have said Amen to. But—and this is the conclusion to which my article draws—Ibsen has said it already, and said it more powerfully. Emma Goldman—who (if among women anyone) should have for us a message of her own, striking to the heart—repeats, in a less effective cadence, what she has learned from him.

The work of Beatrice Webb is the prose of revolution. The work of Ibsen is its poetry. Beatrice Webb has performed her work—one comes to feel—as well as Ibsen has his. And one wonders if, after all, the prose is not that which women are best endowed to succeed in.

A book review (written by a woman) which I have at hand contains some generalizations which bear on the subject. "This is a woman's book [says the reviewer], and a book which could only have been written by a woman, though it is singularly devoid of most of the qualities which are usually recognized as feminine. For romance and sentiment do not properly lie in the woman's domain. She deals, when she is herself, with the material facts of the life she knows. Her talent is to exhibit them in the remorseless light of reality and shorn of all the glamour of idealism. Great and poetical imagination rarely informs her art, but within the strictness of its limits it lives by an intense and scrupulous sincerity of observations and an uncompromising recognition of the logic of existence."

If that is true, shall we not then expect a future more largely influenced by women to have more of the hard, matter-of-fact quality, the splendid realism characteristic of woman "when she is herself"?

July 19, 1912

MODERN WOMAN

Margaret Dreier Robins: The Fifth Paper

The chief work of Margaret Dreier Robins has been in the Women's Trade Union League. It might be supposed that the aim of such an organization was sufficiently explicit in its title: to get higher wages and shorter hours. But I fancy that it would be a truer thing to say that its aim was to bring into being that ideal of American womanhood which Walt Whitman described:

> They are not one jot less than I am,
> They are tann'd in the face by shining suns and
>   blowing winds
> Their flesh has the old divine suppleness and strength,
> They know how to swim, row, ride, wrestle, shoot, run,
>   strike, retreat, advance, resist, defend themselves,
> They are ultimate in their own right—they are calm, clear,
>   well-possessed of themselves.

When Whitman made this magnificent prophecy for American womanhood the Civil War had not been fought and its economic consequences were unguessed at. The factory system, which had come into England in the last century, bringing with it the most unspeakable exploitation of women and children, had hardly gained a foothold in this country. In 1840 of the seven employments open to women (teaching, needlework, keeping boarders, working in cotton mills, in bookbinderies, typesetting and household service) only one was representative of the new industrial condition which today affects so profoundly the feminine physique. And to the daughters of a nation that was still imbued with the pioneer spirit, work in cotton mills appealed so little that they undertook it only for unusually high pay. Anyone of that period seeing the red-cheeked, robust, intelligent, happy girl operatives of Lowell might have dismissed his fears of the factory as a sinister influence in the development of American womanhood and gone on to dream, with Walt Whitman, of a race of "fierce, athletic girls."

* * *

But two things happened. With the growing flood of immigration, the factories were abandoned more and more to the "foreigners," the native-born citizens losing their pride in the excellence of working conditions and the character of the operatives. And all the while the factory was becoming more and more an integral part of our civilization, demanding larger and larger multitudes of girls and women to attend its machinery. So that, with the enormous development of industry since the Civil War, the factory has become the chief field of feminine endeavor in America. In spite of the great opening up of all sorts of work to women, in spite of the store, the office, the studio, the professions, still the factory remains most important in any consideration of the health and strength of women.

If the greatest part of our womankind spends its life in factories, and if it further appears that this is no temporary situation, but (practically speaking) a permanent one, then it becomes necessary to inquire how far the factory is hindering the creation of that ideal womanhood which Walt Whitman predicted for us.

As opposed to the old-fashioned method of manufacture in the home (or the sweatshop, which is the modern equivalent) the factory often shows a gain in light and air, a decrease of effort, an added leisure; while, on the other hand, there is a considerable loss of individual freedom and an increase in monotony. But child labor, a too long working day, bad working conditions, lack of protection from fire, personal exploitation by foremen, inhumanly low wages, and all sorts of petty injustice, though not essential to the system, are prominent features of factory work as it generally exists.

People who consider every factory an Inferno, however, and have only pity for its workers, are far from understanding the situation. Here is a field of work which is capable of competing successfully with domestic service, and even of attracting girls from homes where there exists no absolute necessity for women's wages. Yet at its contemporary best, with a ten-hour law in operation, efficient factory inspection, decent working conditions and a just and humane management, the factory remains an institution extremely perilous to the Whitmanic ideal of womanhood.

But there are women who, undaunted by the new conditions brought about by a changing economic system, seize upon those very conditions to use them as the means to their end: such a woman is Mrs. Robins. Has a new world, bounded by factory walls and noisy with the roar of machinery, grown up about us, to keep women from their heritage? She will help them to use those very walls and that very machinery to achieve their destiny, a destiny of which a physical well-being is, as Walt Whitman knew it to be, the most certain symbol.

* * *

The factory already gives women a certain independence. It may yet give them pleasure, the joy of creation. Indeed, it must, when the workers require it; and those who are most likely to require it are the women workers.

It is well known that with the ultra-development of the machine, the subdivision of labor, the regime of piecework, it has become practically impossible for the worker to take any artistic pleasure in his product. It is not so well known how necessary such pleasure in the product is to the physical well-being of women—how utterly disastrous to their nervous organization is the monotony and irresponsibility of piecework. This method—which men workers have grumbled at, but to which they seem to have adjusted themselves—bears its fruits among women in neurasthenia, headaches and the derangement of the organs which are the source of their different nervous organization. It is sufficiently clear to those who have seen the personal reactions of working girls to the piecework system that when women attain, as men in various industries have attained, the practical management of the factory, piecework will get a setback.

But not merely good conditions, not merely a living wage, not merely a ten or an eight hour day—all that self-government in the shop can bring is the object of the Women's Trade Union League.

* * *

"The chief social gain of the union shop," says Mrs. Robins, "is not its generally better wages and shorter hours, but rather the incentive it offers for initiative and social leadership, the call it makes, through the common industrial relationship and the common hope, upon the moral and reasoning faculties, and the sense of fellowship, independence and group strength it develops. In every workshop of say thirty girls there are undreamed of initiative and capacity for social leadership and control—unknown wealth of intellectual and moral resources."

It is, in fact, this form of activity which to many thousands of factory girls makes the difference between living and existing, between a painful, necessary drudgery and a happy exertion of all their faculties. It can give them a more useful education than any school, a more vital faith than any church, a more invigorating sense of power than any other career open to them.

* * *

To do all these things it must be indigenous to working class soil. No benefaction originating in the philanthropic motives of middle-class people, no enterprise of patronage will ever have any such meaning. A movement, to have such meaning, must be of the working class, and by the working class, as well as for the working class. It must be imbued with working-class feeling, and it must subserve working-class ideals.

It is the distinction of Mrs. Robins that she has seen this. She has gone to the workers to learn rather than to teach—she has sought to unfold the ideals and capacities latent in working girls rather than impress upon them the alien ideals and capacities of another class.

"Just"—it is Mrs. Robins that speaks—"as under a despotic church and a feudal state the possible power and beauty of the common people was denied expression, so under industrial feudalism the intellectual and moral powers of the workers are slowly choked to death, with incalculable loss to the individual and the race. It is easy to kill; it requires a great spirit as well as a great mind to arouse the dormant energies, to vitalize them and to make them creative forces for good."

One is reminded of the words of John Galsworthy, addressed to workingwomen. "There is beginning to be a little light in the sky; whether the sun is ever to break through depends on your constancy, and courage, and wisdom. The future is in your hands more than in the hands of men; it rests on your virtues and well-being, rather than on the virtues and the welfare of men, for it is you who produce and mold the Future."

There are 6,000,000 working women in the United States, and half of them are girls under 21. One may go out any day in the streets of Chicago, at morning or noon or evening, and look at a representative hundred of them. The factories have not been able to rob them of beauty and strength and the charm of femininity, and in that beauty and strength and charm there is a world of promise. And that promise already begins to be unfolded when to them comes Mrs. Robins with a gospel germane to their natures, saying, "Long enough have you dreamed contemptible dreams."

July 26, 1912

MODERN WOMEN

Ellen Key: The Sixth and Last Paper

In these papers a sincere attempt has been made not so much to show what a few exceptional women have accomplished as to exhibit through a few prominent figures the essential nature of women, and to show what may be expected from a future in which women will have a larger freedom and a larger influence.

It has been pointed out that the peculiar idealism of women is one that works itself out, through the materials of workaday life, and which seeks to break or remake those materials by way of fulfilling that idealism; it has been shown that this idealism, as contrasted with the most abstract and creative idealism of men, deserves to be called practicalism, a practicalism of noble and beautiful sort which we are far from appreciating; and as complementing these forms of activity the play instinct, the instinct of recreation, has been pointed out as the parallel to the creative or poetic instinct of men.

Woman as reconstructor of domestic economics, woman as a destructive political agent of enormous potency, woman as worker, woman as dancer, woman as statistician, woman as organizer of the forces of labor— in these it has been the intent to show the real woman of today and of tomorrow.

There have been other aspects of her deserving of attention in such a series, notably her aspect as mother and as educator. If she has not been shown as poet, as artist, as scientist, as talker (for talk is a thing quite as important as poetry or science or art), it has not been so much because of an actual lack of specific examples of women distinguished in these fields as because of the unrepresentative character of such examples.

Here, then is a man's view of woman. And to complete that view, to round off that conception, I now speak of Ellen Key.

The ideas of Ellen Key about love and marriage have been referred to and discussed frequently in this Review, and it must be assumed that they have been done justice to, as it is not specifically those views which I am now going to describe. It is rather the character of Ellen Key as exhibited in them.

* * *

Her writings have had a peculiar career in America, one which perhaps prevents a clear understanding of that character. On the one hand, they have seemed to many to be radically advanced; to thousands of middle-class women who have heard vaguely of these new ideas, and who have secretly and strongly desired to know more of them, her "Love and Marriage" has come as a revolutionary document, the first outspoken word of scorn for conventional morality, the first call to them to take their part in the breaking of new paths.

On the other hand, it must be remembered that America is the home of Mormonism, of the Oneida Community, of the Woodhull and Claflin "free-love" movement of the '70s, of "Dianism" and a hundred other obscure but pervasive sexual cults—in short, of movement of greater or less respectability capable of giving considerable currency to their beliefs. And they have given considerable currency to their beliefs. In spite of the dominant tone of puritanism in American thought our social life has been affected to an appreciable extent by these beliefs.

* * *

And these beliefs may be summed up hastily, but, on the whole, justly, as materialistic—in the common and unfavorable sense. They have converged from one direction or another upon the opinion that sex is an animal function, which, by a ridiculous overestimation, is made to give rise to jealousy, unhappiness, madness, vice and crime.

It is a fact that the Puritan temperament readily finds this opinion, if not the program which accompanies it, acceptable, as one may discover in private conversation with respectable Puritans of both sexes. And it is more unfortunately true that the present-day rebellion against conventional morality in America has found, in Hardy and Shaw and other anti-romanticists, a seeming support of this opinion. So that one finds in America today (though

157

some people may not know about it) an undercurrent of impatient materialism in matters of sex. To become freed from the inadequate morality of Puritanism is, for thousands of young people, to adopt another morality which is, if more sound in many ways, certainly as inadequate as the other.

* * *

So that Ellen Key comes into the lives of many in this country as a conservative force, holding up a spiritual ideal, the ideal of monogamy, and defending it with a breadth of view, a sanity and a fervor that make it something different from the cold institution which these readers have come to despise. She makes every allowance for human nature, every concession to the necessities of temperament, every recognition of the human need for freedom, and yet makes the love of one man and one woman seem the highest ideal, a thing worth striving and waiting and suffering for.

She cherishes the spiritual magic of sex as the finest achievement of the race, and sees it as the central and guiding principle in our social and economic evolution. She seeks to construct a new morality which will do what the present one only pretends, and with the shallowest and most desperately pitiful of pretenses, to do. She would help our struggling generation to form a new code of ethics, and one of subtle stringency, in this most important and difficult of relations.

Thus her writings, of which "Love and Marriage" will here be taken as representative, have a twofold aspect—the radical and the conservative. But of the two the conservative is by far the truer. It is as a conservator, with too firm a grip on reality to be lured into the desertion of any real values so far achieved by the race, that she may be best considered.

And germane to her conservatism, which is the true conservatism of her sex, is her intellectual habit, her literary method. She is not a logician. Anyone who will look at the editorial in the present issue will see that this is not necessarily a defect. She lacks logic, and, with it order and clearness and precision, because of the very fact of her firm hold on realities. The realities are too complex to be brought into any completely logical and orderly relation, too elusive to be stated with utter precision. There is a whole universe in "Love and Marriage"; and it resembles the universe in its wildness, its tumultuousness, its contradictory quality. Her book, like the universe, is in a state of flux—it refuses to remain one fixed and dead thing. It is a book which in spite of some attempt at arrangement may be begun at any point and read in any order. It is a mixture of science, sociology and mysticism; it has a wider range than an orderly book could possibly have; it touches more points, includes more facts, and is more convincing, in its queer way, than any other.

"Love and Marriage" is the Talmud of sexual morality. It contains history, wisdom, poetry, psychological analysis, shrewd judgments, generous sympathies . . . and it all bears upon the creation of that new sexual morality for which in a thousand ways—economic, artistic and spiritual—we are so astonishing a mixture of readiness and unreadiness.

* * *

Ellen Key is fundamentally a conservator. But she is careful about what she conservates. It is the right to love which she would have us cherish, rather than the right to own another person—the beauty of singleness of devotion rather than the cruel habit of trying to force people to carry out rash promises made in moments of exaltation. She conserves the greatest things and lets the others go: motherhood, as against the exclusive right of married women to bear children; and that personal passion which is at once physical and spiritual rather than any of the legally standardized relations. Nor does she hesitate to speak out for the conservation of that old custom which persists among peasant and primitive peoples all over the world and which has been reintroduced to the public by a recent sociologist under the term of "trial marriage"; it must be held, she says, as the bulwark against the corruption of prostitution and made a part of the new morality.

* * *

It is perhaps in this very matter that her attitude is capable of being most bitterly resented. For we have lost our sense of what is old and good, and we give the sanction of ages to parvenu virtues that are as degraded as the rococo ornaments which were born in the same year. We have (or the Puritans among us have) lost all moral sense in the true meaning of the word, in that we are unable to tell good from bad if it be not among the things that were socially respectable in the year 1860. Ellen Key writes: "The most delicate test of a person's sense of morality is his power in interpreting ambiguous signs in the ethical sphere; for only the profoundly moral can discover the dividing line, sharp as the edge of a sword, between new morality and old immorality. In our time ethical obtuseness betrays itself first and foremost by the condemnation of those young couples who freely unite their destinies. The majority does not perceive the advance in morality which this implies in comparison with the code of so many men who, without responsibility—and without apparent risk—purchase the repose of their senses. The free union of love, on the other hand, gives them an enhancement of life which they consider that they gain without injuring anyone. It answers to their idea of love's chastity, an idea which is justly offended by the incompleteness of the period of engagement, with all its losses in the freshness and frankness of emotion. When their soul has found another soul, when the senses of both have met in a common longing, then they consider that they have a right to full unity of love, although compelled to secrecy,

159

since the conditions of society render early marriage impossible. They are thus freed from a wasteful struggle which would give them neither peace nor inner purity and which would be doubly hard for them, since they have attained the end—love—for the sake of which self-control would have been imposed."

* * *

It is almost impossible to quote any passage from "Love and Marriage" which is not subject to further practical modification, or which does not present an incomplete idea of which the complement may be found somewhere else. Even this passage is one which states a brief for the younger generation rather than the author's whole opinion. Still, with all their limitations, her view is one which is so different from that commonly held by women that it may seen merely fantastic to hold it up as an example of the conservative instinct of women. Nevertheless, it is so. It must be remembered that the view which holds that the chastity of unmarried women is well purchased at the price of prostitution is a masculine view. It is a piece of the sinister and cruel idealism of the male mind, divorced (as the male mind is so capable of being) from realities. No woman would ever have created prostitution to preserve the chastity of part of her sex; and the more familiar one becomes with the specific character of the feminine mind, the more impossible does it seem that they will, when they have come to think and act for themselves, permanently maintain it. Nor will they—one is forced to believe—hesitate long at the implication of that demolition.

* * *

No, I think that with the advent of women into a larger life our jerry-built virtues will have to go, to make room for mansions and gardens fit to be inhabited by the human soul.

It will be like the pulling down of a rotten tenement. First (with a great shocked outcry from some persons of my own sex) the facade goes, looking nice enough, but showing up for painted tin what pretended to be marble; then the dark, cavelike rooms exposed, with their blood-stained floors and their walls ineffectually papered over the accumulated filth and disease; and so on, lath by lath, down to the cellars, with their hints of unspeakable horrors in the dark. . . .

It is to this conclusion that this series draws: That women have a surer instinct than men for the preservation of the truest human values, but that their very acts of conservation will seem to the timid minds among us like the shattering of all virtue, the debacle of civilization, the Goetterdaemmerung!

August 2, 1912

160

REALITY

The Lower Depths, A Play in Four Acts, by Maxim Gorky. Plays of Today and Tomorrow. [Duffield & Co.]

In being a free people we suffer a certain disadvantage. We cannot understand the seriousness with which those who are less free take the process of thinking. Provoked as we are by our environment to act without thinking, we cannot comprehend that anybody should ever think without acting. And when we read the writings of philosophic novelists like Turgeniev and Gorky, writings which do not blink the most terrible facts of life, we call them reformers. If "Hamlet" were translated as a contemporary Russian play, we would imagine that it was an attack on Russian tyranny, and set down Shjaigespevr as a communist anarchist. The Russian government would probably take the same view, and make him one by sending him to Siberia! But the fact is that Russian tyranny, however revolutionary it may make its writers, only makes their writings more and more philosophical. Real reform literature—literature designed to move men to action—can only be produced in a country where men are free to act.

The present play is a case in point. Gorky is in his political and social opinions a revolutionist. But he has never written a work intended to arouse men and make them act. He has only written things intended to make them think. Impossible for us to believe this! We take a philosophical work of the first order, "The Night Asylum," and because it deals with thieves, prostitutes and people out of work we imagine that it must be a sociological play; we re-name it—of all absurd titles!—"The Lower Depths." We vaguely fancy that it is devoted to showing how terrible is the lot of the poor and how necessary it is that something should be done about it.

* * *

Well, we are wrong. Let us for once try to see the thing as it is. Gorky is not pleading the cause of the poor, nor suggesting that something be done to abolish poverty. He does not ask us to sympathize with the rags or the hunger of the miserables in this villainous lodging-house. He is not asking for the socialization of property, nor the assassination of the Czar. He does not want us to pass laws, or get signatures to a petition, or lecture from soap boxes. He does not want us to do anything about anything. He only wants us to look into the depths of our human nature and see what we shall see.

The whole point of this play is that it is written about ourselves. Gorky has chosen some thieves and murderers and prostitutes and drunkards to represent us to ourselves, first, because he knows that kind of people better than he does the middle class, and, second, because the readers to which he is accustomed, having none of our pharisaism, are ready to see themselves in these people. We may not be willing to see ourselves in the characters of "The Night Asylum." In that case, Russian literature has no meaning for us.

But let us suppose that we are willing to take Russian literature for what it is. What is it that we find in "The Night Asylum"? To begin with, the play is very different from the plays to which we have been accustomed. There is a minimum of action. The characters sit and talk; and only slowly—to the reader at least—their several personalities and passions emerge from the sodden mass. There is a blacksmith who is out of work, and his wife, who is dying. There is a thief, and a policeman, and a drunken actor, and a street walker, and a man who says that he is a baron by birth and used to have his coffee served to him in bed. There is a woman who wants her lover to murder her husband, and a man who wants to change from an old love to a new. They come and go, play cards, banter each other, quarrel, fight, and some one is killed. After that things go on much as before, only that circumstances are a little bit worse and the people a little more helpless and hopeless in the net of these circumstances.

* * *

But before one has got very far into the play, the incidents show themselves as subordinate to the spiritual state of the characters. It is this spiritual state which is the theme of the play. Everybody is trying to get a little happiness by lying to himself. The facts are too terrible to be faced, and so each one romanticises the facts. The baron tries to cast a glamor over his present existence—he is living on the earnings of Nastya, the street walker—by recalling the dignity of his early life. Nastya herself reads romantic love stories and palms off their contents as autobiography: it comforts her to pretend that she used to be a pure maiden loved by a good man. The actor romanticises his drunkenness, saying proudly: "My organism is poisoned by alcohol." Another one of the riffraff gilds the passing minute by handing out long words, the damaged scraps remaining to him from his youthful education. Even the policeman revels in being called sergeant, muttering that it is true he is not sergeant—as yet. They are all liars to themselves.

But they are not happy, because they can get nobody else to believe the lies they tell themselves. The baron mocks at the pitiful romancing of Nastya, and she cuts in upon his reminiscences with the most pointed allusions to his present basis of existence. They all mock at each other's lies, while trying desperately to keep up their own courage by means of illusion.

To these comes an old pilgrim, Luka—a kind, sweet-natured, generous vagabond. He brings into the little nest of venomous egotisms a strange peace. For he listens to everyone, believes everyone, and has a word of encouragement for everyone. The baron has at last found some one who will

162

believe his story about taking his coffee in bed, and life has a new meaning for him. Poor little Nastya is comforted because old Luka believes her story of Raoul and the pure love that he had for her. The drunken actor is led to believe that he can get cured in an institution and resume his triumphs on the stage. The thief is made to dream of a new and honest life as a settler in Siberia, with a good girl for a wife. For a while they are all happy.

* * *

But their happiness does not last. The benevolent lying of old Luka cannot shut out the truth permanently from their minds. And when the truth does break in, it shatters everything. The actor, the thief, the baron, the street walker, all lose hope, as the world uses them inexorably for its degraded purposes. Things go to smash at the touch of reality.

What of it? The play does not answer that question. Gorky does not undertake to teach us the right attitude toward reality. He only shows us poor wretches, in whom we may surely to some degree recognize ourselves, refusing to face the truth. He shows us the utmost what lying can do in effecting a temporary happiness. And he shows us how terrible truth is to those who have never learned to face it when at last it must be faced—how shattering and devastating it is. More than this he does not do.

Few of us have any faith in lies. The most vigorous part of modern literature has tended to destroy in us the notion that it is good to lie, or to evade the truth. We want to be truthful. We believe, most of us, that in any crisis we would be truthful. We would rise to the occasion with a splendid courage—we think.

Well—it is extremely probable that we wouldn't. We are less strong than we think, we have less courage than we give ourselves credit for. If we save facing reality till some grand occasion, we will never face it then: we will be blinded, crushed, broken to pieces by its impact. We shall prove ourselves weaklings and cowards. For truth is not beautiful; it is as terrible as death. We may think we could die bravely, but when death suddenly comes upon us we find ourselves afraid, unprepared, trembling at the horror of it. Only he who faces death daily in his mind is sure to face it like a man when it comes. And only he who faces reality daily in his mind will be able to look at it with steady eyes when it comes on the great wings of chance or passion.

For those who romanticize life constantly in little things there is no hope of their changing at need. They cannot. They must go on lying, evading, pretending to the end.

Reality is either a poison or a tonic. To those who are not accustomed to the taste, it is a poison, and they do well to put the cup from them. But those who, like Mithridates, have "sampled all the springs to birth From the many-venomed earth," can take the bitter draught, and be renewed and strengthened by it.

And how better learn to face reality than by reading those books in which reality is put before us in all its pain and ugliness! This is the justification of "unpleasant" literature: it teaches us how to live.

> But take it: if the smack is sour
> 'Tis better for the embittered hour.
> It should do good to heart and head
> When your soul is in my soul's stead.
> And I will friend you, if I may,
> In the dark and cloudy day.

For the dark and cloudy day comes; and it requires all the strength that the soul has to keep from being broken by it—to stand erect and walk firmly on an earth which has become so uncertain, under skies that have become so hostile. That day comes, and then one knows what manner of man one is.

August 23, 1912

CONRAD

Almayer's Folly: A Story of an Eastern River, by Joseph Conrad. A New Edition. [The Macmillan Company.]

It is easy to prophesy after the event. Now that Joseph Conrad has become recognized as one of the greatest novelists writing in English, it is not difficult to see in this first novel, "Almayer's Folly," the promise of all his subsequent accomplishment. But seventeen years ago, when it was originally published, what must it have seemed?

The literary skies of 1895 showed different constellations from today's. The brightest stars were Stevenson, Barrie and Kipling, while Hardy had a sensational vogue rather different from the worshipful respect accorded him today. George Moore had achieved a kind of "succes du scandale." S.R. Crockett had set an example in provincial fiction much admired at the time. In America we had Howells and Henry James; but we neglected them for Frank R. Stockton and F. Marion Crawford. F. Hopkinson Smith had already become an institution, and Richard Harding Davis had done his cleverest work. Henry Fuller and James Lane Allen were looked to with increasing confidence. The voice of Lafcadio Hearn had been heard out of the Orient.

But H.G. Wells was still writing "scientific fantasies." Bernard Shaw was doing dramatic criticisms for a London weekly. Arnold Bennet was an insignificant romancer. John Galsworthy was unknown.

Into this world of 1895 let us, if possible, enter, and from there look upon "Almayer's Folly," the first book of an unknown writer.

* * *

We see, first of all, a fascinating romance. "Almayer's Folly" is a tale of hidden treasure, and of the passions and adventures which most naturally come into such a tale. The scene is laid in Sambir, which, wherever it is—and the readers of 1895 would be even less sure than we—is a savage place where there are Malays and Arabs and the moldering remains of a once propserous [sic] Dutch trading post. There lives Almayer, the doting white man, with his savage Sulu wife and their daughter, hating and fearing the one and dreaming great dreams for the other's future; fumbling over the old dead explorer Lingard's maps and papers, and making futile little expeditions up that mysterious river by whose shores lay the wonderful gold mine which was to make all those great dreams of the future come true. And then comes the young Malay chief, Dain Maroola, offering to help Almayer find the treasure; but falling in love with Almayer's daughter, and plotting with her savage mother to take her away to be his wife. And the girl, half European and half savage, convent reared but fallen lately under the influence of her mother, having come to despise what she sees of white civilization and to yearn for the splendid passions of oriental savagery, this girl plots with her lover against her father. An accident precipitates a crisis in this plot, and it is betrayed to Almayer by a jealous slave girl—a betrayal coming too late to do anything but awaken Almayer and make him see the whole fabric of his gorgeous dreams come crashing down in pitiful and terrible ruin. That is the story.

* * *

It is a story which Stevenson might have told—or any one of a dozen other people. It is a romantic, even a conventionally romantic, outline. But it is only that "in the first place"; in the second place it is something wildly different. Into the world of a conventional romance the writer has poured some of the most dazzling descriptive passages ever penned in the English language, and some of the most subtle and profound psychological analysis. He has done things so beautiful and so impressive with words that the romantic theme is cast into the shade. It is not forgotten; it is there to give substance and meaning to the color and depth of the description and psychology; it is not forgotten, but ennobled.

And all this is done not in defiance of the theme, but in a sincere unfolding of it. The writer has simply tried to tell the whole truth about a familiar adventure. In telling the whole truth, in his own way, with the aid of an extraordinarily seeing eye, an extraordinarily understanding heart and a mastery over words which is extraordinary though obviously not yet complete—in seeking to do justice to an old theme he has produced something staggeringly new.

It is as though a writer of genius should set out to tell over again and with all his powers how "at midnight in the month of May a solitary horseman might have been seen galloping down the highway toward a lonely place at the crossroads where a mysterious cloaked and veiled lady awaited him." He makes it real, he makes it vital, he makes it tremendous. It is realism and romance in one. It is a fresh method, giving us a new vision of the world.

Consider his treatment of the jealous slave girl. What is there to say of such a creature which the words that name her do not convey? She is a slave girl. Is not that all? Ah, no! For listen to this:

> In that supple figure, straight as an arrow, so
> graceful and free in its walk, behind those soft eyes
> that spoke of nothing but of unconscious resignation,
> there slept all feelings and all passions, all hopes
> and all fears, the curse of life, and the consolation
> of death. And she knew nothing of it all. She lived
> like the tall palms amongst whom she was passing now,
> seeking the light, desiring the sunshine, fearing the
> storm, unconscious of either. The slave had no hope,
> and knew of no change. She knew of no other sky, no
> other water, no other forest, no other world, no other
> life. She had no wish, no hope, no love, no fear
> except of a blow.

But let us take something that will serve better as a test. All writers, be they realists or romanticists, seek to do justice to the love of man and woman. Here, then, is matter for comparison:

> She drew back her head and fastened her eyes on
> his in one of those long looks that are a woman's most
> terrible weapon; a look that is more stirring than the
> closest touch, and more dangerous than the thrust of a
> dagger, because it, also, whips the soul out of the

body, but leaves the body alive and helpless, to be swayed here and there by the capricious tempests of passion and desire; a look that enwraps the whole body, and that penetrates into the innermost recesses of the being, bringing terrible defeat in the delirious uplifting of accomplished conquest. It has the same meaning for the man of the forests and the sea, as for the man threading the paths of the more dangerous wilderness of houses and streets. Men that had felt in their breasts the awful exultation such a look awakens become mere things of day—which is paradise; forget yesterday—which was suffering; care not for tomorrow—which may be perdition. They wish to live under that look forever. It is the look of woman's surrender.

But if in these passages, so full of color and sympathy, there is the promise of all Joseph Conrad's wonderful accomplishment, there is in it, no less surely, a hint of his limitation. If it shows how by his elemental simplicity he might succeed, it nevertheless indicates how by sheer lack of social theory he might fail. If "Almayer's Folly" presages "Youth" and "Lord Jim," it presages, none the less, "Under Western Eyes."

* * *

For in "Under Western Eyes" Mr. Conrad is judged by some friendly critics to have failed—to have failed, that is, in giving an adequate treatment of his theme, which was that of the struggle in Russia between the autocracy and the revolutionists. It is complained that he has misjudged the cause of the revolutionists, and by his hostile account done them an injustice. If this criticism were expanded it would charge him with failing to appreciate the necessity of the desirability of revolution, of failing to see what is the matter with autocracy.

Of such failure in his own field no other writer of Mr. Conrad's standing could be accused today. It is, indeed, by their very perception of the defects of modern institutions, and by their recognition of the changes necessary or desirable, that Wells, Shaw and Galsworthy have been distinguished. All of these, and many others, have an understanding, not merely of the physical and emotional color of the world, but also of the underlying forces which enable us to interpret for ourselves the values of that emotional coloring. They have, in a word, theoretical knowledge of society as well as actual knowledge of men and women.

Of this theoretical knowledge Mr. Conrad has none, or next to none, and that poor and wrong. He depends upon his ability to see things right with his own eyes. Given the correctness of Conrad's view of Russia, and "Under Western Eyes" is a great novel. But those who should know say it is a wrongheaded view. And yet, guessing badly on fundamental things, Mr. Conrad gives us an account full of physical and emotional truth. It would do for Sambir, since the politics of Borneo do not matter to us; but the politics of Russia do matter to us. The novelist who would write about Russian politics must first convince us that he is politically "right."

In 1895 we should have cared little about this matter; and it is quite possible that in 1925 we shall care even less. For as these changes begin to be effected, we shall be less insistent on sociological orthodoxy. When Russia is freed, we shall not mind a novel's being unfair to the revolutionists. The politics of Russia will be like the politics of Sambir, a thing for the novelist to alter at this own free will! We shall regain our unmixed joy in the vision and sympathy of one of our greatest novelists. We shall not quarrel with his lack of theoretical knowledge; we shall rather marvel at his seeing eye and his understanding heart.

August 30, 1912

WOMEN AND THE WEST

The Wind Before the Dawn, by Dell H. Munger. Illustrated by Thomas Fogarty. [Doubleday, Page & Co.]

Upon one of those maps which enterprising magazines publish from time to time, showing what districts various authors have pre-empted for fictional purposes, "The Wind Before the Dawn" would be credited to Kansas. With regard to the present book, the locale is decidedly more important to discuss than the technique, and one would like nothing so much as a "literary map" to accompany these remarks.

Such maps have a great interest. They show, for one thing, how much our American literature arises out of a genuine desire to express the life of a community, and how little it is founded on mere literary tradition. For there have sprung up, in a hundred places, men and women anxious to describe the life they know, its beauty and dignity and hardship and pathos. Caring little or nothing for what has been done by previous writers, not paying to any predecessor the compliment of imitation, these writers have produced a literature which, if it has its limitations, but none the less its individual triumphs and its general interest—an interest which, in our anxiety to catch up with European fiction in some things, we have been perhaps too ready to underestimate.

168

But one of the chief services which such a map could do for us, if ingeniously enough drawn, would be to show how truly our literature is a frontier literature. A clear-sighted Englishman, A. E. Zimmern, said the other day that the dominant fact in American life, the thing that gave us our specific national quality, was the West. And when we consider how our frontier has moved farther and farther across the continent, we see that Patrick Henry and Abraham Lincoln and William Jennings Bryan have a common quality in representing that West in which mankind is at once in conflict and in alliance with the soil. We see, too, that Cooper and Mark Twain, Bret Harte and Frank Norris have the same task—that of describing frontier life. The frontier changes, the forests and mountains give way to bare prairies and then again to desert plains, and these once more to the fertile slopes of California—but it is always the West.

Indeed, when one considers the matter closely one recognizes that the frontier (if one take the word in a loose sense, as opposed to the old and stable culture of the seaboard) has been the theme of nearly all our writers. Beside those cited above, how many other names might be set! Walt Whitman, W. D. Howells, S. Weir Mitchell, John Burroughs, Thomas Bailey Aldrich, Edward Eggleston, John Hay, Joaquin Miller, James Whitcomb Riley, "Old Ed" Howe, Elia W. Peattie, Mary Hallock Foote, F. Hopkinson Smith, Eugene Field, Hamlin Garland, Octave Thanet, Henry B. Fuller, Robert Herrick, Gertrude Atherton—it begins to be a literary directory!

Yet all these writers owe their particular flavor to that West of which they write—whether it be the comparatively staid eastern West of Mr. Howells or the wild and very western West of Mrs. Atherton. Nor have we finished with this West in our fiction. Now that we have reached the Pacific, we are coming back and opening up neglected bits of territory in between. In particular, it seems that the Mormon colonies must soon attract a writer who will forget most of the Destroying Angel nonsense and do justice to the romance of that extraordinary sect. And for all that the cow puncher has ridden through so many novels, he still waits for the book which shall make full use of the materials which his life, and his phase of civilization, affords.

To this frontier literature the present book belongs. "The Wind Before the Dawn" is a kind of western prose epic, loosely and in part crudely executed, but full of that inspiration which such a theme almost inevitably gives. It is a big book physically, and a big though not a discriminating work spiritually.

It is the story of a young woman who as a farmer's daughter and a farmer's wife experiences all the pleasures and discomforts, aspirations and thwartings and achievements which such a life can hold.

Elizabeth, this young woman, is a 14-year-old child riding horseback and taking care of some cattle on a Kansas prairie when the story opens. The cattle are stampeded by the appearance of that first horde of grasshoppers which scourged the new agricultural districts of the West. Then follows the family council, at which Elizabeth's father announces his determination to stay with the land, no matter what happens. He does stay, and his wife and daughter stay, too, and suffer more than he knows. Elizabeth wants an education. Her father "usually regarded a request from his children as a thing to be denied promptly, and always as a matter for suspicion." But he lets Elizabeth have a little schooling, and then he insists on her taking a country school. Her wages go to help pay off a mortgage he has insisted, in spite of his wife's protest, in giving. But the girl at last revolts, and seeks to free herself from this drudgery by marriage with a man who seems to fulfill her ideal. This man, however, turns out to be the familiar tyrannical male, and after much domestic friction the two separate. Elizabeth, made independent by a fortunate legacy, manages to get her life free from the debts and drudgery in which it had threatened to be swallowed up. In the end of the book there is a foreshadowing of a reunion of husband and wife upon better terms than in the past.

Winter after summer, month by month, this story unfolds, with a wealth of detail which is something very delightful in its simplicity and faithfulness. One remembers such a passage as this one, where Elizabeth has taken refuge from a storm in a "neighbor's" house:

> "Liza Ann! here's Miss Farnshaw, as wet as that last brood of chickens you found under th' corn planter. Give 'er a dry pair of shoes" .
> . . .
> Just then one adventurous chick, which, with the rest of the brood, had been discovered under the corn planter earlier in the day, jumped out of the box in which it had been kept near the fire. Mrs. Chamberlain set the mill on the table and gave chase to the runaway.
> "That's th' peertest chicken of th' lot," she remarked as she again enveloped him in the old woolen skirt, from the folds of which came much distressed cheeping. "They're hungry, I think," she added, reaching for a bowl of yellow cornmeal which she mixed with water. Lifting the skirt off the little brood carefully, and giving it a cautious shake to assure herself that no unwary chick was caught in its folds, she dropped some of the mixture in the middle of the box, tapping lightly with the spoon to call the attention of the chicks to its presence. The chickens pecked hungrily, and there was a satisfied note in the twitterings of the downy little group as Mrs. Chamberlain turned to the preparation of her supper again.

This is, once again, the story of the struggle of human beings with the soil, the weather, grasshoppers and debt; but it derives an individual interest from the fact that it is written from the woman's point of view.

Perre Loti wrote an affecting story called "Les Desenchantees," in which he described the unhappiness that came to Turkish women from the disharmony of their education and their environment. Readers of modern problem novels, these women were completely immersed in a culture centuries behind that of the problem novel. Allowed to discover that they had souls, they were nevertheless treated as chattels, contracted in marriage to men they had never seen. The disharmony was apparent and disheartening. Curiously enough, there is something of a parallel to Loti's novel in this American book. For if from the masculine point of view the conquest of the prairie is a splendid thing, from the feminine point of view it is not nearly so splendid. The man may dream of the future, but the woman experiences the present. And that present is drudgery of a kind more exhausting and monotonous than anything in the lot of man; it includes child-bearing, child-rearing, cooking on a large scale, and all the endless details of rural domestic economy, with the disadvantage of a physique less able than man's to bear this great burden. As well as a report by the Country Life Commission, this book shows that, so far as women are concerned, farming is not by any means all beer and skittles.

* * *

It must not be imagined, however, that the book is couched in terms of complaint. It only shows, by telling the truth, that the desire of a woman to cultivate her personality, to read, to think, to achieve some intellectual distinction, is not quite consonant with the necessities of frontier farming. Or rather—and this is its real meaning—it is not possible for a woman to enjoy her soul on a western farm so long as her father or husband has complete charge of the farm.

The book is a long and faithful chronicle of the wrongs inflicted on such women through a lack of imagination in their mankind. Petty domestic tyranny, exacting ideals of housekeeping, interference, insufficient domestic facilities (though the men have the latest machinery and leave it out all winter to rust), insufficient money for their needs (though the men mortgage the land so as to buy more land), indifference to the social needs of women—all these things are woven into the fabric of this novel. One is left pretty well convinced at the close that what country life needs more than anything else is feminism; more power to women, more opportunity to run things their way. One imagines a life less furiously speeded, with more social intercourse, more of the amenities of civilized life, and all this with a securer economic foundation—no debts, no mortgages—the weight of a great fear lifted from off the soul.

Of some such implications in the book the author is distinctly conscious. The whole story is a forward-looking one, and it is this eager pointing to a better day coming which prevents some pages of the book from being discouraging. What that better day exactly will be there is no chance to say in such a novel. All that is permitted the author is the privilege of declaring that the brave determination of Elizabeth to live an honest and civilized life is the prelude to something clearer and greater—"the wind before the dawn."

September 6, 1912

POETIC JOURNALISM

A Miscellany of Men, by G.K. Chesterton. [Dodd, Mead & Co.]

Piled up on the top of my desk are a lot of London papers, among them the Daily News and Leader, which contains every Saturday a column article by G.K. Chesterton. On the day that Saturday paper comes it is read before anything else is done—read with an unfailing zest. Now that thirty or so of these Saturday articles have been put together in a book—can I infect other people with my own enthusiasm?

Of course, the articles suffer by being put between covers. There is some writing that looks ill at ease between the column rules of a newspaper, and only comes to its own when it has the large type and fair margin of a book page. But these things were written for a newspaper, and some of their flavor vanishes when they are turned into essays. They have lost their old controversial air. Even such a splendid thing as "The New Theologian," in which Mr. Chesterton flays alive a dean who made some silly remarks on the coal strike—this goes much better against a background of headlines telling of the suffering of miners' wives and children. And reading "The Mad Official," in the book, one learns nothing further about the woman who was arrested for not washing her children's faces (when she had no water to do it with, by the way), and was carried away to prison crying, "Lord save me!" Knowing what was done about it, and how hard it was to stop the grinding of the mills of punishment and pull the poor woman out, one feels differently about it, and about Mr. Chesterton. He becomes, not a writer of essays, but a man speaking earnestly and desperately in behalf of beliefs which one shares with him.

* * *

Now he is the Advocatus Pauperis; and now he is the defender of the French Revolution. Here he protests against the defacement of Stonehenge by a barb-wire fence and a policeman—"to keep the place from being spoiled by vulgar 'trippers'"—as though barb wire and a policeman were adornments! Again he takes the photograph as a type of modern scientific falsity, and shows how in the case of the missing poet John Davidson the photograph circulated by the police lied like a thief about the primary facts of the man's appearance. Or he shows just why an ordinary election does not in the least insure the rule of the people. All these things and a score of others he makes clear with all the means at his command—which are chiefly two, humor and noble eloquence. There is a third thing, an amazing and often artificial simplicity; but that is not so much a means deliberately employed as an innate tendency in the writer's mind.

He sees everything in its simplest terms, and when things are not simple his vision distorts them into simplicity. The startling thing is that, recognizing the error, we see that we have not lost so much as we thought. The mass of uncertain opinions, like melting crystals, which is the nearest Mr. Wells (say) can get to the truth, becomes in Mr. Chesterton's hands a hard snowball, capable of being used to knock somebody down with. The vanishing crystals are more interesting to study; but the snowball is more valuable in a fight. Hard truths are sometimes worth more than fine truths.

* * *

It is true that Mr. Chesterton disagrees with us—with some of us—on such questions as religion and woman's suffrage. As to the second question, I must say (not without first a cautious glance around me) that I do not mind. While as to the first question, I am frankly glad that Mr. Chesterton is a Catholic, or, as he calls it, a Christian. There is a large reason which I shall explain later. But there is a small reason, which is that his Christianity gives an intensity to his feeling in such passages as the ones I am about to quote:

> The perpetual public criticism and public change
> which is the note of all our history springs from a
> certain spirit far too deep to be defined. It is
> deeper than democracy; nay, it may often appear to be
> nondemocratic; for it may often be the special defense
> of a minority or an individual. It will often leave
> the ninety-and-nine in the wilderness and go after that
> which is lost. It will often risk the State itself to
> right a single wrong; and do justice though the
> heavens fall. . . . If there was but one slave in
> England, and he did all the work while the rest of us
> made merry, this spirit that is in us would still cry

173

aloud to God night and day. . . . Men must not be busy
merely like a swarm, or even happy merely like a herd;
for it is not a question of men, but of a man. . . . This
is the spirit which makes the Christian poor begin
their terrible murmur whenever there is a turn of
prices or a deadlock of toil that threatens them with
vagabondage or pauperization.

That passage constitutes a rhetorical justification of Mr. Chesterton's
faith. And rhetoric is more important than many people think. I believe that
poetry which can be read aloud and enjoyed is better poetry than that which
must be seen to be understood: that is to say, if the living voice will approve
the poet's verses, they are good. And certainly the living voice approves that
epithet "Christian": almost thou persuadest me!

But there is another justification of Mr. Chesterton's faith, and that
is that it liberates, along with his prejudices, his common sense for our
service. It is not generally recognized how thoroughly implicated most of us
are in modern institutions and movement, and how greatly we have surrendered the faculty of judgment in regard to them. Even when we who are
the boldest start to criticise our own movements and institutions we quickly
enough swerve with a "but of course" into the familiar eulogy. We are such
thorough believers in the public school (for instance) that not one of us dares
say how bad the present American school system is. We believe in sociological experiments too much to admit to ourselves how profoundly our social
settlements have failed. We believe in certain things enough to blunt the
edges of our critical perceptions: and we quite frankly deplore the publication
of the least hint of weakness, lest the enemy should see and flout us.

Such is the inevitable state of affairs in war time, and modernism is
a perpetual guerrilla warfare against the past. But modernism suffers for it,
and its patriotism shades off by degrees into rotten hypocrisy and self-
deception. So that we need some one detached from us to expose our
weaknesses. I, for one, am grateful to Mr. Chesterton.

Mr. Chesterton is not prejudiced in favor of modern science; and
accordingly we owe to him some splendid denunciations of scientific
charlatanism. He is not prejudiced in favor of a benevolent bureaucracy, and
so he has been able to see at what places the benevolence wears through and
the poor man becomes the victim of a terrific conspiracy. He calls this doctor
a dunce and that statesman a knave, and once he has stripped them of their
solemn robes of science and sociology we recognize that he is right. Our
common sense has been paralyzed by our feeling of pride and awe. We let
postal officials take from us fundamental liberties, and we gape admiringly
at their exhibition under the impression that we are seeing the Discomfiture
of Rogues until some one like Chesterton awakes us to our folly. We are the
dupes of Progress.

But this is putting too much to the credit of common sense. Mr. Chesterton is a democrat even before he is a sensible person. And he is a poet almost before he is a sensible person. It is the combination of these qualities, a feeling for the world's overwhelming beauty and an instinctive respect for the desires and opinions of his fellow human beings, together with his common sense, which constitutes his peculiar charm. For his charm does not, I think, lie in his humor. His humor is either a clear or a muddy stream, and one either sees or does not see the truth shining up through—that is all. Usually one does. But Mr. Chesterton is not a "humorist." His humor—to try another metaphor—is like the head of the match one lights one's pipe with: it flares up, and is forgotten all about in the ensuing illumination. Or again—when Mr. Chesterton is funny he is merely raising his voice, as it were, to be heard.

But his poetry—that is a thing in him as enduring as his democracy; indeed, it is when he is a poet that he is most himself. Take this bit about Gothic architecture.

> The truth about Gothic is, first, that it is alive, and second, that it is on the march. It is the Church Militant; it is the only fighting architecture. All its spires are spears at rest; all its stones are stones asleep in a catapult. In that instant of illusion I could hear the arches clash like swords as they crossed each other. The mighty and numberless columns seemed to go swinging by like the huge feet of imperial elephants. The graven foliage wreathed and blew like banners going into battle; the silence was deafening with all the mingled noises of a military march; the great bell shook down, as the organ shook up its thunder. The thirsty-throated gargoyles shouted like trumpets from all the roofs and pinnacles as they passed; and from the lectern in the core of the Cathedral the eagle of the awful evangelist clashed his wings of brass.

There is nothing in the nature of "fine writing" about that. It is Mr. Chesterton celebrating a discovery about the world he lives in. To Mr. Chesterton it is a perpetually enchanting world, and he is never far off from wonder.

But not merely cathedrals are glorious to him: so are cakes and ale. And that, now I come to think of it, is why I like G.K. Chesterton so well. He is the only writer among those who have the task of forming the minds and manners of this generation, who is not, when all is said and done, a Prig.

November 29, 1912

THE NEW POET

The Story of a Round-House, and Other Poems, by John Masefield. [The Macmillan Company.]

John Masefield's latest story—related in verse, after the example of that fine old story-teller, Homer—is the best he has yet done. It is better than that splendid star-splashing "Pilgrim's Progress" tale, "The Everlasting Mercy"; better than that icy-fierce tale of love and death, "The Widow in the Bye-street." "The Story of a Round-House" has neither the exaltation of the one nor the somber passion of the other. But it is superior to both because it deals with a more civilized man. It is easy—for a poet—to make an exciting tale out of primitive materials—out of the white madness of religion or the red madness of love. The saint and the lover, along with the warrior, are the natural heroes of stories. Upon them men's interest naturally centers; into them the listening multitude breathes its breath, and they live. But to take a modern man, a thinker, an artist, and make him, by virtue of his thought and his art, a hero—that is hard!

But that is what Mr. Masefield has done. He has made a protagonist out of an aesthete: which is to find simple and striking terms for the statement of a complex and obscure temperament: which is no small thing!

"The Story of a Round-House" is the alternative title to the poem "Dauber." The "round-house," which at first glance suggests a railroad, is what appeared in Captain Marryat as the "fo'c's'le." Dauber is a painter who has shipped as a sailor, in order to learn the sea so that he, first of all men, may truly paint it. One sees him in the first chapter—or canto, if you prefer—standing on the deck, watching the sunset. It is four bells, and for an hour there is no work on board ship. Some of the men sing, others play checkers or mend clothes. Dauber, so named by the crew in derision, watches till the light grows dim. He is not yet 22, and young for his years, "sickly and not yet brown with the sea's tan."

* * *

Si, the apprentice, comes over and asks, "Why did you come to sea, Dauber?" "I want to be a painter," Dauber tells him. He wants to know the sea and ships from A to Z, and "paint great ships at sea" before he dies. It's not been done yet, from the inside, by one who really knows.

> Even as he spoke his busy pencil moved
> Drawing the leap of water off the side,
> Where the great clipper trampled iron-hooved,
> Making the blue hills of the sea divide,
> Shearing a glittering scatter in her stride,

And leaping on full tilt with all sails drawing,
Proud as a war horse, snuffing battle, pawing.

"I cannot get it yet, not yet," he says. "O if I could, O if I only might!" Just then the suns sets, the wind cuts chill, and there is a call: "Out sidelights." Dauber is the lampman. Of course he is late. Art doesn't go any better with seamanship than poetry with bookkeeping. The bos'n "gives it to him" later. And the cook starts a popular movement when he remarks that Dauber's paints are "poisoning all the air." So Dauber takes his sketches, the fruits of his first six weeks' work, up on deck and hides them under the ship's long boat—where, of course, they have no business to be—

He stayed a moment, leaning on the boat,
Watching the constellations rise and burn,
Until the beauty took him by the throat
So stately is their glittering overturn;
Armies of marching eyes, armies that yearn
With banners rising and falling and passing by
Over the empty silence of the sky.

He gives a last look, a painter's look, at the great moonlit sails, the sidelight dripping green light as it passes over the water, the on-rushing "fire-bright bows." He sighs. "I'll do't," he says, and goes below.

*   *   *

Then some reefers who have been watching go and get the sketches, and by way of a joke rub them with turpentine and a knife until the six weeks' work is effectually effaced—

. . . every trace
Of quick perception caught by patient skill
And lines that brought the blood into his face . . .

Next day is Sunday—"his free painting day." He gets up at 5 o'clock, and scrubs the deck, hurriedly, so as to get to his real work. At breakfast the bos'n points out that he has skimped his work; and some one else says, "Look at his hands, all oil still to the wrists." So they make him "strip and scrub." Meanwhile they pass remarks on his appearance—scraggy neck, sloping shoulders, narrow chest, thin arms and unmuscular hands—

So precious time was wasted, bell by bell,
Before the washing and the breakfast ended.
The artist's leisure which the wise gods sell
Only for life paid down and spirit spended.

But at last Dauber is free. He goes to get his drawings. He finds them ruined. A lump comes in his throat, for he is "vain of his attempts, and tender-skinned." Dauber tries to find out who did it, and only gets himself hazed, terribly and yet not unkindly, by everyone on board from the captain down. A sailor trying to paint! The apprentice, Sails, gives him advice. It is more racy in diction, but in substance is the same that every artist, of whatever kind, hears from his practical friends:

"Lord Dauber, be a man, and take a joke"—
He puffed his pipe—"and let the matter rest.
Spit brown, my son, and get a hairy breast;
Get shoulders on you at the crojick braces
And let the painting business go to blazes.

But there is no use trying to turn a fool from his folly. Dauber pulls out his easel, his paints, his stool—

He dipped his brush and tried to fix a line.
And then came peace, and gentle beauty came,
Turning his spirit's water into wine,
Lightening his darkness with a touch of flame;
O joy of trying for beauty, ever the same,
You ever fail, your comforts never end;
O balm of this world's way, O perfect friend.

A little afterward Dauber finds a friend—for an hour—in Si the reefer. Si tells the story of his life, and asks for Dauber's. Dauber gives it at length. His father had been a farmer, and idealized farming, and it broke the old man's heart when the boy left home to be a painter. At last Dauber turns to Si, and finds him asleep! For chumming with Dauber that one hour, however, Si—a young gentleman, learning to command—is disciplined by his companions on the half-deck: and he speaks to Dauber no more.

* * *

But when it come to rounding the Horn, Dauber has to lock up his paints, join the watch, and go aloft with the others—

Drenched, frozen, gasping, blinded, beaten dumb.
High in the night, reeling great blinded arcs
As the ship rolled, his chappy fingers numb,
The dock below a narrow blur of marks,
The sea a welter of whiteness shot with sparks . . .

Ah! the story of that rounding of the Horn! Never in prose has it been so tremendously described. The "marching silences," the fog, the fog-horn baying "like a solitary hound," the mournful answer of the whales riding that desolate sea, and always the fog—"a wall of nothing at the world's last edge"; the cackling sea-birds, the polar snow—and then the storm. And "painting and art and England were old tales told in some other life."

* * *

Dauber, trying to help furl sail, is a pitiful figure in a terrific picture—a picture that grows more like a nightmare every moment. Frozen, half-drowned, aching with hour on hour of paralyzing toil, cursed, kicked—

> Death would be better, Death, than this long hell
> Of mockery and surrender and dismay,
> This long defeat of doing nothing well,
> Playing the part too high for him to play.
> "O Death, who hides the sorry thing away,
> Take me. I've failed. I cannot play these cards."
> There came a thundering from the topsail yards.
>
> And then he bit his lips, clenching his mind,
> And staggered out to muster, beating back
> The coward frozen self of him that whined.
> Come what cards may, he meant to play the pack.

It is the beginning of probation for Dauber's soul. For the next month the ocean teaches him, and in that month he is "never warm, nor dry, nor full, nor rested." Then, after thirty days, a ghostly sun gives "sickly promise" that the storms are over. "So long, Cape Stiff!" cry the sailors, and Dauber sings as he scrubs. He has endured the worst, and is done with fear. He is tanned and "plumped" and made new all over. The men respect him. The bos'n offers to teach him "square sennit." Dauber feels "promoted into man"—

> It was his warrant that he had not failed,
> That the most hard peak in his difficult climb
> Had not been past attainment; it was scaled
> In spite of perilous ways and slippery slime.
> He had emerged out of the iron time
> And knew that he had compassed his life's scheme;
> He had the power sufficient to his dream.

Dauber is congratulated by the mate on having become a sailor and learned sense—

> "So throw your paints to blazes and have done.
> Words can't describe the silly things you did,
> Sitting before your easel in the sun,
> With all your colors on the paint-box lid.
> I blushed for you . . . and then the daubs you hid.

179

My God! you'll have more sense now, eh? You've quit?"
"No, sir." "You've not?" "No, sir." "God give you wit..."

But the Horn "flicks her tail," and there is another storm before they
reach Valparaiso Bay. The sails go, and the hands run to clear away. "Three
to the mast they ran; it was a race." The mate is ready to bet on Dauber. The
gale roars at them, a gust tears the sail from Dauber's hands, and he sees a
man falling. . . .

No, it is he himself that falls. They kneel about him. "His pain was
real enough, but all else seemed." He murmurs, "It will go on," and colors
and sounds seem mixing in the air; and again: "It will go on"—

> Not knowing his meaning rightly, but he spoke
> With the intentness of a fading soul
> Whose share of nature's fire turns to smoke,
> Whose hand on Nature's wheel loses control.
> The eager faces glowered red like coal;
> They glowed, the great storm glowed, the sails, the mast.
> "It will go on," he cried aloud, and passed.

Masefield does not point the moral. He merely tells what the seamen
said, and how Dauber was buried at sea, and how the ship sailed into
Valparaiso Bay, where "the pointed mountain pointed at the stars, frozen,
alert, austere," and the falling stones fill the gorges with echoes . . . He lets
the story stand for itself, and we may make what we like of it.

* * *

This, then, is what I make of it: a declaration of belief in life.
Masefield lets his hero die before accomplishing his ambition, in order to
show that it makes no difference. "It goes on"—the desire, the effort, the
enjoyment. We go out like lamps, but the flame lives. The desire, the effort,
the enjoyment—that is life. The race will-to-live effloresces in our thousands
of little lives, yours and mine, and we have sights and sounds and friendships
and the glory of talk: we plan a little, we taste a little, and we fall asleep.
But—"it goes on."

It is the "golden instants" when life becomes "more splendid than
its husk" in which we transcend mortality, being by virtue of our ecstasy
united with that which endures. "The days that make us happy make us
wise," as Masefield says in another fine poem in this volume, "Biography."
Or, as he says in another of these poems, "Laugh and be proud to belong to
the old proud pageant of man." How much better it sounds in poetry than in
prose!

Nevertheless, if any reader insists that the death of the Dauber was wholly unnecessary I will make him that handsome concession. It is true that success is likely to be a little vulgar; nevertheless, it is time that poets and dramatists and novelists found some other way out of the difficulty. Death is too easy a solution. One is ashamed in real life to add a specious dignity to one's striving by getting run over by a street car; one continues to strive, it is no great matter to what final end. So do all we Daubers, and so should Masefield's.

Nevertheless, Masefield has given us a great poem. There is no use making any bones of that fact. "Dauber" is great because it gives a vision of life, in its outer semblance and in its inner significance, vividly, poignantly, simply, truthfully—and rhythmically. For Masefield is a master of rhythm. He knows the time for dulcet melodies, and the time for discords. He knows how to create the overtones of narrative poetry.

* * *

Despite the surprised air of some of Masefield's critics, there is nothing novel or doubtful in his use of colloquial language for serious poetry. In this he but follows the precept of Wordsworth in the preface to the "Lyrical Ballads" and the practice of Byron in "Don Juan." Masefield has brought back the story-poem just when it seemed that poetry was becoming exclusively lyrical (and unpopular); but the first English poet was a story-teller, and probably the last will be. What Masefield has given us that is new is a poetic personality of first-rate importance.

Masefield is not a new edition of Kipling, or of Keats; he is himself. He did not learn from the pages of his favorite author how to look at the world, and what to think about what he saw: his own soul taught him. He took his stanza from Shakespeare, but he poured into it poetry white-hot from the crucible of his imagination. One feels that Masefield has worked hard at poetry; but not trying to make it resemble some model: no, only to make it express his thought and feeling about the world in which he lives.

January 17, 1913

DORA MARSDEN

Dora Marsden is a new figure in the feminist movement. Just how she came into being is hard to tell. Her family were Radicals, it seems, smug British radicals; and she broke away, first of all, into a sort of middle class socialism. She went into settlement work. Here, it seems, she discovered what sort of person she really was.

She was a lover of freedom. So of course she rebelled against the interference of the middle class with the affairs of the poor, and threw overboard her settlement work and her socialism together. She was a believer in woman suffrage, but the autocratic government of the organization irked her. And, besides, she felt constrained to point out that feminism meant worlds more than a mere vote. The position of woman, not indeed as the slave of man, but as the enslaver of man, but with the other end of the chain fastened to her own wrist, and depriving her quite effectually of her liberties—this irritated her. Independence to her meant achievement, and when she heard the talk about "motherhood" by which the women she knew excused their lack of achievement, she was annoyed. Finally, the taboo upon the important subject of sex exasperated her. So she started a journal to express her discontent with all these things, and to change them.

* * *

Naturally she called her journal the Freewoman. "Independent" expresses much of Dora Marsden's feeling, but that word has been of late dragged in a mire of pettiness and needs dry cleaning. It has come to signify a woman who isn't afraid to go out at night alone or who holds a position downtown. A word had to be chosen which had in it some suggestion of the heroic. Hence the freewoman.

The Freewoman was a weekly. It lived several months and then suspended publication, and now all the women I know are poring over the back numbers while waiting for it to start again as a fortnightly. It was a remarkable paper. For one thing, it threw open its columns to such a discussion of sex as England had never known before. Poor dear Mrs. Humphry Ward wrote a shocked letter to the Times about it. Of course, a good many of the ideas put forth in this correspondence were erroneous or trivial, but it must have done the writers no end of good to express themselves freely. For once sex was on a plane with other subjects, a fact making tremendously for sanity. In this Miss Marsden not only achieved a creditable journalistic feat, but performed a valuable public service.

Her editorials were another distinctive thing. In the first issue was an editorial on "Bondwomen," from which it would appear that even such advanced persons as you, my dear Madam, are still far from free. She went on to attack all the things which bind women and keep them unfree. As such she denounced what she considered the cant of "motherhood." Listen!

"Considering, therefore, that children, from both physiological and psychological points of view, belong more to the woman than to the man; considering, too, that not only does she need them more, but as a rule, wants them more than the man, the parental situation begins to present elements of humor when the woman proceeds to fasten upon the man, in return for the children she has borne him, the obligation from that time to the end of her days, not only for the children's existence, but for her own also!"

When asked under what conditions, then, women should have children, she replied that women who wanted them should save for them as for a trip to Europe. This is frankly a gospel for a minority—a fact which does not invalidate it in the eyes of its promulgator—but she does believe that if women are to become the equals of men they must find some way to have children without giving up the rest of life. It has been done!

*   *   *

Then, having been rebuked for her critical attitude toward the woman suffrage organization, she showed herself in no mood to take orders from even that source. She subjected the attitude of the members of the organization to an examination, and found it tainted with sentimentalism. "Of all the corruptions to which the woman's movement is now open," she wrote, "the most poisonous and permeating is that which flows from sentimentalism, and it is in the W. S. P. U. that sentimentalism is now rampant. . . . It is this sentimentalism that is abhorrent to us. We fight it as we would fight prostitution, or any other social disease."

She called upon women to be individuals, and sought to demolish in their minds any lingering desire for Authority. "There is," she wrote, "a genuine pathos in our reliance upon the law in regard to the affairs of our own souls. Our belief in ourselves and in our impulses is so frail that we prefer to see it, buttressed up. We are surer of our beliefs when we see their lawfulness symbolized in the respectable blue cloth of the policeman's uniform, and the sturdy good quality of the prison's walls. The law gives them their passport. Well, perhaps in this generation, for all save pioneers, the law will continue to give its protecting shelter, but with the younger generations we believe we shall see a stronger, prouder, and more insistent people, surer of themselves and of the pureness of their own desires."

*   *   *

She did not stick at the task of formulating for women a new moral attitude to replace the old. "We are seeking," she said, "a morality which shall be able to point the way out of the social trap we find we are in. We are conscious that we are concerned in the dissolution of one social order, which is giving way to another. Men and women are both involved, but women differently from men, because women themselves are very different from men. The difference between men and women is the whole difference between a religion and a moral code. Men are pagan. They have never been Christian. Women are wholly Christian, and have assimilated the entire genius of Christianity.

"The ideal of conduct which men have followed has been one of self-realization, tempered by a broad principle of equity which has been translated into practice by means of a code of laws. A man's desire and ideal has been to satisfy the wants which a consciousness of his several senses gives rise to. His vision of attainment has therefore been a sensuous one, and if in his desire for attainment he has transgressed the law, his transgression has sat but lightly upon him. A law is an objective thing, laid upon a man's will from outside. It does not enter the inner recesses of consciousness, as does a religion. It is nothing more than a body of prohibitions and commands, which can be obeyed, transgressed or evaded with little injury to the soul. With women moral matters have been wholly different. Resting for support upon a religion, their moral code has received its sanction and force from within. It has thus laid hold on consciousness with a far more tenacious grip. Their code being subjective, transgression has meant a darkening of the spirit, a sullying of the soul. Thus the doctrine of self-renunciation, which is the outstanding feature of Christian ethics, has had the most favorable circumstances to insure its realization, and with women it has won completely—so completely that it now exerts its influence unconsciously. Seeking the realization of the will of others, and not their own, ever waiting upon the minds of others, women have almost lost the instinct for self-realization, the instinct for achievement in their own persons."

*   *   *

Whether she is right is a moot question. Certainly in such matters as testimony in court, the customs-tariff, and the minor city ordinances, women show no particular respect for the law. Ibsen sought in "The Doll's House" to show that her morality had no connection with the laws of the world of men. Even in matters of human relationship it is doubtful if women give any more of an "inner assent" to law than do men. Woman's failure to achieve that domination of the world which constitutes individuality and freedom—this Dora Marsden would explain on the ground of a dulling of the senses. It may

184

be more easily explained as a result of a dulling of the imagination. The trouble is that they are content with petty conquests. Inevitably one argues with Dora Marsden. That is her value. She provokes thought. And she welcomes it. She wants everybody to think—not to think her thoughts necessarily, nor the right thoughts always, but that which they can and must. She is a propagandist, it is true. But she does not create a silence, and call it conversion.

She stimulates her readers to cast out the devils that inhabit their souls—fear, prejudice, sensitiveness. She helps them to build up their lives on a basis of will—the exercise, not the suppression, of will. She indurates them to the world. She liberates them to live. She is the Max Stirner of feminism.

Freedom! That is the first word and the last with Dora Marsden. She makes women understand for the first time what freedom means. She makes them want to be free. She nerves them to the effort of emancipation. She sows in a fertile soil the dragon's teeth which shall spring up as a band of capable females, knowing what they want and taking it, asking no leave from anybody, doing things and enjoying life—Freewomen!

January 17, 1913

OF O. HENRY

Rolling Stones, by O. Henry. Illustrated with original photographs, drawings by the author, reproductions of letters, etc. [Doubleday, Page & Co.]

More interesting than the good stories in this book are the bad ones which it contains. These are some early things of his, and they are interesting because of the view they afford of O. Henry's background. When as a youth he went from North Carolina to Austin, Texas, he was already filled with literary ambitions. He speaks in letters to a friend of a play he has written. Here are poems, found in his handwriting, some humorous, some serious, a boy's experiments in rhyme and meter. Articles and stories flow from him in a gradually increasing stream. A comic newspaper occupies his energies for a while. One can see dimly through the thin fabric of this early work, the young man's reading. He hardly trusts himself to use the life about him for material—he parodies Anthony Hope and Gaboriau. This early work is indicative of a career, of some sort, as a writer.

Why didn't O. Henry ever tackle anything big? Perhaps the best answer is that he never got around to it. He suffered from the mediocrity of his fellow story-tellers, for he had to do ten men's work in order to satisfy the editors. He projected a book which was to be "nothing but the truth." He was going to take his hero "through all the main phases of life—wild adventure, city, society, something of the 'under world,' and among many characteristic planes of the phases . . . and have him tell the truth about everything." Yes, that might have been a big thing. But he did not get to finish even the letter in which he set the project forth. He speeded himself up to meet the obligations to his publishers. Always short stories, and more short stories. One letter to an editor is given:

> I owe Gilman Hall $175 (or mighty close to it) pussonally—so he tells me. I thought it was only about $30, but he has been keeping the account.
>
> He's just got to have it today. McClure's will pay me some money on the 15th of June, but I can't get it until then. I was expecting it before this—anyhow before Gilman left, but they stick to the letter.
>
> I wonder if you could give me a check for that much to pay him today. If you will I'll hold up my right hand—thus: that I'll have you a first-class story on your desk before the last of this week.
>
> I reckon I'm pretty well overdrawn, but I've sure got to see that Hall gets his before he leaves. I don't want anything for myself.
>
> Please, sir, let me know right away, by return boy if you'll do it.
>
> If you can't, I'll have to make a quick dash at the three-ball magazines; and I hate to tie up with them for a story.

It may be suspected that I am not an O. Henry enthusiast. But this does not mean that I am "superior" about O. Henry. It means merely that I have never predicted for him a glorious immortality of fame, nor called him "the American De Maupassant," nor subscribed for a collected edition of his works. Every copy, in fact, that I ever owned I gave away—but not before I had read it with unaffected enjoyment.

Two things, I suppose, may be said without contradiction about O. Henry. One is that he had no preoccupation with ideas. The other is that he had no preoccupation with style. The first of these I count a serious limitation. The second is a glorious virtue. The lack of "style" is what makes me read every O. Henry story I see. The lack of ideas is what keeps me from ever reading the same story twice.

Of course, in the patois of the writing trade, he had "ideas." He was full of them. He with his teeming brain was the despair of a hundred thousand laborious short-storyists with their scrapbooks and card-catalogues. He not merely used his eyes and his memory, he used his wit, and lo! there were stories where before there had been nothing. He knew that an "idea" was worth a dozen plots any day, and so he accomplished continually the miracle of making literary bricks without straw.

But he had no general ideas. He listened eagerly enough to the rough music of life, but he had no ear for its overtones—for the large abstractions of philosophy or politics or ethics. There is not to be discovered from the perusal of his stories any view of what love or friendship, or art or money, or success or failure, or birth or death mean. He has not reflected upon these things: he has only observed them, and arranged them in striking sequences. He has no theories of life to offer. And so it is that while one always reads these stories, one never remembers them. They offer nothing to that eager questioning which is the specific attribute and function of the human soul. The truth is that while they deal with human incident they do not deal with human life.

* * *

That is one reason why O. Henry never wrote a novel. For a novel inevitably presents a view of life. It is a revelation of its author's attitude toward the universe. It is a discussion of first and last things. It is a confession of faith—or of unfaith. But O. Henry had no confession to make. He had only tales to tell.

However, the profession of the teller of tales is an ancient and honorable one. If O. Henry was no philosopher, neither was that ingenious and beloved lady, Sheherezade [sic]. Suffice it that he had the mastery of his trade. He knew how to attract the idle attention, to hold it fast, and to let it go in time. He knew how to arouse curiosity, to engage sympathy, to amuse, divert and at last—with that unfailing trick of surprise which he kept for the last page—to shock. He was a real story teller.

And in his mastery of the craft of story-telling he was aided enormously by that virtue alluded to above: his indifference to style. Let me not be misunderstood. I use the word style deliberately in a bad sense. There is of course a sense in which style is one of the great things of literature, but that is when manner is identical with matter—when the style is the man. But style as an adornment has been the bane of American literature. Our writers have been hag-ridden by it. They have paid so much attention to their literary dress that they have turned themselves out in their books as dressmakers' dummies, wickerwork affairs covered with fine clothing of a distinctly antiquated pattern.

There was Hawthorne: a romantic soul, a kind of pale progenitor of Edgar Allan Poe, with a penchant for the supernatural. He was a talented writer, very well in his way; but the trouble is that we his naive fellow-countrymen regarded him too seriously. We mistook his fantastic concatenations of impossible events for novels. His romantic descriptions of the pangs of guilty conscience we mistook for psychological insight. Worst of all, we mistook his affected archaisms of rhetoric for the hall-mark of literature. God forgive us, we imitated him. We learned to say things in a gracefully unnatural way.

But we were rescued from that abomination of desolation, that gracefully unnatural way of saying things, by the practical necessities of politics. When it became necessary to convince people that you were right, and not merely to have them admire you, the orotund oratory of Webster gave way to the anxiously clear explanations of Lincoln. Lincoln never let eloquence interfere with argument. When he had stated his case in exact terms, he sometimes summed it up in poetic terms, as when he said: "A house divided against itself cannot stand." People ask why Lincoln never made another speech like that one at Gettysburg. The answer is that while the men were alive over whose graves he spoke those memorable sentences, they wanted to hear, and he wanted to tell them, something else: to wit, what should be done to save the new West from the grip of the economic feudalism of the South. He had to tell these farmers and storekeepers exactly what was his policy for the preservation of the Union.

Journalism followed suit, and newspapers became marked by a real desire to make clear what it was that had happened. The lights were turned up, and poetic obscurities fled away to the corners presided over by music and art critics, where they still remain. But elsewhere there was manifest an intention, at least, to be exact.

* * *

In this healthy atmosphere there grew up some of the best writers yet produced in America: Howells, Mark Twain, the brothers James, and Theodore Dreiser. It may seem that the case of Henry James in not one in point. But it is an admirable example of just this thing, the anxiety to say what one has to say, with a comparative indifference to grace. Henry James is not graceful. He is triumphantly exact. One may not be interested in the subject matter, but if one is, it is all there. Having a great deal to say about what his characters think and feel, he calmly sets it all down, regardless of everything, even at times of grammar. Hawthorne would not have known what to make of a page of Henry James. He would have said that it lacked "style." And so it does—in the Hawthornian sense. But it is—Henry James.

In the writings of William James, too, there is always perceptible a kind of dogged intention to say his say, not to be estopped from precision by anything. "And all that niceness would forbid, Superb, he smiled upon and did."

Of Theodore Dreiser, one may say much the same thing. Desiring to set forth a life which has for him and should have for us interest and significance, he goes about it "like a river-god building a wall at three francs a day," as Bernard Shaw said of Rodin. He puts it all down. There it is, honest, complete, exact. Mark Twain's province had different boundaries, but his methods of exploiting it were the same. He did not, by means of vaguely droll combinations of words, seek to make his readers credit him with a sense of humor. But there is a point of view from which anything, however familiar, or however sacred, may seem funny; and to this point he brought his readers, by the most careful manipulation of language. He left the acquisition of a "kommical style" to Artemus Ward. He never bothered about having a cap-and-bells literary manner; he was very gravely intent on bringing out the full humor of his subject.

* * *

O. Henry—whose writings William James said he "loved"—had something in common with all of these. He did not worry about his literary manners, but set about making his point in every story as best he could. He had one convention—the "surprise" ending. But he found a different sort of beginning for nearly every new story, a start that was calculated to prepare for this particular story and no other. Having started, he went along with his story, following its peculiar pattern. Whatever the notion upon which he built it, the whole story was built to bring out that notion. One finds him, in a letter included in this oddly assorted final volume, telling a friend, who had in his youth held up trains, how to make an article out of his experiences:

"Put in," writes O. Henry, "as much realism and as many facts as possible. Where you want to express an opinion or comment on the matter, do it as practically and plainly as you can. Give it life and the vitality of facts.

"Now, I will give you a sort of general synopsis of my idea—of course, everything is subject to your own revision and change. The article, we will say, is written by a typical train hoister—one without your education and powers of expression (bouquet), but intelligent enough to convey his ideas from his standpoint—not from John Wanamaker's. Yet, in order to please John, we will have to assume a virtue that we do not possess. Comment on the moral side of the proposition as little as possible. Do not claim that holding up trains is the only business a gentleman would engage in, and, on the contrary, do not depreciate a profession that is really only financiering with spurs on. Describe the facts and details—all that part of the

189

proceedings that the passenger sitting with his hands up in a Pullman looking into the end of a tunnel in the hands of one of the performers do not see. Here is a rough draft of my idea; Begin abruptly, without any philosophizing, with your idea of the best times, places and conditions for the hold-up—compare your opinions of this with those of others—mention some poorly conceived attempts and failures of others, giving your opinion why—as far as possible refer to actual occurrences, and incidents—describe the manner of a hold-up, how many men is best, where they are stationed, how do they generally go into it, nervous? or joking? or solemnly. . . ?''

* * *

This letter is sufficiently indicative of the bent of O. Henry's mind. He was the sort of writer who would not fail to make his point clear. If his writing is not of permanent interest to the public, it will not be because O. Henry ever lost sight of the thing he was at the moment trying to do. The only question—but never mind!

January 24, 1913

THE BOOK OF THE WEEK

Post-Impressionists

The Post-Impressionists, by C. Lewis Hind. (George H. Doran Company.)

At the performance of ''The Yellow Jacket'' the other night (as Mr. Hind would have said, had he seen that delightful play when he wrote this very personal and subjective book of criticism), I saw a Chinese ''property man.'' It was his duty to assist at the performance by arranging tables and chairs and attending to certain of the scenic effects—all of which he did with the utmost nonchalance in the midst of the action, his half-smoked cigarette depending meditatively from his lips as he worked. In the last act, when the hero whose fortunes I had been following with the deepest concern, was dying in a snowstorm, he placed a cushion under the head of the actor, spread a white sheet over him, and overturned in the most casual way, a tray

190

of white confetti on the recumbent form . . . I laughed with the rest of the audience, but for me the situation was far more emotionally affecting than it would have been in the laborious hands of Belasco. The illusion was too complete to be shattered even by the intrusion of the efficient property man with his cigarette. But he made me think of Matisse.

* * *

Mr. Hind, though an enthusiast, declines to commit himself as to the absolute artistic value of the work of Matisse. And very discreetly, one thinks, after seeing the examples of it in the International Exhibition of Modern Art. But he is keenly interested in the spirit of the painter—and anyone who has attended the exhibition will not be surprised at that. For Matisse is shocking, in the real meaning of the word.

We have the advantage, or disadvantage, of Mr. Hind, in having heard about the new art long enough to have become prejudiced for or against it before we see it. Mr. Hind visited the exhibit in London, he tells us, with a virgin mind. But we, after the exploitation of the "cubists" and "futurists" by the newspapers, are likely to be even a little disappointed if we go in search of sensation. There is a strong flavoring of experimental and questionable work in the international exhibition shown here, along with a great deal of what, if we know anything about art, we must recognize as indisputably good painting.

One goes to the Art Institute, with appetite whetted by the newspapers to sup full of horror. But if it were not for Matisse, one would have to go away hungry. To be sure, there is a roomful of cubist pictures, patient studies for the most part, in "planes of movement"—excellent illustrations for a PH.D thesis on the laws of vision, but, to one who has no head for mathematics, decidedly dull. There are Cezanne and Gauguin, looking like very respectable and interesting old masters. There is Van Gogh, youthful in spirit and full of splendid vitality, but never going far beyond his familiar bounds, and always justifying himself so completely in his achievement as to leave no matter for argument. There is "The Two Friends," by Alexandre Blanchet, as consciously reversionistic as a pre-Raphaelite picture, and yet as young as tomorrow morning in Montmartre: a composition illustrating with subtlety and reserve the post-impressionist tenets as to spirit and form and color, and yet capturing the imagination from the first glance and dominating it like a classic. Then there are the very earnest Americans, among them Glackens and Bellows are distinguished by apparently knowing why they are there. . . . But it is the wall filled with Matisses that gives one the prescribed "frisson."

But it is, as Mr. Hind indicates, an impatient mind, too; one not so much chafing at restraints as ignoring them; never stopping to secure the good will of the spectator by giving him anything he has already learned to like; a mind that goes straight to the point in every matter and flings over its left shoulder, as it were, paintings which settle to its own satisfaction this or that problem with a splendid ease and an outrageous simplicity.

And one sees their creator, nonchalant, preoccupied, careless—intruding into the midst of his effects his cold, harsh, almost cynical interest in experiment, indifferent as to whether he spoils them for you or not. He does not care whether you thrill or snigger, he will not waste a stroke to please you. In each picture is felt the presence of Matisse, already bored with this creation and thinking of something new. . . . And that is why, when I saw that Chinese property man in "The Yellow Jacket," I thought of Matisse. You take it or leave it, he says, walking indifferently between you and the picture, and puffing away at his speculative cigarette: but there it is!

* * *

Yes, there it is; but what is it? Mr. Hind does not undertake to tell us, and his example may be for the present, well emulated. One thing seems certain: that his treatment of the nude will for a generation hinder any general appreciation of his real artistic qualities. His nudes, we say, are so ugly! That is but an incident in his work; but to Americans, unacquainted with the more recent continental tendencies in the treatment of the nude, it bulks large. The preoccupation of painters for the last 2,000 years with the nude, and particularly with the female nude, means that they shared the general belief that it is beautiful. But it was inevitable that sooner or later there would be a revolt among artists against the idea. The revolt has come, and many artists are declaring that, while from the sentimental point of view a woman's body may be beautiful, from the artist's point of view, in point of form and color, it is less beautiful than trees or cattle! The reaction (predicted by Schopenhauer) came long before Matisse, and he has only carried it on with particular insistence—by exaggeration or caricature—as to its structural ineptitude. One might imagine that if he felt that way about woman he would stop painting her. But that is not the psychology of the artist. Any truth, even an ugliness, has a beauty for him, and so he exploits her mercilessly as a sprawling, deformed and etiolated mass, rejoicing brutally in her discords of form and color. He says these things more violently than anyone else has dared to say them, that is all. He is worlds away from the delicate sensuality of Bourguereau, the sentimental prurience of a thousand painters of Susannah at the Bath. He is cold, hard, restless—and as such repugnant to us. It is with relief that we turn from his horrific nudes to those of Gauguin, warm with the sympathy of their creator.

* * *

Should the repugnance toward one aspect of an artist's work check our admiration for his power? Perhaps it should not, but it does. At least with the ordinary spectator. But here is what Berenson, perhaps the greatest of art critics, thinks about Matisse. It is quoted by Mr. Hind from a letter published in the New York Nation:

"I have the conviction that Henri Matisse has, after twenty years of earnest searching, at last found the great high road traveled by all the best masters of the visual arts for the last sixty centuries at least. Indeed, he is singularly like them in every essential respect. He is a magnificent draughtsman and a great designer. Of his color, I do not venture to speak. Not that it displeases me—far from it. But I can better understand its failing to charm at first; for color is something we Europeans are still singularly uncertain of—we are easily frightened by the slightest divergence from the habitual."

"Death, I fancy," says Mr. Hind, more modestly, as becomes him, "will still find me trying to explain Matisse." But—to return a moment to the question of his nudes—it is certainly more interesting and more stimulating to look at Matisse's devastating mockeries of woman's body than to look at Marcel Duchamp's painful geometrical tribute to her ability to descend a staircase. The one is the product of a mind which works out its problems through the medium of art—the other the effort of a mind, incapable of enjoying the liberties of that art, to extend it in an impossible direction.

Monet painted haystacks as they were at one particular moment of the day. Van Gogh painted the hills at Arles as they were, are and shall be evermore. Duchamp paints a person as he is in seventeen successive seconds of time—surely the most violently trivial task which an artist could set himself. Besides, we have the moving pictures.

* * *

It is perhaps unfortunate for the spectator seriously interested in the new art that there are not a greater number of examples of the work being done quite soberly under the direct influence of that revolution in creative taste which has in its vanguard the extremities of Matisse. I should have like to have seen some of the work of Bror Nordfeldt, for instance, who is investing his talents of post-impressionism currently with an extraordinary judiciousness and success. But there is Auguste Chabaud, whose "Flock After the Rain" is one of the best things in the exhibition. Henri Manguin, an excellent example of conservative post impressionism; and Augustus John, who is forcing a distinct path of his own. If disregarding the more experimental examples of Matisse himself, one takes the other half together with the work of the great forerunners, Cezanne, Van Gogh and Gauguin and the magnificent painting of Blanchet's and adds the work of Chabaud, Manguin and Augustus John, one should be able to arrive at some conclusions concerning the significance of post-impressionism.

"I have wanted to make an impressionism," said Cezanne at the end of his career, "something solid and durable, like the art of the museums." To achieve some such end as this, to fulfill a need achingly felt more and more in the last ten years, one artist after another has struggled for the quality of permanence, with the method of the impressionists. Some with a new sense of form, some with a new sense of color, some with deliberate primitiveness. They have striven to use scientific knowledge hithertofore dedicated chiefly to a subtle, impermanent vision of the world, to turn this knowledge to a larger purpose. Impressionism was analytic. Post-impressionism is synthetic. That much at least, even in face of this bewildering variety of new schools, can be stated.

* * *

Mr. Hind tries to define the spirit of this movement in these words: "Expression, not beauty, is the aim of art. Beauty occurs. Expression happens, must happen. Art is not beauty. It is expression; it is always decorative and emotional. There is as much intellect as emotion in the Parthenon and the Sistine Vault. Art is more than the emotional utterance of life. It is expression of personality in all its littleness, in all it immensity. A man who expresses himself sincerely, can extract beauty from anything. There is a beauty of experience lurking within all ugliness. For ugliness does not really exist. We see what we bring. He who expresses his emotion rhythmically, decoratively, seeking the inner meaning of things, is an artist. He who represents the mere externals is illustrator."

One reason for the extraordinary stimulus which such painting has upon an open mind is the implication which one cannot but follow from painting into the other arts. Arnold Bennett expressed this sense of disturbance when he wrote: "I have permitted myself to suspect that supposing some writer were to come along and do in words what these men have done in paint, I might conceivably be disgusted with nearly the whole of modern fiction, and I might have to begin again. . . . This awkward experience will in all probability not happen to me, but it might happen to a writer younger than me."

* * *

But enough of didacticism. I search through Mr. Hind's volume for some frivolous remarks with which to conclude my review. Not finding any, I am compelled to make them up myself, apropos of some of the painters in the international exhibition.

Picasso—The stormy petrel, but the weather man says "continued bright and fair."

Marcel Duchamp—A geometrician strayed from the schoolroom.

Odilon Redon—A Blake whose mysticism is annoying rather than profound; a quaint and charming anthologist.

Henri Matisse—If at first glance you think you like him, you are mistaken; if at first glance you think you don't like him, think again.

Francis Picabia—The seismograph record of an earthquake which has not yet been located.

William Lembruck—A pedantic cribber from the primitives.

Amadeo de Sousa Cardoza—No skeletons in his closet.

Constantine Brancusi—Villanelles in stone.

Andre Derain—An artist among cubists.

Maurice Denis—Should have illustrated "Recondite."

Charles Conder—A delicate decadent; a superficial Watteau; the antithesis of modernity.

Andre Dunoyer de Segonzac—The greatest living cattle painter.

George Roualt—Forget him if you can; his ancestry is Hogarth and Goya; on the literary side, Tourneur and Baudelaire.

Felix Vallotton—Should be triumpantly acquitted of having attempted anything new.

Eugene Zak—Hurry up and decide which!

The Americans (or most of them:) Que diable font-ils dans cette galere?

March 28, 1913

THE SOUL OF SHAKESPEARE

The Women of Shakespeare, by Frank Harris. (Mitchell Kennerley.)

It is true that Mr. Harris is the best Shakespearean critic we have, and the best, for that matter, since Morgann, whose essay on Falstaff is just beginning, after a hundred years or so, to be appreciated. Mr. Harris is—it would be stupid to deny it—a man of critical genius. But he is not necessarily on that account right. One reads the present volume with a clearer sense of his violent and beautiful wrongness—a clearer sense than "The Man Shakespeare," dazzling us with its illuminating flashes, permitted. It is not exactly ungrateful for us to disbelieve all of Mr. Harris' main contentions: for we concede to him at once that the "professors"—against whom he has so odd and unnecessary a grudge—are much more wrong than he. At all events, Mr. Harris got his information about Shakespeare out of Shakespeare's own writings, not out of the imaginings of a dull and provincial mind.

Nevertheless, Mr. Harris is wrong. And in regard to one point, the most unimaginative of the professors could set him right. It will be remembered that in "The Man Shakespeare," besides showing us (a wonderful piece of criticism it was, too) how Shakespeare had revealed his own character again and again, in Hamlet, in Othello, in Antonio, in Macbeth—this latter being not at all the bloody villain which bad actors make him but a gentle soul, rightly despised by his sterner spouse!—besides this he revealed to us the love story of Shakespeare, as indicated in the Sonnets. Well, this has been done often enough before; and it really makes no difference whether Mary Fitton was the Dark Lady or not. The point is that Mr. Harris shows us the Dark Lady all through Shakespeare's plays. It is to this part of his task that he returns in "The Women of Shakespeare," though, indeed, he had been almost too thorough to be convincing in the previous volume. A case as well proved as this begins to look like the Baconian heresy. It is here that we part company with Mr. Harris, thanking him and assuring him that he is the best of companions, though a trifle ill-tempered at times.

* * *

And here it is that we perceive a fundamental mistake in Mr. Harris' criticism. His elevation of the Dark Lady to the position she occupies in this volume, as the original of every effective female character in the whole of Shakespeare's work—this is achieved only by misreading the importance of her position in the Sonnets. One would think the Sonnets were mainly concerned with her. But the plain, pedantic fact is that she is involved in only the last twenty-six of the 152 sonnets. It is a fact, moreover, that the most poetically distinguished and interesting sonnets are to be found in the other group. For reasons which are at the base sentimental and not critical, Mr. Harris has deprecated the earlier sonnets and exalted the latter. He has found it necessary to say that Shakespeare was a snob, addressing adulatory verses to a young nobleman in the hope of patronage, and meaning none of the extravagant things he said. All of which is ridiculous, quite as ridiculous as anything the professors have ever done. It is true that in this sonnet sequence we feel that we are close to the heart of Shakespeare; but that heart is not snobbishness, nor yet the rather commonplace infatuation he displays for the Dark Lady. It happens to be something much more dignified than either.

To preface these remarks upon a mooted subject, it must be said that the form in which these revelations appears is significant. The sonnet-sequence, as the Elizabethans found it in Italy, was a form devoted to the expression of a philosophy, not in purely abstract terms, but rather in vivid, concrete instances. This is but a crude way of saying that Dante and Petrarch were not trying to tell a story in their sonnets; they were trying to express an attitude toward the world. Nor was Shakespeare trying to tell a story in his sonnets; he could tell a story, when he chose, magnificently, as in his two great narrative poems. No, Shakespeare, like Petrarch and Dante, was trying to express a philosophy of life.

* * *

Not that he was doing anything so absurd as trying to state a new philisophic [sic] theory in verse. He was but seeking, as every writer must seek, to express that feeling about life which life itself has impressed upon his heart. Such feelings are not impressed upon the heart save through the medium of definite personal experiences. Nor are they expressed in verse save through the medium of definite personal experience—true or false in detail, true or false to fact, but essentially true.

There may never have been any Dark Lady; or there may have been a dozen. It is, on the whole, probable that a good many sheer facts are preserved in the amber of the verse, however. And it seems quite certain that there was one definite young man about whom all of Shakespeare's feeling about youth and beauty, and age and death, crystallized with some emotional violence.

What was Shakespeare's philosophy? Bernard Shaw says he had none. That only means, of course, that Shaw does not like Shakespeare's philosophy. Nevertheless, Shaw is a good critic, and his analysis of Shakespeare's philosophy is accurate enough. The vanity of life, the certainty of death, the ultimate futility—all this is not robust enough for G.B.S. But it is what Shakespeare thought about life. "Out, out, brief candle!" Not very encouraging! No heroics about the importance of every life in the vast cosmic scheme of which we are part. . . . No wonder Shaw doesn't like it! I don't like it either; I worship in the same church as Shaw. But Shakespeare, not having the advantage of the broad view of things which reconciles Shaw and myself to the universe, was a pessimist. He thought it was a sad thing to grow old and lose one's curves and complexion and teeth and hair, and the absolute tragedy to die.

The best things in all his work, the most deeply felt things, are expressive of this attitude. His most sincere utterances about life were of this cast. It was to him a tale told by an idiot, full of sound and fury, signifying nothing. . . .

It was inevitable that such a man should make of youth the symbol of all that was fleetingly and poignantly beautiful—in his verse as in his life. That the youth was a young man in Shakespeare's sonnets was an accident of time and place. For Omar there sufficed the casual cypress-slender minister of wine, the girl for whom every hyacinth the garden wears is a memorial of her once-living loveliness. In the Elizabethan period the fashion was masculine friendships, together with a frankness which we should now deem unmanly, in the expression of the emotions of friendship. In these sonnets there is apparent a very passion of affection; but more apparent still, and more nobly expressed, is the poet's deep feeling about life and death.

*　*　*

To him the boy is not merely his beloved friend, he is the symbol of all that passes from loveliness to decay. He has seen the whole world go along that tragic path, and he knows that this youth, too, must tread it to the end. Images of decay haunt and torment his mind. He celebrates the beauty that exists, and his chant of praise turns into a cry of pain at the sick thought of what must be. He turns every way to avoid the thought and seeks for some escape that will permit him peace. He thinks of two things—two answers to the terrible riddle of mortality. They are "breed" and poesy—the begetting of another form into which this loveliness may steal as it ebbs away from his decaying self; and the preservation of it in immortal verse. These two things antiphonally ring through the sonnet sequence, the answer of Shakespeare to the perpetual threat of death which hangs over the blossoming world.

Mark the first sonnet—the first line:

From fairest creatures we desire increase
That thereby beauty's rose might never die.

This is not the snobbish tribute of an aspiring literary man to a wealthy young patron; nor is it the speech of personal passion: it is the utterance of a high philosophic idea—the cry of a spirit sick with the thought of mortality.

It is only a man desperately in love with the idea of youth, hopelessly revolting against the thought of age, who could plead in sonnets of such singular force and loveliness that a youth should marry: it is the idea behind the sonnets which informs them with beauty and vigor.

> When forty winters shall besiege thy brow,
> And dig deep trenches in thy beauty's field . . .

Morbid, if you like; it was written by one who had never heard of the city Beautiful, but was in love with loveliness.

> Thou art the mother's glass, and she in thee
> Calls back the lovely April of her prime.

That is the way of escape, the way to defeat the coarse plans of Time, to cheat the envious dust.

> Then let not winter's ragged hand deface
> In thee thy summer, ere thou be distilled:
> Make sweet some vial; treasure thou some place
> With beauty's treasure . . .

We cannot mistake what he has to say when he says it so clearly, summing up in the splendid twelfth sonnet his indictment against the universe. Everything speaks to him of decay and death. The clock that strikes the hours tells him of the dying of brave day; the violet past prime, curls silvered o'er with white; lofty trees barren of leaves, and summer's green horne on the bier with white and bristly beard.

> Then of thy beauty do I question make
> That thou among the wastes of time must go . . .

And nothing can make defense against Time's scythe save only "breed, to brave him when he takes thee hence."

But no, there is another way; this youth shall live twice, if he beget a child: "in it, and in my rhyme." A new hope, this, and a braver one:

> But thy eternal summer shall not fade
> Nor lose possession of that fair thou owest;
> Nor shall Death brag thou wanderest in his shade,
> When in eternal lines to time thou growest.

Henceforth the old note is sounded, I believe, no more. It is the new cry—"Not marble nor the gilded monuments Of princes shall outlive this powerful rhyme." What though everything that grows holds in perfection but a little moment; let Time do whate'er it please to the wide world and all its fading sweets—

199

.... Despite thy wrong My love shall in
my verse ever live young.

From this point also the verse, being charged with the preservation of this lovely youth forever, grows more personal; and there is a touch of humor and of malice in the recording of the fact that the youth, being addressed in such terms, likes it very well and, like any pretty girl with a poet for a lover, demands more praise of the same sort. Here it is that the poet's personal feelings become the most definitely implicated in the verse. He deserts his philosophical vantage ground, returning to it only for a few noble utterances, and devotes himself to a minute, almost photographic, picture of the fluctuating moods of love. These sonnets are the precursors of the modern psychological novel of D'Annunzio and Strindberg. With an astonishing frankness they tell all the humiliations, the abasements, the suspicions, the angers, the recantations which are, after all, inevitably a part of any passionate relation, whether it be friendship or love. But now and again he remembers his original intention, even though it be only to doubt his power, and his speech grows grave and extraordinarily sweet:

Since brass, nor stone, nor earth, nor boundless sea,
But sad mortality o'ersways their power,
How with this rage shall beauty hold a plea,
Whose action is no stronger than a flower?
O, how shall summer's honey-breath hold out
Against the wrackful siege of battering days,
When rocks impregnable are not so stout,
Nor gates of steel so strong but Time decays?
O fearful meditation! where, alack,
Shall Time's best jewel from Time's chest lie hid?
Or what strong hand can hold his swift foot back?
Or who his spoil of beauty can forbid?
O, none, unless this miracle have might,
That in black ink my love may still shine bright.

It is this idea which binds the whole sequence together: the last sonnet, like the first, strikes that solemn note of warning and of fear. Despite the unparalleled wealth of psychological detail concerning the poet as friend and lover, and the poet, standing more sheerly forth as man—despite all this the poem finds its real significance when read in the light of this idea. Another sequence (and a sadly inferior one) begins where this leaves off. Of that I say nothing save that it shows how dull Shakespeare could be in dealing with a trite theme—the falsity of woman: and how unilluminating. But this sequence stands by itself, an artistic whole, dominated and swayed by a single thought: the sick thought of decay and death.

In the face of this universal doom the poet does not feel like being rhetorical; he does not say sententiously that the flower's life suffices the flower and that it has all been worth while, but he snatches the fading loveliness of the world and sets it forever in his verse. He celebrates us who are about to die. It is a song that turns to a cry, a cry that turns to a song—the joy and pain of a soul that tastes in the April breezes the subtle poison of mortality.

April 18, 1913

THE BOOK OF THE WEEK

THE CASE OF MR. HOWELLS.

New Leaf Mills: A Chronicle, by W. D. Howells. (Harper & Brothers.)

The interest which one has in this new novel by Mr. Howells is not so much in the book itself as in the questions it brings up concerning its author. "New Leaf Mills" is the story of an idealist and his wife who attempt to establish, in the America of the '50s, a communistic kingdom of God on earth. The book is taken up with a rather minute record of the activities of daily life. There is a certain charm in this detail, but there are no general outlines of sufficient interest to make it easy to talk about the book. However, it is not the book but the author about which, in this instance, one desires to talk!

For it has become the fashion to dispraise Mr. Howells. Not that it is any new thing to renounce the Dean of American Letters and all his works. But it used to be done only in private conversation: or if in print, then strictly by implication. So much respect was due our greatest living author.

But now it is different. In a book on "The Spirit of American Literature" an ex-English instructor in Harvard, and an ex-editor to boot, John Albert Macy, utters all the things that have been proscribed in print.

Charged With Obstructing Traffic.

He was in the first place, says Mr. Macy, a victim of the "Dead Hand in Literature." To explain: "There was in his vicinity no live literature to sustain him, to keep him in a state of courageous contemporaneity with the world about him. He fell back on the past: and even the seven or eight

201

modern European literatures with which he is familiar are, as he speaks of them, remote, romantic, misty. He writes of Tolstoy as he writes of Jane Austen or Dante.''

Thus it was, according to his critic, that he, like Henry James, mistook the nature of the method which he formally adopted, the method of Realism. ''The realistic novel,'' says Mr. Macy, ''grew up naturally from historic roots in France and Russia. It was nurtured by a veracity of mind and a social freedom utterly alien to the hypocrisy and the superficial optimism of America. Mr. Howells and Mr. James, alert to fine achievement, admired this great Slavic and Gallic performance, and they seem to have said: 'Go to! realism is the real right thing: we will be realists.' They thus accepted the self-imposed limitations of realism, but they could not accept its profound privilege of telling the truth. America would not perhaps have tarred and feathered a man honest and intrepid enough to write as Balzac, Flaubert, Tolstoy, Dostoievski wrote, but it would not have permitted him to be Dean. Mr. Howells' realism is like a French play adapted for our stage, the point of the original is missed, and we wonder, as we watch the Frohmanized translation, how Frenchmen can be so dull. To take the method of realism without its substance, without its integrity to the bolder passions, results in a work precise in form and excellently finished, but narrow in outlook and shallow.''

Enough! The intent of the charges is sufficiently clear. Mr. Howells is accused of fencing off the turbulent highway of realism, sodding it down and turning it into a suburban park.

Establishing an Alibi.

We are past the day when a writer could be held responsible for the tendencies of a period. We cannot blame Mr. Howells for the tameness of American literature. If American literature is ''precise in form and excellently finished, but narrow in outlook and shallow'' (as indeed much of it is), not one writer, not one school, not one literary center, but the whole of American life must be held to blame.

Boston and Mr. Howells have been made the scapegoats for the sins of American literature long enough. It is well enough to realize what Boston is: the chief city of a desperately commercial region—the region which created and still strives to retain the protective tariff—the region where one of the most terrible of ''famine strikes'' was only the other day fought out to a bitter finish: a region, withal, of the sincerest and most genuine aspirations toward the perfection of the soul. Ad astra plus laisser faire!

This, you say, might be Moscow. Yes. But add one thing more—Puritanism, that spiritual myopia which prevents a frank recognition and confession of the situation, and you have Boston; you have New England; you have America.

For Boston is but the type city of that American culture which has

202

created the American literature of the past. We in America have genuinely aspired to the stars. And we have indubitably groveled in commercialism. And we have, above all, lacked the saving grace of sincerity. So it is not Boston that is to blame, it is not Mr. Howells, it is the American spirit.

Nevertheless, we are learning to be candid, to confess our sins. And Boston, as the type city of our American culture, has furnished us some of our ablest teachers. If the satire of Dr. Holmes seems dull to us now, that does not signify that the last generation was not touched to the quick by it. And if the novels of W. D. Howells seem too suave and gentle in their renderings of this life of ours, it does not mean that this writer has not greatly helped us to see ourselves.

As Mild a Man as Ever Jabbed a Lie!

He has helped us. He has done for us what no other writer could have done. We listened to Mr. Howells when we would have shut our ears to a harsher voice. So pleasantly has Mr. Howells made game of us that we have paid attention. We have been a little checked in our boisterous self-complacency. We have learned to laugh at ourselves a little. Now perhaps the time has come to draw more bold and mordant pictures of life. We have Theodore Dreiser; we have Albert Edwards. There was a time when it would have been a tactical error to express gratitude for a writer like Mr. Howells, lest thereby one should seem to disparage cruder, truer, more courageous and more vital work, such as "Sister Carrie" and "A Man's World." But now that Mr. Howells has ceased to be an influence and has become a tradition, now that he is being taught in the public schools, one need not scruple to do him justice.

And justice to Mr. Howells compels one to the admission that he is not merely a technical artist of great skill, but a philosopher. He has what is essential to every real writer, a distinct attitude toward life. And he is able to express it through the medium of incident, never being forced—as the best writers are sometimes forced—into downright preaching.

The Creed of Quiet Disillusion.

In a memorable passage in one of his books—I forget which—there is a chapter dealing with the visit of a friend to the home of Bartley Hubbard (if that was his name!). Bartley and his wife have gone through the astringent comedy (quietly enjoyed by Mr. Howells) of newly married life—the rapture, the looking forward, the overweening confidence, and then the inevitable friction and the gradual estrangement hastened in this case by Bartley's drunkenness: all these have been set forth. Bartley and the girl put on their company manners for the guest's sake, and bring out the baby to be praised. The house is neat, the dinner table is bright and cheerful—but underneath all one sees the seething misery of wife and husband. The final touch is given by the comment of the guest, a romantic bachelor. "By Jove," he says to

Bartley, "you know all this makes me want to get married myself."

Or the last chapter of "April Hopes": a young man and young woman of utterly alien and irreconcilable temperaments have successively disliked each other, fallen in love, become engaged, quarreled, made up, and quarreled again; everybody knows they simply cannot get along; yet in a vein of gay mockery Mr. Howells chronicles their final reconciliation, which is to lead immediately to marriage.

A real realist, a writer of profundity as well as charm, a truth-seeker, and an artist—such must be our verdict upon Mr. Howells.

The life that he satirized, and the life that made him what he was, is passing. New writers are here to interpret for us the new life; others are coming. We shall not be so stupid as to demand from them the peculiar excellence of Mr. Howells. Nor shall we be so absurd as to ask of him that he take the measure of the new time. The exponent of a vanishing epoch, we make him his own monument, setting him carefully on a pedestal, out of the way of traffic; we make him president of the American Academy of Arts and Letters—a gentle irony that he should be the first to appreciate.

May 9, 1913

THE BOOK OF THE WEEK

GLORIA MUNDI

The Gods Are Athirst, by Anatole France. Authorized translation. (John Lane Company.)

In some French illustrated paper there appeared last year a characteristic photograph of Anatole France: somewhere in an African desert, with Bedouins in the background, himself sitting at the feet of that "tres jolie" American woman aviator who was afterward killed, the first of her sex, while attempting some daring feat of aeronautics. Anatole France, a worshiper still, at almost 70 years, of beauty and of daring.

It is this quality which transpires from every page of this his latest novel. Anatole France is in love with life. He has not, like Tolstoy, turned Puritan and moralist in his latter years. He has become, it seems, more warmly human; his cynicism is gentler, his irony more suave. He does not hesitate to confess his enthusiasms.

And so he gives us an old man's vision of life, in a book full of wisdom and of humor, lighted by a benevolent skepticism and a benign mockery; a little terrible in its clarity and its candor, but calm and sweet and unfailingly just. Such a book makes us fall in love with old age. One would willingly grow old, if one might grow old in the manner of Anatole France.

"The Gods Are Athirst" is a story of the last terrible days of the French Revolution, of the days when Paris, or a few of its heroic and merciless souls, saved the Revolution by the Terror, sending to the guillotine the inefficient generals, the royalist conspirators, the reactionaries, the malcontents—purging the nation of patriotic ardor which has made them ever since execrated by their beneficiaries. This Terror, necessary, successful and horrible, is the background of the story. One of the jurors of the revolutionary tribunal which sent the enemies of the Republic by the thousands to the guillotine, and some of these more-or-less enemies of the Republic, are the characters. It is the distinction of Anatole France that he should have found in this theme the materials for—not by any means a tale of horror—but for an ironic idyl, full of beauty and pathos and quiet charm.

For Anatole France is not to be taken in by even the greatest historical event of modern times. He can see through even the French Revolution. He knows of what revolutions are made. And he reduces this one to simple elements of spiritual and physical passion, the proper materials for the story-teller and the artist. In the cold patriotism and the hot love of Evariste Gamelin, revolutionary juror, you have the whole revolution.

It is not that Anatole France does not believe in the French Revolution. Not to believe in it, not to be thankful for it, is a thing impossible to an intelligent man today. And if one hopes for another revolution as vast, one is left with one's faith intact—only one prays to die on the first barricade lest, sick to loathing with its terrible success, one blaspheme against it and perish rather than see it go on.

The bloody-minded Gamelin is the servant of a righteous cause: and he is disgusting. Brotteaux, the ex-farmer of taxes; Pere Longuemare, the Barnabite monk; Athenais, the bedraggled little courtesan—these are useless persons all, having no right to stand in the way of the Revolution, deserving death at its hands for even seeming or threatening to impede it for a moment: yet when these three, proscribed and in danger of their lives, are gathered together for a night under the same roof, one comes to love them—and something more. That something is the secret of the power of Anatole France.

For Brotteaux, the former aristocrat, now reduced to a maker of marionettes, carrying about with him a worn copy of Lucretius; he and the devout and gentle Barnabite monk represent, after all, a rich achievement of the human race, an achievement which we are not willing to sacrifice to any cause, howsoever just. We know with Anatole France that a revolution which succeeds by destroying these is, for all its rightness, wrong. We realize that humanity is greater than revolutions. And we share the feelings of the little kind-hearted, foul-mouthed Athenais when, finding her friends and protectors arrested, she cried out "Vive le roi!" so that she might die with them. For they, and she, too, in that moment are the human race in flower; and the Revolution is only—a revolution.

Athenais, slightly sketched as she is by the author, is one of the most charming figures to be met with in a lifetime of reading. And, indeed, the book offers a very garland of delightful women. There is Gamelin's sister, Julie, whose lover the bloody patriot inexorably sentences to death; vivacious, light-hearted even in her fears, she adventures in boy's clothing, knows how to starve or to fling money away, and enjoys life with a healthy appetite.

Then there is Rose Thevenin, the actress: pale and voluptuous, faded and pretty, tired and indefatigable, "she filled the earth with movement, color and harmony": she was "a woman of ever-varying moods, but always gay, sensitive, quick-tempered and yet easy-going and accommodating, a sharp tongue with the most polished utterance, vain, modest, true, false, delightful." After the Revolution was over Rose Thevenin remarked of the marionette-maker Brotteaux, "I was not indifferent to him." She had in mind, perhaps, that day in prison, when she had said the same words to this man on the edge of death and all too willing to be done with life: "I have only seen you once, for a day, and yet you are not indifferent to me. And if what I am going to tell you can renew your attachment to life, oh! believe my promise—I will be for you . . . whatever you shall wish me to be"—and they exchanged a kiss on the mouth through the bars.

*　*　*

And Elodie, the patriot's sweetheart, who unwittingly provides him a human motive for his bloody reprisals against the aristocracy; she is almost a perfect picture of what has been called the "typical" woman. Her practicality, her devotion, her unscrupulousness, her intense femininity, all the things that evoke the heavy satire of less sophisticated writers, are indicated here with a light, sure, just touch. One smiles at her, and continues to love her, as in real life. For is she not woman?

It is Elodie to whom Anatole France most devotes himself, using her as the figure by which to tell us most directly, though still in symbols, what he thinks of life. He illustrates well the words of John Galsworthy, which we pause to quote: "Nothing," he says, "is more dubious than the way in which the two words 'pessimist' and 'optimist' are used: for the optimist is he who cannot bear the world as it is, and is forced by his nature to picture it as it ought to be, and the pessimist one who can not only bear the world as it is but loves it well enough to draw it faithfully." In such wise does Anatole France love the world, and that love he expresses, not obscurely, in the figure of Elodie.

*　*　*

When she sent Gamelin forth from her house one night at the very beginning of their love, she whispered to him in the darkness: "Good-by, sweetheart! . . . To have the street door opened, give three raps on the concierge's window. Good-by, my life, good-by, my soul!" And when he found himself in the street, "he saw the window of Elodie's chamber half unclose, and a little hand pluck a red carnation, which fell at his feet like a drop of blood."

When Robespierre fell, and Gamelin was being taken to the guillotine to which he had sent so many others, he passed the house of Elodie:

> As the cart passed in front of the window of the blue chamber, a woman's hand, wearing a silver ring on the ring-finger, pushed aside the edge of the blind and threw toward Gamelin a red carnation, which his bound hands prevented him from catching, but which he adored as the token and likeness of those red and fragrant lips that had refreshed his mouth. His eyes filled with bursting tears, and his whole being was still entranced with the glamour of this farewell when he saw the blood-stained knife rise into view in the Place de la Revolution.

And only a few months later, when the Revolution is ended, Elodie sent another forth from her house into the night, saying: "Good-by, sweetheart! . . . To have the street door opened, give three raps on the concierge's window. Good-by, my life, good-by, my soul!"

She is a symbol of the life that flows on, past all the revolutions, forgetfully, from joy to joy.

May 23, 1913

NEGLECTED MASTERPIECES

"ROUGE ET NOIR"

To say that "Rouge et Noir" is neglected is not in this case to plead for it. "Rouge et Noir" can afford to be neglected for a long time to come. Written early in the nineteenth century, and left alone until nearly the end of that century, it is finding its proper readers; and it will be another century before it comes to the fate which sooner or later overtakes all great works, the fate of being popular.

Popularity and Stendhal are incompatible. One does not desire it for him. One regrets that it must come about. . . . When I reflect that this little ebullition of gratitude is a part of that gradual process which is to bring "Rouge et Noir" to annotated editions of use in the schools, and prefaces by the Hamilton Wright Mabies of the future, I almost desist. But it is inevitable. First the keen and critical appreciation that is accorded to Turgeniev; then the gross approval that is lavished upon Balzac; by such degrees will "Rouge et Noir" descend until it is revered by the mandarins and hated and despised by every man of independent mind.

But that will not be for a long, long time. We have a hundred years or so to read and praise Stendhal and to say among ourselves (when there are no stupid and disputatious persons present, for there is no use arguing about the thing: you either see it or you don't!) that "Rouge et Noir" is the greatest novel ever written.

* * *

"Rouge et Noir" is a book with only one fault: it comes to an end. Bitterly one regrets this fact even in the midst of one's pleasure. After a mere 200,000 words or so it is finished, and there is no more of the greatest novel ever written. . . . One sips it in slow, delicious mouthfuls, as one might, in some sad, Shavian, teaified Utopia of the future, the last wine in the world.

I suppose, after these remarks, that I really ought to go on and tell the story of "Rouge et Noir." Perhaps, before I get thru, I shall. But I do not promise. In the first place, as will already have been perceived, this is not a review: it is a serenade. And, in the second place, it does not matter what "Rouge et Noir" is about. Not in the least.

It is the way he does it. Stendhal writes like the Mississippi River—broad, calm, powerful, unending.

Broad: for his book carries with it a sense of the whole of human life. His characters are extraordinarily few, his canvas never overcrowded, and he seems always intent on the matter in hand, without reference to any of the other affairs of the universe. But, life-size tho these figures are, and minutely as their thoughts and actions are considered, they are all seen down a long perspective—thru the pillared corridors of a noble mind.

* * *

Calm: for Stendhal never grows excited, never tries to induce excitement in his reader. This doesn't mean that the reader never gets excited; he does. But Stendhal disdains the use of any tricks of style, even the most legitimate, to work his reader up to a proper appreciation of what is about to happen. His is a plain, pedestrian method, without ornament, without a trace of poetry. Instead of describing the landscape, he is likely to tell you what the principal crops of the region are. He does not talk about his characters, he tells about them, stopping to explain every time an explanation is needed, putting you in possession of all the facts (carefully selected facts, but plain and straightwardly presented); he never tries to make words do more than they will, neither asking them to carry the reader into the clouds nor to burrow into the secret depths of the earth. He deploys his sentences in open order, never hurling them sensationally against embattled heights, but sweeps the plain in a succession of easy skirmishes. It may not be magnificent, but it is writing!

Powerful: what is it that gives his work such an air of magnitude, so that one trusts oneself to his pages as to the pages of the book of life itself? It is perhaps that in the presence of a mind so keen one is impressed as by sheer physical strength. The phrases that move lazily yet swiftly across the page are like the ripple of great muscles under a velvet skin; to read a chapter is like being picked up between the thumb and forefinger of a friendly giant. It is an intellectual greatness which looms and lowers like the landscapes of Jotunheim.

* * *

Unending: for in order to bring his book to a close Stendhal had to kill his hero. He killed him well, none has done it better. But it should have been hereafter; there would have been a time for such a word, when the boy had reached 40 years of age: but to kill him in his twenties, when life was still interesting—that was a piece of cruelty! The book is not built to such an ending; it is built to go on and on, in twenty or thirty volumes, and never to be finished at all. These first two volumes were well devoted to the young man's love affairs; the next should have told of his career in diplomatic intrigue.

Such a continuation would have displayed more effectively the theme suggested in the title. . . . By the bye, when H. G. Wells wrote in "The

New Machiavelli'' of the struggle between ''the white passion and the red,'' between the white passion of statecraft and the red passion of love, did he think of ''Rouge et Noir''? Did he deliberately turn the black passion of political intrigue which festers in the heart of Stendhal's hero into the white passion of utopian scheming which ennobles Remington's? It is not very likely. Yet the likeness in theme and the contrast in treatment are sufficiently striking as one thinks of the one and of the other. Politics has changed since Stendhal's day—perhaps. It has changed enough to be ranked so high by Wells that when his hero has eloped with Isabel he still wonders whether he ought not to have stayed in parliament: Stendhal's view is different. Like Wells, he presents the story of a man who desires power and whose career is wrecked by love. Nowhere in his story does he express any view of the merits of the two passions, but he sets above it the title: ''Rouge et Noir.''

* * *

All the first part of Stendhal's novel is the prelude to something which he never wrote. The young peasant's tormenting ambition, his hypocrisies, his first steps in those devious paths that led thru the priesthood into politics—the only way possible to an ambitious young man since the downfall of Napoleon—all these seem to announce a motif to be worked out fully later. It is inconceivable that Stendhal should have told us so much about his hero's ambition, if it were not to show this ambition operating in fields of action greater than any the boy had reached by the end of the book as it stands. A second part is demanded by the first.

Stendhal's other novel, ''The Chartreuse of Parma,'' with its picture of the life at an Italian court, gives us an indication of what this second part would have been like. What a wonderful book it would have been, this ''New Machiavelli'' which Stendhal did not write! As for the succeeding volumes, I know what they would have been about, too; but I have perhaps called up enough imaginary masterpieces from the vasty deep. . . .

No, I shall not tell the story of ''Rouge et Noir.'' It is enough to say that if Stendhal did not write the book about politics he did write the one about love, and this is it; and it contains two of the most interesting—no, let us tell the truth—THE two most interesting women in fiction. One is Mme. de Renal, with a love too high for pride and too deep for shame; and the other is Mathilde de la Mole, a young girl with a heart like an eagle's. Nobody has ever written about women as Stendhal has about these. . . . Nevertheless, I wish he had gone on to write that book about his hero in politics. For it is only when we have seen the black passions at work that we know the truth about the red.

July 5, 1913

210

NEGLECTED MASTERPIECES

"BLIX"

When anyone selects one of Frank Norris' books to be enthusiastic about, it is usually "McTeague." For it is generally agreed that "The Octopus," that huge chaotic mass of eloquence, realism, mysticism and adventure, does not bear very well the test of re-reading: as for "The Pit," his friends never mention it; "A Man's Woman" and "Moran of the Lady Letty" are melodrama; and "Blix"—in the current view—is merely a pretty story. It is always "McTeague" that is selected for the honors. So if I elect to praise "Blix" as a masterpiece, I shall have to explain.

In the first place, then, "Blix" is not a masterpiece: not really. But it is one of the most American books ever written, a delightful idyl of love-out-of-doors, and the most genuine piece of work that Norris ever did.

* * *

Frank Norris was the most promising, the most brilliant of all our heritors of unfulfilled renown: and "McTeague" is one of the most astonishing of his performances. It sums up the naturalistic tendencies of a whole literary period, the period of Zola: it is a firework that explodes in flashes of superb brutality. Do you remember the ends of Trina's fingers? Do you remember the cat that stands with tail nervously flicking to and fro outside the fatal door? Do you remember that silent struggle in the desert of two men handcuffed wrist to wrist? Delightful horrors, for those who care to sup on them. But that is all they are.

It is not as tho Frank Norris really believed that life was like that. If these things had represented the vision he had of life, they would have by some subtle access of power which can come only from sincerity been turned into literature. But as it is they are only the splendid "stunts" of a young man bent on showing that he could go Zola one better.

* * *

Frank Norris did not think that life was like that. His view of life was that it was a scene of tumultuous and vivid activities which could be observed with endless pleasure. His world was one in which there was satisfaction for the adventurous spirit: hardships to be endured heroically, difficulties to be overcome. It was a place, too, where one laughed at one's fellows while loving them—at their habits, their manners, their speech, their ideas. In short, it was a place where a decent young fellow of ability, ambition and good intentions could have a very good time. He would have

211

his work and his play. And likely enough he would meet some nice girl, with a mind of her own—one who was going off to study to be a doctor or nurse, and who didn't care about "dolling up" and going to tea parties, but who liked to tramp around in old clothes with a man, and all that sort of thing. And when he fell in love with her and she with him, that would awake them both to a sense of the seriousness of life. But it would all be great fun.

It is a clean world, a green world, this of Frank Norris': a world of ambition, and struggle, and a not too dubious kind of love: a world into which the soul with all its maladies has not yet passed. Deficient, truly enough, in subtlety and depth of emotion, it is a world in which the American temperament is happy and at home.

* * *

And it is out of such materials that Frank Norris made his honestest book. "Blix" does not pretend to epic greatness, but it has a lasting charm. One may object to the limitations inside which this story moves; but they are pretty much the restrictions of the American consciousness itself. The love story of Blix and Condy as Frank Norris wrote it will always possess a freshness, a sweetness and a zest, like a wind from off the snow-fields.

Condy is a reporter on a San Franciso paper, who sells a story once in a while to an eastern magazine; he is crude in manner, extravagant in speech, hard-working, full of enthusiasm for Kipling and De Maupassant. Blix is a girl with ambitions of her own, sensible, tender, unsentimental, a rare companion. She is the sort of girl who, as Walt Whitman says, can ride, swim, shoot and generally enjoy the outdoors. She has, like Frank Norris' best creations, something fiercely virginal about her, a cold, hard indifference that only gradually melts into something maternal and wifely. Thruout their whole relationship sex is diffused as a vague sweetness. It is a strange and an interesting courtship, with not a word or gesture of passion in it. Comrades they are, and friends to the very end, when the girl calmly informs the man that they are in love with each other: he is half incredulous and wholly delighted. A remarkable courtship!

* * *

But it is all the more delightful for that. The adventuring of these two unconscious lovers thru San Francisco and its environs, the things they see and do together, the people they meet, the healthy animal enjoyment they take in the sun and the air, the things they talk about: these make an idyl of "togetherness," of all that which is so much longed for and so infrequently achieved by lovers. It is a sort of "down the world with Marna" feeling that is disengaged by the story of these innocent adventures. One envies them their happiness, their frank, free comradeship, their blithe sharing of a wonderful world, the gay communion of their untroubled spirits. It is a picture at which one may smile a little, but which one is glad to remember.

July 11, 1913

THE BOOK OF THE WEEK

ART VERSUS LIFE

The Letters of a Post-Impressionist: Being the Familiar Correspondence of Vincent Van Gogh. Translated by A. M. Ludovici. Frontispiece. (Houghton Mifflin Company.)

The interest of this volume does not depend on the opinion one holds of Van Gogh. One may regard him as the great forerunner of a great movement in art; or one may regard him as a self-deluded fanatic—tho a mention of the sums his pictures fetch today might do a good deal to dissipate that notion; or one may be gloriously ignorant of the very word Post-impressionism. In any case this volume of letters, brief and fragmentary, contains the inner history of an artist as it has perhaps never before been written. It is a rare piece of self-revelation: it reveals more than the writer himself was aware of. Looking into it idly to see what Van Gogh thought about art, one becomes gripped by the fascination of the man's perilous aspirations, his tragic adventuring.

His outer history is easily set forth. Vincent Van Gogh was born in Holland sixty years ago, the son of a clergyman. Dissatisfied with the profession of art dealer, for which he was intended, he became successively a schoolmaster, a theological student and an evangelist among the Belgian miners. At the mines he began to draw. He did not give his attention wholly to painting until he was 29 years old. Eight years later he died. In the meantime, supported by the generosity of his younger brother Theodor, to whom many of these letters are addressed, he painted hundreds of pictures, thought of nothing but painting, ruined his health and went insane. In a lucid moment he ended his life in the year 1890.

The letters begin with his first experiments in painting. He writes enthusiastically to his brother, who has given him carte blanche for materials at the art dealers', saying: "You must not take it amiss if I write to you again so soon. I do so only in order to tell you how extraordinarily happy painting makes me feel." He has slaved so hard that he is dead tired—seven color studies straight off! "I literally cannot stand, and yet I can neither forsake my work nor take a rest."

Thus in the first letter is revealed that fury of work which takes account of nothing. Beside that intensity of will-to-create there was no place for lesser desires, for pleasure, rest, love, health, or life itself. Of his health he is utterly reckless. The protests of his body against overwork he disregards with the mistaken insolence of the artist. "I have just decided," he says in his second letter, "to pay no further heed to my indisposition, or, rather, all that is left of it. Enough time has been lost, and I must not neglect my work. Therefore, whether I am well or not, I shall again draw regularly from morn till night. . . . Art is jealous; she will not allow illness to take precedence of her. And I given in to her."

Who was this man, that he should defy Life in such a fashion? He was a revolutionist of art. The thing is perhaps a little hard to conceive. We thrill to the revolution in music or in drama, but of the great war that has gone on in the last fifty years in the world of painting we generally know nothing. Yet there was a war, and Vincent Van Gogh, whether a fanatic or a hero, was certainly a victim.

* * *

"The thing I have set my mind on as the goal of all my efforts is devilish difficult, and yet I do not think that I am aiming too high," he writes. But that requires "resolute and unremitting industry, as well as constant observation." He had made another study of a child's cradle, he tells his brother, and adds: "I trust I may yet be able to draw the little cradle a hundred times over resolutely." The task he has set for himself, if one has the imagination to conceive it, is cruel, heart-breaking, appalling. He has renounced all right to life, to the amenities of social intercourse, the beauty and wonder of love, the dignities and decencies of civilized life. He has become a monster with a palette, a terrible machine that toils and toils, and feels within its heart "a calm, pure harmony and music." He has no right to stop, not even to save his body or his soul. "Men like myself," he writes grimly, "really have no right to be ill."

Only his work matters. "I am deriving great pleasure from my work just now," he says, "altho from time to time I feel the after effects of my illness somewhat severely. As to the market value of my pictures, I should be very much surprised if, in time, they did not sell as well as other people's. Whether this happens directly or later on does not matter to me."

He is forever attempting the impossible in his painting, and almost succeeding in accomplishing it. In his magnificent ignorance, he invents new methods. "In a sense I am glad that I never learnt to paint," he confesses. "If I had I should perhaps have learnt to overlook such effects. Now I say: 'No!—this and only this must I have, and if it is impossible, well then, it is impossible, that's all. I will have a shot at it, altho I do not know the right way to do it.' "

He had ideas, ideas which are not so startling now as they were when he uttered them. "Tell Seurat," he says, "that I should despair if my figures were correct; tell him that if you take a photograph of a man digging, in my opinion, he is sure to look as if he were not digging; tell him that I think Michelangelo's figures magnificent, even tho the legs are certainly too long and the hips and pelvic bones a little too broad; tell him that in my opinion Millet and L'Hermitte are the true painters of the day, because they do not paint things as they are, dryly analyzing them and observing them objectively, but render them as they feel them; tell him it is my most fervent desire to know how one can achieve such deviations from reality, such inaccuracies and such transfigurations, that come about by chance. Well yes, if you like, they are lies; but they are more valuable than the real values." Again he says: "What impressed me most on looking back at the old Dutch pictures, was the fact that in the majority of cases they were painted rapidly, and that great masters like Hals, Rembrandt, Rysdael, and many others, painted as much as possible du premier coup and avoided overmuch retouching." "I believe it is better to scrape an unsuccessful portion of one's picture completely away and to begin again, than to keep on trying to improve it."

* * *

And then he remarks: "Thank Heaven! my digestion has so far recovered that I have been able to live on ships-biscuit, milk and eggs for three weeks. The beneficent heat is restoring my strength to me. . . . I am now as healthy as other people. . . ." He goes to work with renewed vigor—"like mad, as if the devil himself were at one's back, until the canvas is covered." He has no choice between work and play, no choice between comfort and despairing exertion. "I can only choose between being a good and a bad painter. I choose the former."

To his friend, E. Bernard, who is indulging himself in the melancholy incidental to an unhappy love affair, he says gravely: "To paint and to love women are incompatible. This is really," he adds, "a confounded nuisance." He returns to the subject, saying regretfully: "The Dutchmen were married,

215

and begat themselves children. That is a fine, in fact a very fine way of filling a life, and quite a natural way, too!'' But he praises Delacroix in the next breath, Delacroix, who ''had very little to do with women, and indulged only in amours faciles, so as not to waste any of the time consecrated to his Life's task.''

He cannot escape the tragic knowledge that he has shut himself outside the house of life. ''And even if the feeling that one has no share in real life remains a melancholy one (for it would surely be preferable to deal with living flesh and blood than with color and clay, and one would sooner beget children than work at art or at the commerce of art), one feels, notwithstanding, that one does at least live, for among one's friends are there not numbers who also have no share in real life?'' To this pass, and to such pitiful arguments, is reduced the revolutionist. ''One feels exactly like an old cab-horse, and one knows that one must always return to the same old shafts, when all the while one would love to live in the fields, in the sun, near the river, in the country, with other horses, also free, and have the right to procreate one's kind.'' It is not enough to be a painter. There comes the desire, insistent, inappeasable and tragic, to be a man.

The artistic life, he tells himself, artificial tho it is, seems so vigorous and vital that ''we should be ungrateful not to be satisfied with it.'' Besides, a love affair, even a light one, might lead to a binding relationship. ''One must be content to paint pictures, which is by no means real happiness or real life.'' . . . The end draws near.

* * *

Meanwhile he dreams of the art of the future, that art so beautiful and so young, to which he and his fellows sacrifice their youth, health and freedom. ''I cannot imagine,'' he says bitterly, ''the painter of the future leading the life I lead. He would not have to go to small restaurants and wear false teeth''. . . . nor adopt desperate and pitiful makeshifts for love. No! the artist of the future will not have to starve, to deny himself all human joys save that of painting ''like a lion devouring a piece of flesh,'' to break down the health of his body and his soul, and to be packed off at last, like Van Gogh, to the insane asylum.

For that was the end of the tragic path along which Van Gogh climbed, his eyes on the stars even while his feet stumbled at the edge of the abyss. . . . In a period of sanity he said to his friend Gauguin: ''My dear master, after having known you and grieved you, it is more dignified to die while I am fully conscious of what I am doing than to take leave of this world in a state which degrades me.'' So he fired a bullet at himself, and ''a few hours later, while lying in bed smoking his pipe, with all his wits about him, full of passionate love for his art, and without any feelings of resentment toward humanity, he quietly passed away.'' So Life revenged herself on him who had denied her.

July 18, 1913

THE BOOK OF THE WEEK

A GOOD NOVEL

O Pioneers! by Willa Sibert Cather. (Houghton Mifflin Company.)

This book provides an opportunity for the American Academy of Arts and Letters to justify its existence. One of the functions of an academy—a function which the recently created British Academy has not hesitated to assume—is the discovery and recognition of genius. A committee including Bernard Shaw not long since selected a certain prose work for the honor of a prize, as containing that specific and peculiar promise which attaches to the early productions of genius. Well! it would be a gratifying result of the enterprise of our American academicians if a committee headed by W. D. Howells should discover this novel by Willa Sibert Cather. It has that specific and peculiar quality. It is touched with genius. It is worthy of being recognized as the most vital, subtle and artistic piece of the year's fiction.

Why is it all that? I despair of being able to show why. The book does not deal with any of the large ideas which, rightly enough, agitate this generation. It has no palpable finesse of style. It does not stun nor dazzle. It only tells the story of a girl and her younger brothers who live on a Nebraska farm: the story of their struggle with a stubborn land which almost crushes them to death before it suddenly smiled and yielded; the story, moreover, of such friendship and love as came, sometimes with wistful autumnal sweetness and again with tragic passion, into their lives. It is not an extraordinary story. Everyone knows a dozen like it.

* * *

The book opens rather unpropitiously in the little town of Hanover, anchored on a windy Nebraska tableland, and ''trying not to be blown away.'' The Swedish and Bohemian farmers who are engaged in the fierce and almost despairing effort to reclaim the land from its prairie wildness—it was thirty years ago—are in to trade at the general store. Among them is the girl Alexandra, a fine, resolute, man-minded, thoughtful young creature, with her little brother Emil; and Carl Lindstrum, a thin, frail boy with an artist's sensitiveness and skepticism in his face; and the little Bohemian girl, Marie Tovesky, a pretty child with a coaxing little red mouth and eyes with golden glints in the brown iris.

These are seen for a moment in a setting of men drinking raw alcohol to protect themselves against the cold, and women pinning red shawls about their heads, and all talking loudly in a room reeking with tobacco smoke and kerosene. Then they set out, and the town vanishes behind them "as if it had never been." Alexandra goes back to the side of a father who is dying in the shadow of debt and failure, to her brothers to whom she must bear the difficult part of a mother, to a friendship that is cut short by separation, and to the terrible struggle with the land.

That is all there is to the whole first part of the book. And yet one does not stop reading. There is something in her calm yet vivid narrative that seems so profoundly true, a faithfulness not merely to the exterior of life, but to its intimate soul, that it has an extraordinary zest. And there is something more. One feels thru this narrative the spirit of the author, and comes to trust oneself completely in her hands. It is a spirit, an attitude toward life, that in its large and simple honesty has a kind of nobleness. Life, the course of events, as traced by such a mind, loses the taint of commonplace and becomes invested with dignity.

* * *

So one follows the story, seeing the struggle with the land, carried on inexorably by Alexandra against the poorer judgment and the feebler will of the two older boys, her brothers, at last successful: the gray prairie turned into a vast checkerboard of wheat and corn. The two older boys are married. Emil is away at college. Alexandra has a big house, in which the most interesting room is the kitchen, where three pretty, young Swedish girls chatter and cook and pickle and preserve all summer long. To be sure, they always wasted a good deal of time getting in each other's way and giggling at each other's mistakes. But, as Alexandra had pointedly told her sister-in-law, it was to hear them giggle that she kept three young things in her kitchen; the work she could do herself, if it were necessary.

Alexandra is unmarried. When Carl, after all these years, comes to see her, he is a painter, and in the eyes of her staid and prosperous brothers a vagabond. In his own eyes he is that, too. "Our landlady and the delicatessen men are our mourners," he says, "and we leave nothing behind us but a frock coat and a fiddle, or an easel, or a typewriter, or whatever tool we got our living by. All we have ever managed to do is pay our rent, the exorbitant rent that one has to pay for a few square feet of space near the heart of things. We have no house, no place, no people of our own. We live in the streets, in the parks, in the theaters.''

But Alexandra sees more clearly the values of his life and the one he left behind. "I would rather have Emil grow up like that than like his two brothers. We pay a high rent, too, tho we pay differently. We grow hard and heavy here. We don't move lightly and easily as you do and our minds get stiff. If the world were no wider than my cornfields, if there were not something besides this, I wouldn't feel that it was much worth while to work. No I would rather have Emil like you than like them.''

As for Emil, he has grown up into a handsome young man. He is a nice boy, and when he finds himself falling in love with Marie, the Bohemian girl, who is now the young and pretty wife of Frank Shabata, he goes away to Mexico City thinking to make matters all right that way. . . . Alexandra reads his letters to Marie. "Marie knew perfectly well that Emil's letters were written more for her than for Alexandra. They were not the sort of letters that a young man writes to his sister. They were both more personal and more painstaking. . . . In short, they were the kind of letters a young man writes to a woman when he wishes himself and his life to seem interesting to her, when he wishes to enlist her imagination in his behalf.''

Marie had eloped with Frank Shabata, who had dressed to hit the eye and was the desire of every Bohemian girl in the district. In a few years his gayety had turned to sullenness, his bravado to black misanthropy. In particular, he was jealous. He would nurse vague grievances in his mind until he grew capable of furious rages. He had little sympathy for his wife's attempts at friendship. But Marie met the situation with what seemed an inexhaustible fund of good fun. Carl Lindstrum, looking at her dancing eyes, thought to himself, "What a waste. She ought to be doing all that for a sweetheart. How awkwardly things come about.''

* * *

As for Carl, he goes away, seeking a fortune in the Klondike. Alexandra's brothers are afraid she is going to marry him. "Can't you see he's just a tramp and he's after your money? He wants to be taken care of, he does.'' Alexandra says: "Well, suppose I want to take care of him. Whose business is it but my own?'' Even Emil, just starting off for Mexico, couldn't see why she should want to. He wouldn't, of course: his sister was 40. And Carl will not accept happiness on these terms; off to the Klondike he goes.

Emil returns, and the dangerous friendship with Marie is recommenced. It is here, in conjunction with a remarkable restraint, that the writer's sympathy is most limpid-clear in its showing of life. It is the story of Youth. . . . One turns back to the little poem set in between the title page and the table of contents, telling of the somber land and the unresponsive sky—

Against all this, Youth,
Flaming like the wild roses,
Singing like the larks over the plowed fields,
Flashing like a star out of the twilight;
Youth with its insupportable sweetness,
Its fierce necessity,
Its sharp desire.
Singing and singing,
Out of the silence,
Out of the earthy dusk.

A song too soon, too tragically ended. But of that ending, nor of the delayed happiness of Alexandra and Carl, I shall not go on to speak. Either I have conveyed some sense of the richness, the charm and the dignity of this novel, or I have not. But I have done all I can, and—now it is up to the Academy.

July 25, 1913

THE NEW CHARLOTTE BRONTE LETTERS

It is not necessary, in order to be a good citizen, to be acquainted with Charlotte Bronte's biography. And even if one does know the general events in the life of this plain little consumptive governess whose novels are among the glories of English literature, one may not have attached special importance to her stay at the Heger *pensionnat* in Brussels, nor her friendship for Constantin Heger, professor of rhetoric. Her biographers, it is true, have speculated daringly on the matter (tho most of them have been inclined to accept the fact that Professor Heger was married and had five children as a sufficient alibi for Charlotte's heart). But despite the obvious portraiture of Professor Heger in one of her novels, and her frank admiration for him as expressed in her letters home, nothing definite has been known of her real feelings for him, until the publication the other day in the London Times—as related in another column by Mr. Bullock—of four of Charlotte Bronte's letters to him. But these letters do more than satisfy a special and specific curiosity. They are documents of first-rate interest, revealing to us as they do the mainspring of Charlotte Bronte's career: a frustrated but passionate love, a love impossible and rejected, a love that crushed and exalted her, that destroyed all her happiness in life and made of her a great novelist.

220

* * *

In the light of these letters one may interpret more easily that obscure misery which descended upon Charlotte Bronte during her second year in Brussels, when she returned there to teach without her sisters. "I returned," she wrote later, "against my conscience, prompted by what then seemed an irresistible impulse. I was punished for my selfish folly by a total withdrawal, for more than two years, of happiness and peace of mind." It must have been pain of the bitterest sort for her to realize, as she must soon have been forced to do, that love, the one possible consolation for her restless and unconfinable spirit, had come to her in no ideal guise, but in its most vulgar if not criminal form. "It is madness in all women," she wrote in "Jane Eyre," "to let a secret love kindle within them which if unreturned and unknown must devour the life that feeds it; and, if discovered and responded to, must lead, ignisfatuus-like, into miry wilds whence there is no extrication." We may well imagine then, that Charlotte Bronte took care to keep her secret—care which seems to have deceived everybody except Mme. Heger who had a woman's clairvoyance in such matters. She taught, read, tramped by herself along the streets of Brussels, suppressing her feeling and working herself into a state of nervous tension.

One September day she found herself in the shadow of a cathedral; she slipped in and stayed thru vespers. She watched the penitents kneel at the confessional, and at last in the morbid and irresistible desire to communicate to someone this secret that was poisoning her soul, she, too, knelt down before the little grating. But she did not know the formula of confession, and was obliged to admit to the priest that she was a Protestant. He kindly let her go on, however, and, as she wrote to her sister Emily, she made "a real confession." The priest invited her to come to his house the next day, hoping to convert her. But that was not what she wanted. She went back to the school and shortly afterward gave notice. Dissuaded from going, she remained a few months longer. "I suffered much before I left Brussels," she said, on her return. "There are times now when it appears to me as if all my ideas and feelings, except a few friendships and affections, are changed from what they used to be: something in me, which used to be enthusiasm is tamed down and broken. I have fewer illusions; what I wish for now is active exertion—a stake in life." She found her stake in literature. Two years later she wrote one of the finest of English novels, a book in which she distilled the bitterness of her knowledge of life into intoxicating prose.

* * *

But the compensations of art were slow to manifest themselves. The two years after she left Brussels were years of loneliness, of perpetual thinking on one forbidden subject, of the struggle of pride with passion. Out

221

of this period, like lightning flashes that light up the black depths of a stormy sky, come these letters—letters which reveal while they do not state her love, and which are the clew to the desperation which subjugates even if it does not stifle her sense of shame.

It is characteristic that it should have been in Bernard Shaw's organ, the New Statesman, that a critical article appeared which referred to the "emotional mendicancy" of these letters. It is sufficiently clear that Charlotte Bronte is not made of the stuff which Shaw, and the young and intellectually vigorous generation which calls him Master, would approve. To them it is an offense against human dignity to confess a loss of self-centricity. That one's happiness should be in the power of some one else they consider ridiculous. Pitiful, truly, it is to see this strong spirit turning and twisting in the steel-toothed trap: but pain has also its dignity.

"I tell you frankly that I have tried meanwhile to forget you," she writes. "When one has suffered that kind of anxiety for a year or two, one is ready to do anything to find peace once more. I have done everything; I have sought occupations; I have denied myself absolutely the pleasure of speaking about you—even to Emily; but I have been able to conquer neither my regrets nor my impatience. That indeed is humiliating—to be unable to control one's own thoughts, to be the slave of a regret, of a memory, the slave of a fixed and dominant idea that lords it over the mind."

To be unable to control one's own thoughts. . . to be the slave of a regret, of a memory . . . In these words Charlotte Bronte touched upon the fatal weakness of the mind by virtue of which we are at once higher and lower than the brutes: the self-distilled poison by which the haughtiest will is corroded and destroyed.

* * *

All of the letters, with the exception of the postscript to the last, are in the language of the recipient. "I greatly fear that I shall forget French," she writes, "for I am firmly convinced that I shall see you again some day—I know not how or when—but it must be, for I wish it so much, and then I should not wish to remain dumb before you. To avoid such a misfortune I learn every day by heart a half a page of French, written in familiar style; and I take pleasure in learning this lesson, Monsieur; as I pronounce the French words it seems to me as if I were chatting with you."

For a reason that we do not know, whether one connected with what are called moral scruples or from mere indifference, Professor Heger replied unsympathetically when he replied at all. Mostly he did not reply at all. The first letter begins: "I am well aware that it is not my turn to write to you. . . ." A little farther down she says, "I refrain from uttering a single complaint for your long silence"—for she knows he is overworked and in ill health. "Ah, Monsieur! I once wrote you a letter that was less reasonable, because sorrow was at my heart; but I shall do so no more—I shall try to be selfish no longer; and even while I look upon your letters as one of the greatest felicities known to me I shall await the receipt of them in patience until it pleases you and suits you to send me any. Meanwhile I may well send you a little letter from time to time—you have authorized me to do so."

* * *

She adds by way of postscript: "I have not begged you to write to me soon as I fear to importune you—but you are too kind to forget that I wish it all the same—yes, I wish it greatly. Enough; after all, do as you wish, Monsieur. If, then, I received a letter, and if I thought that you had written it *out of pity*—I should feel deeply wounded."

It seems that he does not write even out of pity. In the second of the letters that are preserved to us, Charlotte inquires anxiously if he has heard from her at the beginning of May and again in the month of August. "For six months I have been waiting a letter from Monsieur—six months waiting is very long, you know!"

This plea effects nothing. The visitor from Belgium who delivered her letter returns without a reply. "Neither letter nor message." She writes it all down for him:

> Having realized the meaning of these words, I
> said to myself what I should say to another
> similarly placed: "You must be resigned, and above
> all, do not grieve at a misfortune which you have
> not deserved." I strove to restrain my tears, to
> utter no complaint.
> But when one does not complain, when one seeks
> to dominate oneself with a tyrant's grip, the
> faculties start into rebellion and one pays for
> external calm with an internal struggle that is
> almost unbearable.
> Day and night I find neither rest nor peace.
> If I sleep I am disturbed by tormenting dreams in
> which I see you, always severe, always grave, always
> incensed against me.
> Forgive me, then, Monsieur, if I adopt the course
> of writing to you again. How can I endure life if I
> make no effort to ease its sufferings?

"I shall not re-read this letter," she says, further on. "I send it as I have written it. Nevertheless, I have a hidden consciousness that some people, cold and common-sense, in reading it would say—'She is talking nonsense.' I would avenge myself on such persons in no other way than by wishing them one single day of the torments which I have suffered for eight months. We should then see if they would not talk nonsense, too."

There is more in the same vein. The interested reader may have a translation of the whole by procuring the London Times Weekly edition for Aug. 1, from which these excerpts are taken. Enough has been quoted to give the flavor of these letters, salt with tears and bitter with the peculiar anguish of loneliness. Four letters out of the black void of those two years; and, representing in some sort Professor Heger, "some commonplace notes in pencil on the edge—one of them the name and address of a shoemaker."

Then silence, and then "Jane Eyre"—the story of a tragic love that flowers late into happiness and peace. That which she could not ever know for herself she made real for others with swift and passionate pencil. She had once written to Professor Heger that if it were not for her failing eyesight, she would write a book and dedicate it to him—"to the only master I ever had—to you, Monsieur." All her books were truly dedicate [sic]—a romantic proceeding of which Shaw would certainly not approve—to the memory and the dream of him.

August 15, 1913

THE ALCOHOLIC MEMOIRS OF JACK LONDON

John Barleycorn, by Jack London. (The Century Company.)

When, a week ago, I sat up all night to read "John Barleycorn" I was paying a tribute not so much to a tract against alcohol as to one of the most interesting adventure stories I had ever read. For "John Barleycorn" is the saga of drink, and of all the splendor, perhaps a meretricious splendor, that drink brings into man's life. It is a swift and impassioned story of adventure, drawn with the hard lines of realism but lighted by all the colors of romance. It is harsh with truth and bitter with the taste of life, yet alluring with the splendid vigor of youth. It was not at all as a total abstinence tract that I read it.

* * *

But it got in its sad work nevertheless. The next day when I sat down to dinner I had to refuse the friendly cocktail that my host provided. It occurred to me that I had never really liked cocktails; that I thought they tasted like nothing so much as gasoline . . . "I've just been reading 'John Barleycorn,'" I explained apologetically. "Yes," answered my host. "I read it halfway thru and then stopped—on purpose."

But it is not for its rather questionable effect upon the habits of its readers that the book, after all, is notable: questionable, for if it did not convert its author ("No," he concludes on the last page, "I shall take my drink on occasion" . . .) it can then hardly be expected to have any permanent influence in that direction on us. However, it does something else to its readers which is perhaps far more profound and significant.

It is a habit of mind, as Jack London says, for us to conceive the world as a place with good drinking in it. "I like the bubbling play of wit, the chesty laughs, the resonant voices of men, when, glass in hand, they shut the gray world outside and prod their brains with the fun and folly of an accelerated pulse." So, perhaps, most of us feel. We could not shape any sort of future, any utopia worth living in which was not lighted at intervals by the golden glow of drink.

Thus I have imagined myself surviving into a dull teaified universe presided over by Bernard Shaw, in which the manufacture of alcoholic drinks had been utterly stopped; a universe in which there remained, nevertheless, by some happy accident, one single bottle of wine, at the secret consumption of which I was permitted to assist. It was, as I saw it in imagination, a solemn, almost a religious, ceremony, which we, poets and artists all, conducted by thus pouring down our throats amid high talk this wine, the last wine in the world. It was as tho, watchers at a deserted and desecrated shrine, we had seen flicker and go out the flame of a sacred torch. A magic was forever gone out of our human life, a wild beauty lost forever. It is indeed hard to think of life as having the same values, the same color and fragrance, without drink. When we think of a pleasant world, it has alcohol in it. And this conception is always in the background of our mind, of our thinking in regard to what is called the "drink question."

* * *

But Jack London's book is capable of changing that, of shattering that conception, of remaking the background of one's thoughts. He can make one conceive of a world without alcohol as being a very fine place to live in. He suggests to us a world in which the "adventure stings and the genial predispositions, the social man-impulses," which are so bound up with drinking today, flourish freely without the stimulus of any subtle and delightful poison. "The overwhelming proportion of young men are so normally nonalcoholic that, never having had access to alcohol, they will never miss it. They will know of the saloon only in the pages of history, and they will think of the saloon as a quaint old custom similar to bull baiting and the burning of witches."

Disconcerting to me, who have been accustomed to resent, on behalf of the cause of woman suffrage, the charge that women were committed to the folly of prohibition legislation, is his prediction of their part in this great change. "The women," he says, "are the true conservators of the race. The men are the wastrels, the adventure lovers, the gamblers, and in the end it is by their women that they are saved. About man's first experiment in chemistry was the making of alcohol, and down all the generations to this day man has continued to manufacture and drink it. And there has never been a day when women have not resented man's use of alcohol, tho they have never had the power to give weight to their resentment. The moment women get the vote in any community the first thing they proceed to do, or try to do, is to close the saloons. In a thousand generations to come, men of themselves will not close the saloons. As well expect the morphine victims to legislate the sale of morphine out of existence."

I really intended to write of this as an exciting personal narrative, for there are some of the finest pages of excitement in it that I know of. The story of young Jack London's exploits as an oyster pirate in San Francisco Bay, when he won his title afloat and ashore as "Prince of the Oyster Beds"; of mad deviltry along the Oakland water front with "Young Scratch" Nelson for a partner; of orgies in Japan punctuated by a daring swim out to the schooner that was the talk of the harbor for days ("I remember it today, twenty years afterward, with a secret glow of pride"); of orgies of physical and intellectual effort almost beyond credence—these make the book, as I have said, an adventure story. But, after all, the real adventure for the reader is to have his well-based and well-cherished notions on the subject of drink knocked into a cocked hat. So let us not try to escape the argument to which all this exciting narrative tends. Jack London is bound to prove his point.

* * *

And there is no denying that he knows, as he says, "the drinking game from A to Zed." He gives the psychology of the drinker as it has never been done before: literally never, I am assured by those who know both the game and the literature of drinking far better than I ever expect to. He tells the story of his drinking experiences from the time when, a child of 5 years, he got drunk on the beer he was carrying to his father out in the plowing field, down thru his water front and sailor days to the time when he found that he couldn't get down his customary thousand words of a morning before he had a cocktail. There are a hundred touches that anyone who is acquainted with the psychology of drinking will recognize as keen and true. For he gives John Barleycorn his rights, never stinting the praise that is due him for the loan (on well-known loan-shark principles) of energy, the added joys of comradeship (which will not bear critical observation, it is true, from the outside), and the razor edge it sometimes gives to the mind (thus enabling it

226

to cut thru the protective illusions of life to the deadly truths beneath): for all these things praise is rendered generously. The book leaves one in no doubt why men drink. "All ways led to the saloon. The thousand roads of romance and adventure draw together in the saloon and thence led out and on over the world."

But one is not permitted to assume that his is a special, nontypical case, the case of the born alcoholic. "It is the accessibility of alcohol that has given me my taste for alcohol," he writes. "I did not care for it. I used to laugh at it. Yet here I am, at the last, possessed with the drinker's desire. It took twenty years to implant that desire; and for ten years that desire has grown. And the effect," he adds mildly, "of satisfying that desire is anything but good."

The effect, visited upon this strong man with "land, money, power, a consciousness that I do my meed of good in serving others, a mate whom I love, children that are of my own fond flesh"—is peculiar to its victim, "the imaginative man who is lusty with life and desire to live." It is what Jack London calls the White Logic—"the urgent messenger of truth beyond truth, the antithesis of life, cruel and bleak as interstellar space, pulseless and frozen as absolute zero, dazzling with the frost of irrefragible logic and unforgettable fact. John Barleycorn will not let the dreamer dream, the liver live. He destroys birth and death, and dissipates to mist the paradox of being, until his victim cries out, as in 'The City of Dreadful Night': 'Our life's a cheat, our death a black abyss.' And the feet of the victim of such dreadful intimacy with Truth take hold of the way of death."

* * *

Of his intellectual dealings with "the Noseless One" Jack London tells in some detail. If the account is not as impressive as he would like to make it, he has his excuse: "Take Hasheesh Land, for instance, the land of enormous extensions of time and space. In past years I have made two memorable journeys into that far land. My adventures there are seared in sharpest detail on my brain. Yet I have tried vainly with endless words to describe any tiny particular phase to persons who have not traveled there."

But if this part of the book, for whatever reason, seems to me lacking in impressiveness, the effect of the whole is shattering. It is not the effect of logic, but of confession. It shakes us, as such extraordinary candor always must. And in a period and a country when respectability is rated so dear, candor is peculiarly disturbing. "John Barleycorn" is an inescapable document. One is half charmed, half repelled by his moral, but peruse it one must, whatever the results to one's established notions. Jack London is, now as always, "Yours for the Revolution."

August 22, 1913

THE BOOK OF THE WEEK

HIS GREAT ADVENTURE

His Great Adventure, by Robert Herrick. (The Macmillan Company.)

[With every possible apology to Mr. Herrick, this attempt at sympathetic interpretation of the mood in which a book like "His Great Adventure" might be written by the author of "One Woman's Life," is offered instead of the conventional review.]

It probably happened something like this—

The author sat in his study, writing. On the shelves above him were the works of Flaubert, Dostoievsky, Turgeniev. A little clock somewhere in the room struck the hour.

He stopped writing, and read over with gusto what he had just written. It was the last chapter of a novel. In this novel he had set forth the career of an American woman. He had stripped her soul of its romantic pretenses, and shown her up for what she was—a pretty grafter. He had followed her from her girlhood days on to her second marriage, showing her the same in all phases—a parasite. No sentimental deviation from the path of her destiny, no romantic conversion was allowed her. As in the beginning, so in the end.

He lingered fondly upon the page he had just written. Those somber geniuses of Realism whose works looked down upon him from the shelves might have inspired it, so filled was it with the sense of stern, unswerving truthfulness. He had left her as he found her, the same beautiful, hard, materialistic creature, walking in the path foredoomed to her by her nature. For her there was no change possible, no genial redemption, no magical right-about-face. Like an aroma, the sense of fatality lifted itself from the written page. This, with its inexorable and tragic consecution, was Life, as understood by the great Realists there on the shelves.

He finished reading, and laid down the manuscript. "Well," he said, "I think that just about does for Millie!"

* * *

At that moment a faint sound came to his ears—the sound to which every American soul vibrates in willing or unwilling sympathy. It was the sound of a fire engine, clanging its way out of the dark along this quiet street.

He frowned, took up his pen, and then put it down. He rose, hesitated, and went to the window in time to see the whole fire company rage past. A crowd began to follow. He looked after them down the dark street.

228

"Only a block away!"

Curious thing, a fire engine! There are no fire engines in Flaubert—none in Dostoievsky. In the works of the great Realists, one does not run to fires. Life, as they see it, is different. One feels in their writings the slow, resistless force which impels a character along the path of his destiny. The end one perceives afar, but there is no avoiding it. The sense of fatality is heavy in the atmosphere. . . . But a fire engine changes all that. No one can feel the inexorableness of destiny when a fire engine has just gone past. A fire engine is a crude and blatant piece of romanticism. It turns one into a boy, with all of a boy's illusions about the mysterious depths, the odd corners, the hidden secrets and the magical gifts of life.

* * *

Abruptly he went out the door and followed the crowd down the street.

A fire destroys far more than it touches; it destroys, recreates, renews the whole world. The known universe shrivels up and disappears; and the new universe, tho it may seem very like the old, is nevertheless new and mysterious, and friendly, and charming.

It was not at all strange when he found himself talking to a young woman who stood, bare of head and eager-eyed, beside him in the crowd. She had a soft southern voice. He found himself inventing a name for her. "Melody," he said to himself. "Not a bad idea."

(You understand, do you not, that all this is purely imaginary?)

The young woman was staring in one direction, away from the flare of the engine, to where some roofs and chimneys were oddly silhouetted against the sky. "It reminds me of a certain view, from a bridge, in Paris."

"It isn't, by chance, the Pont Neuf?" he asked. The comparison was ridiculous, but he felt glad when the words struck a light in her eyes. "Yes," she said. "Do you know it?"

So they talked about Paris, while the efficient fire company subdued the adolescent blaze. He found himself in an expectant attitude, toward the whole world and her, and was not at all surprised, only regretful, to learn that they had been in Paris at the same time, and had even lived in adjoining pensions. It was one of those delightful coincidences of which Flaubert and Dostoievsky make so little account, but with which American life is well seasoned.

"What are you doing?" she asked.

"Finishing a novel. Don't you want to come and hear the last page or two? I'm just around the corner."

When she had disposed herself comfortably in a large chair, he took up the manuscript. But he no longer felt the same glow of approval toward it. Instead, he was distinctly anxious to discover the opinion—the "reaction," he called it—of his auditor. So he read, while she looked at him with grave eyes.

When he came to the last page, he read it slowly; it still seemed, tho less certainly than before, good. A mist, an aroma of fatalism, rose from the written words. It had the acrid flavor of Life, as it is understood by the great Realists. Finishing, he looked up anxiously.

"What do you think?" he asked.

She gave a little start. "Is that the end?" she asked blankly. Then she smiled candidly, and said, "I beg your pardon. But something you wrote reminded me of something else, and I wasn't listening to that last page. Won't you read it to me again, please?"

"No," he said, "that is the criticism I wanted." He stuffed the manuscript into the desk. "Perhaps you are right."

* * *

He commenced walking up and down the room. At last he stopped before her. "Tomorrow," he said, "I shall put the finishing touches on that last chapter, and send the book away. Then, the very next day, I commence another. I have just invented it. It is different from anything I have ever done. It is to be called—yes—'His Great Adventure.' "

" 'His Great Adventure'?" she repeated, smiling.

"It is to be a story of adventure. A young man, an unsuccessful playwright, is in New York—broke. He befriends a dying man, who gives him the combination of a safe in San Francisco, and tells him to get the contents and take them to Berlin. He mentions a girl. Her name—I think her name will be Melody."

"Pretty name," murmured the young woman.

"The young man goes to San Francisco, robs the safe, takes the contents to Berlin and sells them for $2,000,000. Then he starts to look for Melody."

"Of course he finds her!" she mocked.

"Not at once. First he goes to Arizona, exploits a sulphur mine and becomes very rich."

"What does he do with his money?"

"I think he tries to found a people's theater," said the author, his tone slightly tinged with bitterness—"and gets universally roasted for it. No—no—this is a romance, and I shall have him succeed. Succeed splendidly! Melody, now that I think of it, shall be the star of the people's theater."

"How very simple!" said the young woman.

"I know it is crude," he said defensively. "But that is only the husk. It is the kernel that I am after. And that is the sense of life that I have tonight: a sense of the magical quality of life—its sudden turns, its generosity, its surprises, its essential friendliness. I want to show somebody doing—not what he has to do, but what he wants to do. I want to celebrate the will of man, the will that conquers obstacles instead of being defeated by them. I want to celebrate man's unconquerable soul."

"You run the danger," said the young woman, "of becoming a best seller."

He braced himself spiritually, and stood tense and upright in the face of those bleak winds that rave about the pinnacles of the soul. "I can bear even that," he said simply.

The little clock somewhere in the room struck again. The author turned gravely to the young woman. "Will you go down to the drug store and have an orange ice with me?" he asked.

As they went out the shock of the door's closing dislodged a volume of Flaubert which was standing loosely in the shelf, and the masterpiece of that great Realist fell to the floor, unheeded. . . .

—At least that is how it might have happened!

September 19, 1913

LITERARY EDITORS.

All the good literary editors go. Mr. Francis Hackett, who founded the *Friday Literary Review* four years ago last March and who, as its editor, established a reputation for himself as a critic, left after a time to do "independent literary work." He continues to view the progress of this paper from the vantage point of London, which, if it is not the place where all good literary editors go, is certainly the place where all literary Irishmen go.

Mr. Floyd Dell, who has been associated with the *Review* since its inception and who has been in editorial charge of it for more than two years, goes this week to New York to pursue (need we add?) "independent literary work." Those who are familiar with the *Review* are aware of the intelligence and the enthusiasm which he brought to the consideration of contemporary literature and the unfailing courage and vivacity with which he exercised his critical gifts.

It is then with a certain awareness of London and New York, as well as of Chicago, that this promise is made: the standards for which the *Friday Literary Review* has been known in the past will continue to be maintained.

Lucian Cary, Literary Editor
October 3, 1913